LABOR ORGANIZATIONS
IN THE UNITED STATES
AND MEXICO

Contributions in American History

Series Editor: Stanley I. Kutler

LABOR
ORGANIZATIONS
IN THE UNITED STATES
AND MEXICO

*A History
of Their Relations*

Harvey A. Levenstein

Contributions in American History
Number 13

Greenwood Publishing Company

1971

Library of Congress Catalog Card Number: 79-98708
ISBN: 0-8371-5151-1   13349 P

Greenwood Publishing Company
A DIVISION OF GREENWOOD PRESS, INC.
51 Riverside Avenue, Westport, Connecticut 06880

Printed in the United States of America

For Mona

Contents

Acknowledgments

I WOULD LIKE TO express my appreciation to the Henry L. and Grace Doherty Foundation for the fellowship that allowed me to spend a year in Mexico doing research for this study. The Graduate School of the University of Wisconsin provided a travel grant to enable me to do research in Washington. Many Mexicans took the time to help me overcome some of the difficulties inherent in doing research on twentieth-century Mexican history. Among them I would especially like to thank Sr. Rosendo Salazar for helping me find my way about at first, granting me interviews about his experiences, and joining me in some stimulating discussions about the Mexican labor movement in general. The late Lic. Vicente Lombardo Toledano took time out from his busy schedule to grant me interviews and answer a questionnaire. Sr. José Ortiz Petricioli of the CROM, and Professor Bernardo Cobos and Lic. Luis Macías of the CTM were of aid in helping me deal with the later period. Dean David A. Shannon of the University of Virginia, who guided this book at the dissertation stage, helped push it through many shoals. He provided valuable advice and encouragement when it was sorely needed. Professor James D. Morris of the Cornell University School of Industrial and Labor Relations and Professor James Gilbert of the University of Maryland read parts of the manuscript in earlier stages and offered useful comments and suggestions. Finally, I would like to thank the editors of the *Hispanic American Historical Review* for permission to use in chapter 8 material that first appeared in my article, "The AFL and Mexican Immigration in the 1920's: An Experiment in Labor Diplomacy," *Hispanic American Historical Review* 47, no. 2 (May 1968).

New York, New York
September 1969

LABOR ORGANIZATIONS
IN THE UNITED STATES
AND MEXICO

1

Introduction

ALTHOUGH MUCH attention has been devoted to the activities of such nongovernmental institutions as American business corporations and political pressure groups in Latin American affairs, the activities of labor organizations, which have a tradition of internationalism, have received very little scholarly attention—especially in the United States. The international activities of American labor unions are often relegated to a short separate chapter in histories of American labor and written as a catalog of dates and many-lettered, always changing, international organizations, which American labor groups are either forming, disbanding, joining, leaving, or attacking. Excessive concentration upon the mechanics of the rivalries among international labor organizations, although often necessary, also serves to obscure the reasons for their existence and the interest of the national labor organizations in international affairs in the first place. In the case of Latin America, the relative paucity, until post–World War II years, of imposingly named international organizations competing for dominance had led to the downgrading of the prewar activities of U.S. labor organizations there into mere notations that Samuel Gompers was interested in Mexico, formed the Pan-American Federation of Labor, but that when he died, so did it, along with the interest of the American Federation of Labor in Latin America.

Much more attention is devoted to the subject in non-scholarly works, but these usually take the form of political tracts that purport to give the histories of the hemispheric labor organizations they are defending or attacking. The attacks and defenses generally fall into two categories, revolving around the motivation of the U.S. labor organizations seeking closer ties with Latin American labor. The U.S. labor organizations are pictured either as tools of the American government, attempting to aid and supplement American economic and political imperialism, or as completely altruistic, seeking only to help their underdeveloped Latin brothers obtain the high living standards enjoyed by American workers by helping them develop the same tools—"free trade unionism." The truth lies in neither of these stereotyped categories. It presents a much more complex picture.

The propaganda pamphlets are right on one point. The major question is that of motivation. As always, it is also the most difficult to answer. The motivation of the individuals concerned with shaping policy can never be pinpointed exactly without resorting to forms of historical psychoanalysis—a dubious proposition in biographies, let alone in studies of this nature. However, individual leaders must be able to justify their policies on some rational basis, and this aspect is the important one. Samuel Gompers might really have wanted to cultivate close relations with Mexican labor because he liked Mexicans as people, but he could hardly justify the expenditure of AFL funds on that basis. Whatever his own proclivities, he had to come up with a rationale for doing what he wanted, and it is on the basis of the rationales presented, not their personal origin, that policy in any organization is usually discussed and decided.

On both sides of the border, the most common ideological basis for justifying close relations between the Mexican and American labor movements was the belief in the identity of interests of the working classes of the world and the need for international labor solidarity.

The ideal of international labor solidarity probably reached its apogee in the nineteenth century. It is hard to think of a nineteenth-century European labor ideology that did not rely heavily upon it. By the early twentieth century, it was generally accepted by the labor movements of the world as a good in itself, although there were differences over its practicality, usefulness, and the modes in which it should be employed. The achievement of close and harmonious relations with foreign labor movements became an end in itself. World War I exposed the hollow nature of much of the rhetoric surrounding European labor solidarity. Nevertheless, the myth of international labor solidarity, although weakened, continued to be an operative one. Indeed, it continues to affect policies to this day.

Internationalism was not endemic to the American labor movement. Although many U.S. labor leaders before the twentieth century were affected by foreign ideas, they seldom had much interest in cultivating close international ties. This was natural, for not only was the United States geographically isolated from Europe, but the mainstream of American radicalism and unionism was also intellectually isolated from European currents. The two great streams of radical thought that affected European unionism so greatly, Marxism and anarcho-syndicalism, had little effect on American labor organizations of the nineteenth century.

In spite of its generally conservative tactics, the AFL was somewhat affected by socialist thought. Samuel Gompers himself had started his career as a Socialist. His differences with the Socialists in the AFL were more over tactics than over general ideals. Once the AFL had achieved some strength at home, Gompers tentatively took steps to bring it out of its isolation from the rest of the world's labor movements. In doing this, he espoused the ideal of international labor solidarity.

In Mexico, influenced as it was by anarcho-syndicalist

thought, the labor movement from the very beginning found it hard not to respond to the ideal of international solidarity. It was almost endemic to anarcho-syndicalism in any of its forms. Throughout the period dealt with, the necessity for international labor cooperation was accepted by unionists on both sides of the border. It was either accepted as a given, and therefore not even mentioned, or relegated to the realm of platitudinous oratory. This is understandable, for the ideal itself, separated from specific interests, becomes almost inoperative. Once the ideal is accepted as a good thing in itself, if the various organizations neither need nor want anything from each other, the demands of the ideal are easily satisfied by ritual exchanges of greetings and convention delegates and by membership in powerless international labor organizations.

Thus, although the ideal did play a role that varied in strength, depending on the individual labor leaders and the nature of their organizations, it was never strong enough in itself to sustain a close relationship between two labor organizations. More tangible benefits were needed to do that. It was around the possibilities of achieving practical benefits that the relationship between U.S. and Mexican labor movements waxed, waned, and waxed again in the period dealt with in this study. It is on them, therefore, that the study concentrates its attention.

The expression "practical benefits" does not merely refer to "bread-and-butter" issues, such as preventing the importation of strikebreakers, restricting immigration, and eliminating discrimination, which have directly affected workers' pocketbooks and have traditionally concerned unionists on both sides of the border. There also were benefits that the labor movements as a whole hoped to gain—in the case of the American labor movement, the protection of their back door against revolutionary unionism; in the case of both movements at different times, the hope of improving or retaining their positions in the power structures of their respective countries by demonstrating their usefulness to their governments in foreign affairs. This does not necessarily imply a form of labor imperialism, for it usually did not involve trying to influence the nature of labor unionism in the other country. More often, it involved attempting to demonstrate one's influence and importance to the government by drumming up the support of the labor movement of the other country for a particular government policy.

There was an interrelationship between the ideal of international labor solidarity and the practical benefits to be achieved from it. Aside from providing an ideological basis for cooperation by its universal acceptance as a good in itself, the idea of labor solidarity tended to lead labor organizations into overestimating the strength and influence of their united forces. Labor organizations on both sides of the border felt that in international labor relations one plus one equaled two-and-a-half, that the strength of two united labor organizations was greater than the sum of their strength taken individually. There was also an undercurrent of feeling that close relations with a foreign labor movement added strength to a labor group's domestic position. This was certainly valid if one was thinking of international working-class revolution, which, for the most part, unionists on both sides of the border were not. Despite having lost much of its relevance to Mexican-American labor relations, this myth persisted and exercised subtle influence. However, like the idea of the innate goodness of international labor cooperation as a whole, from which it was derived, this corollary was never strong enough in itself to sustain continued close contact among labor organizations on both sides of the border. Its effects were felt more by the Industrial Workers of the World (IWW) and the Mexican labor organizations, which had ingrained traditions of anarcho-syndicalism and Marxism, than by the American labor movement. In general, Mexican and American labor unionists tended to feel that international solidarity was a good thing, but more important were the practical benefits to be derived from it.

Before being relegated to the realm of rhetorical overlay, the ideal of international labor solidarity did play a role in Mexican-American labor relations. In its anarcho-syndicalist form, it provided the basis for the first major contacts between the labor movements of the two countries: the contacts between the IWW and the Mexican Liberal party.

Labor unions were prohibited in Mexico under the dictatorship of Porfirio Díaz, but the period just before his fall from power in 1910 saw various attempts to found them. The IWW, and especially its ideas, played an important role in these conflicts. The first, and most important, strike broke out early in 1906 in Cananea, a small mining town in the Sonora Desert, just across the border from Arizona. Cananea's proximity to American mining towns in southern Arizona, which at that time were rife with organizers for the newly founded IWW, made its labor force particularly receptive to IWW ideas. The Mexican miners organized and demanded various improvements in their miserable wages and working conditions. When the American-owned company dismissed their demands out of hand, 3,000 of them went out on strike.

The strike was led by a fusion of IWWs and members of the local Liberal Club, followers of Ricardo Flores Magón and Enrique Flores Magón, and IWW organizers who came down from Arizona and California to help keep it going. After a riot in which the two American managers and ten Mexican miners were killed, the governor of Sonora ordered Yaqui Indian troops of the Mexican Army to Cananea to help crush the strike and appealed for aid from across the border. A detachment of U.S. soldiers arrived, along with armed American miners from Arizona, recruited on the pretext that Mexicans were slaughtering Americans on the streets of Cananea. A short bloody battle with the virtually unarmed strikers ensued. Twenty strikers lay dead on the streets, and the strike was over.[1] The strike at Cananea failed to achieve its objectives, but it had provided an example of how the IWW and the Mexican Liberal party could work together—an example that would be followed four years later with the invasion of Lower California.

The Mexican Liberal party had been founded in St. Louis, Missouri, in September 1905, by Ricardo and Enrique Flores Magón, two exiled opponents of the Díaz regime who pubblished an anti-Díaz Spanish-language newspaper there. Throughout its short-lived existence, it remained almost wholly the creature of Ricardo Flores Magón, a brilliant intellectual revolutionary of the nineteenth-century European breed. The party's first manifesto, published on July 1, 1906, just one month after the Cananea strike, called for far-reaching social reforms such as lay education, better working conditions, and the distribution of untilled lands to the peasantry. But in general, it was more in the mold of nineteenth-century European liberalism than a far-reaching type of socialism.[2] This soon changed. By 1910, Magón had moved far to the left and had become a full-fledged libertarian anarchist during one of his frequent stints in prison.[3]

It was one of Magón's terms in an American prison that first drew Samuel Gompers, president of the AFL, into the involvement with Mexico and the Mexican Revolution that was to last the rest of his life. Magón and two other Liberal party leaders had been imprisoned by the U.S. government in 1907 as a preliminary to allowing the Mexican government to extradite and punish them for their revolutionary activities. By this time, they had moved their headquarters to Los Angeles, where they were able to arouse a powerful movement among Socialists and trade unionists to defend them against extradition. The defense movement succeeded in enlisting the aid of Gompers and soon reached national proportions.[4] Gompers had the 1908 AFL convention pass a resolution extending its sympathy toward the imprisoned three in their fight against extradition and pressured Congress to conduct an investigation of the persecution of Mexican political refugees in the United States. In 1910 a congressional committee got around to doing so.[5] Although the defense movement helped prevent their extradition, the three remained in a federal prison until the middle of 1910.

When the revolution against Díaz broke out on November 20, 1910, Magón and the Liberals organized an invasion of Lower California. In January 1911, they crossed the border and soon found themselves fighting both federal troops and troops who supported Francisco Indalecio Madero, the authentically "liberal" presidential candidate.[6]

The Magóns had maintained contacts with West Coast radicals and unionists and appealed for help. It was soon forthcoming, mainly from their old friends, the IWW.[7] In April 1911, Magón asked Gompers for aid. Gompers, suspicious of Magón's goals and friends, asked for a statement of aims. When Magón gave an evasive reply, Gompers promptly dropped the matter.[8] It is surprising that Gompers even went so far as to ask for a statement of aims. It was obvious by then that Magón was not simply the battler for a liberal welfare state that he had been in 1907. It was becoming clear that he was trying to set up a true anarchist state in Lower California.[9]

If Magón's anarchism was distasteful to Gompers, it was very appealing to West Coast IWWs. In response to his calls for aid, he soon had a motley battalion of IWWs and soldiers of fortune fighting alongside him. Some financial help also came from West Coast union locals and socialist groups, but it was not enough.[10] Ricardo Flores Magón's dream of bringing anarchism to Mexico and the IWW's hopes of setting up a "cooperative commonwealth" in Lower California [11] soon were ignominiously dashed by military might.

Cananea and the invasion of Lower California were both unsuccessful, but to anyone north of the border who had an interest in combating the IWW, there were lessons to be learned and storm warnings to be heeded. They showed the IWW's interest in organizing in Mexico and demonstrated their ability to do so. They also showed the natural affinity between the IWW and anarcho-syndicalist ideas that many Mexican radical intellectuals were moving toward.

The triumph of Madero in mid-1911 only served to heighten rather than allay these warnings. In the wave of union organization that followed the rescinding of the ban on labor unions, many IWW locals were founded in Mexico. Throughout the period 1911 to 1920, IWW locals were born and died in many parts of Mexico. Although many of them were ephemeral and their actual organizational connection with the IWW in the United States either tenuous or dubious, during this period of growth and flux in the Mexican labor movement there were always enough of them to worry AFL unionists in the United States. If Mexican unionism in this formative stage had moved left, rather than right, it would have moved further in the direction of anarcho-syndicalism and developed into at least a Mexican counterpart of the IWW. Until it was crushed during World War I, the IWW in the United States, weak as it was, represented the only real rival of the AFL. Samuel Gompers could certainly not look with equanimity upon the possibility of a strong ally of the IWW sitting just across the border.

NOTES

1. Luis F. Bustamante, "La Huelga de Cananea hace 28 años," *CROM*, July 1, 1934; Charles C. Cumberland, *The Mexican Revolution, Genesis Under Madero* (Austin: University of Texas Press, 1952), pp. 16–17; Jesús Silva Herzog, *Breve historia de la Revolución Mexicana* (Mexico: Fondo de Cultura Económica, 1960), I, pp. 45–49.

2. For the complete text of the program, see Francisco Naranjo, *Diccionario biográfico revolucionario* (Mexico: Imprenta Editorial Cosmos, 1935), pp. 249–263.

3. Alberto Morales Jiménez, *Hombres de la Revolución Mexicana* (Mexico: Instituto Nacional de Estudios Históricos de la Revolución Mexicana, 1960), pp. 11–13.

4. Grace H. Stimson, *The Rise of the Labor Movement in Los Angeles* (Berkeley and Los Angeles: University of California Press, 1955), p. 227.

5. Samuel Gompers, "United States–Mexico–Labor—Their Relations," *American Federationist* (August 1916): 637; American Federation of Labor, *Proceedings of the 28th Annual Convention, Celebrated in Denver, Colo., Nov. 9–21, 1908*, p. 153 (hereafter referred to as AFL, *Proceedings*).

6. Morales Jiménez, *Hombres de la Revolución*, p. 14.

7. Lowell Blaisdell, *Desert Revolution, Baja California, 1911* (Madison: University of Wisconsin Press, 1962), p. 41.

8. Ibid., p. 96.

9. Morales Jiménez, *Hombres de la Revolución*, p. 14.

10. U.S., Senate, Committee on Foreign Relations, *Investigation of Mexican Affairs*, S. Doc. 285, 66th Cong., 2d sess., 1919–1920, p. 2502.

11. *Industrial Worker*, June 8, 1911, in Blaisdell, *Desert Revolution*, p. 101.

2

The AFL
and La Casa del
Obrero Mundial

ASIDE FROM the rather prosaic threat of rival unionism gaining a foothold in Mexico, Samuel Gompers had other reasons for interesting himself in the course of affairs south of the border. As a boy, he had emigrated from England to New York, where he worked in a cigar shop and became involved in the cigarmakers' union. He rapidly rose to the leadership, which placed him in touch with Latin unionists among the cigarmakers of Tampa and Puerto Rico. This contact imbued in him a special interest in Latin America, which he frequently interpreted as a certain degree of expertise with regard to its affairs.

Also, Gompers in his younger years had flirted with socialism and its frequent concomitant in the later nineteenth century, an internationalist, humanitarian form of pacifism. By 1886, when he helped found the American Federation of Labor and became its first president, he had abandoned most of his socialist beliefs, replacing them with a firm belief in strictly "economic" trade-union action as the road to well-being for the working classes. The early years of the AFL, when the Socialists, who wanted the AFL to expand into "political" action (i.e., support for a socialist political party), emerged as his main rivals within the federation, served to strengthen Gompers's antisocialist tendencies. Although he had abandoned socialism, Gompers clung to its inherent internationalism and pacifism. He retained an interest in international affairs and did what he could to promote contacts and cooperation with the European trade-union movements. In this pursuit, he was severely hampered by his antisocialism, for the main organ for international trade-union contact was the Second International, which was also the organ for cooperation among the socialist parties affiliated with the European movements. They were usually much too far to the left for him, and he was much too far to the right for most of them. The only European labor movement to which Gompers developed relatively close ties before World War I was the British Trades Unions Congress, which, unlike the continental unions, was not Marxist, did not talk about "revolution," and was not excessively "political."

Thus Mexico, and the great revolution that broke out there, gave Gompers an opportunity to combine many activities. He could indulge his personal interest in Latin American affairs, work to promote liberty and democracy in a country that had just overthrown an oppressive dictatorship, strive for peaceful relations between the new governments and the United States, and aid the emergence of a trade-union movement in Mexico that would align itself with the AFL. Aside from closing the door to the IWW, this would help the AFL break out of the encirclement of Marxist unions in international labor affairs and provide Gompers with a stage upon which he could prove that he and the AFL still retained a deep commitment to the welfare of workers throughout the world—in other words, that "economic" unionism did not preclude international labor solidarity.

Before 1910, Gompers consistently opposed the Díaz dictatorship in Mexico, hoping for a liberal, democratic revolution. When the revolution erupted, he tried to peer through the clouds of dust and propaganda obscuring the various factions to decide which was the most liberal and democratic and worthy of AFL support. In early 1913, when Gen. Victoriano Huerta, an alcoholic right-winger, betrayed President Madero and led a successful coup against him, having Madero and his Vice President assassinated and setting up what was in fact a de facto government, there was no thought in AFL head-quarters in Washington of asking President Woodrow Wilson to recognize Huerta.

However, neither do there seem to have been any attempts during 1913 to place pressure upon Wilson to recognize Venustiano Carranza, who had emerged as the leader of the liberal opposition to Huerta, pronouncing against him in March 1913 and setting up a rival constitutional government in October 1913.[1] In November 1913, while Carranza and his supporters controlled a sizable part of Mexico, the AFL convention simply resolved against armed intervention in the conflict on the part of the U.S. government.[2] Although the resolution was aimed at the prointervention efforts of "American and foreign corporations and certain jingo newspapers,"[3] at that time it was much more likely that Wilson would intervene to depose Huerta than to support him.[4]

Part of the blame for Gompers' being a bit behind the times with regard to the situation in Mexico can be placed on Carranza and his agents in the United States. Although Carranza had so many agents in Washington in 1913 that they were interfering with one another,[5] there are no indications that any of them were in regular contact with Gompers, who could have been an influential voice on their side.

Carranza's failure to see the advantages that might accrue from labor support abroad is not surprising, for, at least until late 1914, he appears to have been unaware of, or wary of, the possibilities of drumming up labor support within Mexico. A stiff, pompous man from the north of Mexico, the Mexican extension of the American West, he displayed little insight into, or sympathy toward, the problems faced by the land-hungry peasants or urban workers of central Mexico. He usually had to be dragged into approving formulas that would improve their lot by military or political exigencies. In opposing Díaz and Huerta, Carranza had acted more as a rebel than as a revolutionary. In power, he was more like an old-fashioned *caudillo* than a man presiding over a vast social revolution. The only consistent political commitment that his career reveals is an intense nationalism, amounting to, if not xenophobia, then at least anti-Americanism.

Although he struck a temporary alliance with the fledgling Mexican labor movement in 1915, Carranza was always regarded with suspicion by most labor unionists. His contacts with labor leaders usually took place through intermediaries, people such as Gen. Álvaro Obregón, who had a greater appreciation of the value of a militant, if small, labor movement in a society in political flux. In the end, in 1919, Carranza discovered that the revolution could no longer be ridden by old-fashioned *caudillos* such as he. He was ousted and forced to flee to the hills, where he was hunted down and killed by the soldiers of the new-style "revolutionary" *caudillos*. These men, General Obregón and Gen. Plutarco Elias Calles, were also "Men of the North," but they had a much greater awareness of the problems of central Mexico. Most important, they displayed much greater finesse in manipulating both the rhetoric of the revolution and the new social forces it had given birth to. The labor movement was the most important of these.

Although there is no indication that Carranza ever asked him for his support, by mid-1914, when the Constitutionalist forces had defeated Huerta, Gompers felt that he was enough of a Carranza supporter to be able to proffer him advice on how to handle the situation in Mexico. In a letter to Rafael Zubaran Campmany, U.S. representative of the Mexican Constitutionalist government, Gompers asked Zubaran to tell Carranza of his support for the Constitutionalist government and his hopes for land reform and a declaration of mercy toward the defeated Huertistas. In his inimitable style, Gompers wrote:

> What I have in mind is, that since the American Federation of Labor, as no other instrumentality outside the government of the United States, has aided for the success of the prospective government, we have the right to suggest to those who represent General Carranza and the victorious revolutionary army that the higher humanitarian consideration be given, aye, even to those who have been guilty.[6]

There is no indication that Carranza ever bothered to answer this appeal. The Huertistas were shown as much mercy as any side usually showed the other throughout the Revolution, which was not much.

In November 1914, with the Constitutionalist front splitting apart and Carranza preparing to abandon Mexico City to the superior forces of Generals Francisco Villa and Emiliano Zapata, the AFL convention finally came out in support of the Carranza government.[7] The reasons for AFL support at this time are uncertain. However, convention resolutions were usually prepared some time in advance, which would indicate that the resolution probably was drafted when it seemed that Carranza had settled into power in Mexico City, before the rift between him and Villa and Zapata erupted into open warfare.

Until early 1915, in dealing with Mexico, Gompers and the AFL Executive Council were primarily dabblers. They were kibitzers at a poker game being played for very high stakes but had no stake in the game and little acquaintance with any of the participants. Occasionally, they voiced support or opposition to some of the participants and gave not-very-welcome advice. Although they ended up supporting Carranza, Carranza himself had little interest in their support. However, two of his aides, General Obregón and Rafael Zubaran Campmany, were more perceptive. It was the pact which they negotiated for Carranza with the Casa del Obrero Mundial (House of the World's Worker) that proved to be one of the decisive points of the struggle against Villa, a turning point in Mexican labor history, and the spur to the establishment of formal contacts between the Mexican and American labor movements.

Of all the local labor unions that the revolution of 1910 gave birth to, undoubtedly the most important was the Casa del Obrero Mundial. Founded by a group of foreign and Mexican left-wing intellectuals in 1912, the Casa was not a labor union in the American sense. It was a meeting ground for exchanging ideas and organizing concerted action by the individuals and local labor unions belonging to it. From its founding it was dominated by the anarcho-syndicalist beliefs that exiled Spanish intellectuals had brought to Latin America.

The guiding lights of the Casa were Bakunin and Proudhon rather than Marx. The general aim of the Casa was to organize the working class into unions and instill them with class consciousness. Once organized into revolutionary unions, the workers would be in a position to use their economic power (i.e., the general strike) to bring down the whole bourgeois capitalist economic and political structure and set up an anarcho-syndicalist state, based on ownership by workers of their places of employment. The ideological position of the Casa was basically antipolitical. Whereas Marx had urged the proletariat to organize into revolutionary political parties to take over the bourgeois state and set up the dictatorship of the proletariat, the Latin anarcho-syndicalists would have nothing to do with revolutionary political parties, or the thought of a centralized political structure of any kind. Instead, they placed their faith in revolutionary unions and the potential power of the general strike.

It was for this reason that from 1912 until 1915, in spite of

the political turbulence surrounding it, the Casa took no formal part in the Mexican Revolution. However, it tacitly supported Madero while he was in power—at least to the extent
of not being overly critical of him—and attacked Huerta in a
public meeting in Mexico City in 1913, a display of bravery
that met with the expected answer—the suppression of the
Casa. Its headquarters were confiscated, many members were
killed, imprisoned, or fined, and foreign members were deported. Still, until 1915 the Casa kept to its apolitical path,
looking upon the Mexican Revolution as essentially a bourgeois revolution with different *caudillos* engaged in another one
of their struggles over control of the capitalist state structure.
They refused to ally with any of the factions, preferring to
continue organizing the workers for the day when their time
would come.[8] The Casa, then, like the AFL, was against
"political" unionism. It was non-Marxist, but from a completely different vantage point. To the Mexican anarcho-
syndicalists, "economic" unionism was revolutionary unionism,
and the economic power of the workers was to be directed, not
to the extraction of "bread-and-butter" gains from the capitalists, but toward the overthrow of the capitalist system and
its replacement by a form of anarchist socialism.

By late 1914, with the division of the revolutionary camp into
factions supporting Carranza, Villa, and Zapata, the country
was in economic and social chaos. With the revolution itself
moving leftward, awakening more of the social and economic
aspirations of the lower classes with each passing day, it was
becoming almost impossible for the Casa to adhere to its policy
of not supporting any side and still continue to remain a relevant force among Mexican workers, who rapidly were taking
sides. It was also becoming obvious that, ironically perhaps,
only with the approval or support of a political power would
they be able to organize workers on a mass scale. Although at
first the Casa was almost evenly divided between supporting
Villa and Carranza, Carranza's decrees of December 1914 and

January 1915, promising legislation to improve the lot of the working classes, and some assiduous behind-the-scenes persuasion by his aide General Obregón, succeeded in swinging the Casa over into a formal alliance with Carranza.[9]

In February 1915 the negotiations were completed, and a formal pact was signed by representatives of the Casa and Zubaran Campmany, Carranza's representative. The agreement stipulated that the Casa would organize workers into "Red Battalions" to fight on Carranza's side. In return for this armed aid, Carranza's military officers were to help the Casa organize branches in newly conquered towns, and Carranza reiterated his promise of December to enact legislation to improve the lot of the workers.

An interesting aspect of the pact is that it included the first recognition by the Constitutionalists of the desirability of arousing sentiment for their cause by the "workers of the world," as they were known in those days. In the sixth clause of the pact, the Casa promised to propagandize among both Mexican and world labor to raise support for the Constitutionalist cause.[10]

The Casa kept its word and rapidly recruited six "Red Battalions," which soon were engaged in battles against Villa. In the areas occupied by the Constitutionalists, Casa leaders took advantage of the pact by organizing strikes for higher wages, shorter hours, and better working conditions. With the support of the local military commanders, these strikes were usually successful, and many workers were recruited into the branches of the Casa.[11]

It was in trying to carry out their agreement to swing foreign labor to the support of Carranza that the Casa had to face the reality of what they had given up by signing the pact. By agreeing to take part in a struggle for control of the bourgeois state, they had, in fact, abandoned revolutionary anarcho-syndicalism. Though they might still sympathize with it, their actions were now going completely contrary to it. If anything, they had now taken either a Marxist or a reformist path. According to Vicente Lombardo Toledano, the pact meant the end of "the thesis of the non-recognition of the juridicial order created by the *bourgeoisie* and the State created by it" in the ideology of Mexican unionism.[12]

Thus at the same time as the leaders of the Casa had contracted to establish contact with foreign labor movements, their own ideological base, and therefore the basis from which they would judge foreign labor organizations, had changed radically. This produced a conflict, one which was most apparent in attempting to decide which of the organizations north of the border they should ally with—the IWW or the AFL. Their previous course had run closely parallel to that of the IWW, and their sympathies naturally lay more with the Wobblies than with the reformist AFL, which seemed to have sold out completely to the capitalist system. However, they themselves had abandoned the IWW path and therefore should have had no compunctions about dealing with the AFL. This, plus the obvious fact that the AFL was strong and in a position to influence the U.S. government, whereas the IWW was weak and in no position to influence government policy, induced the Casa to jump at the first opportunity to establish contact with the AFL.[13]

The opportunity was not long in coming. Early in the spring of 1915, soon after the Casa-Carranza agreement was signed, two foreign correspondents arrived in Veracruz, headquarters of the *Carranzista* forces. One was George Bremond, the correspondent for *L'Humanité;* the other was John Murray, acting as correspondent for the *New York Call,* organ of the Socialist party of America.[14] Murray soon became a key man in promoting closer relations between the Mexican and American labor movements.

Murray was born in 1865 into the upper-class New York family for whom the Murray Hill section is named. In his youth, he had moved to Los Angeles because of the tuberculosis that was to plague him all his life. In the 1890s, supposedly after reading Tolstoy, he became interested in reform and was active in Los Angeles Socialist and trade-union circles. He was a member of the trade-unionist wing of the Socialist party and a strong proponent of cooperation between Socialists and the AFL.[15]

In his activities in left-wing circles, Murray had been involved in organizing Mexican workers and had become friendly with many local anti-Díaz Mexicans. Through Job Harriman, his friend and their lawyer, he met the Magón brothers in 1907. In 1908 he made a trip to Mexico with credentials supplied by them.[16] By 1915, he was again in the East, writing for the *Call*.

Before leaving for Mexico, Murray visited Gompers and discussed the possibility of his meeting Mexican labor leaders there. Gompers asked him to investigate the state of relations between the Casa and the Constitutionalist government, to express his sympathy for Mexican labor, and to explore the possibilities of entering into relations with them.[17]

Murray arrived in Veracruz, Carranza's headquarters. He made an excellent impression there, describing Gompers and his interest in Mexican labor in glowing terms, and succeeded in quelling a lot of the innate suspicion that the Casa leaders felt toward the AFL. He told them that Gompers, although opposed to the IWW, would do nothing irresponsible or underhanded in opposing them. He invited two members of the Casa to return with him to the United States on an information-gathering trip. The invitation was accepted, with Rosendo Salazar and Alejo Fernandez as appointed delegates, but the visit later had to be abandoned. In all, Murray spent close to three weeks in Mexico, establishing contacts with the Casa and familiarizing himself with the current labor and political situation. By the time he left, he had done much to change the attitude of the Casa concerning relations with the AFL from one of negative resignation to one of positive anticipation.[18]

The Casa leaders, in turn, had succeeded in convincing Murray of the prolabor nature of the Carranza government, and he returned to the United States determined that the AFL should put pressure on the U.S. government to recognize Carranza.

Upon his return to the United States, Murray, by now a partisan of a formal Mexican-American labor alliance, went to AFL headquarters in Washington to press his ideas on Gompers. There he met Santiago Iglesias, a veteran socialist who was the Puerto Rican organizer for the AFL. Iglesias had become convinced of the necessity for a formal Pan-American labor organization to counteract the recently formed Pan-American Financial Congress. Murray told him of the Casa-Carranza agreement and the possibility of establishing close relations with the Casa. The two succeeded in convincing Gompers that the AFL should enter into some kind of a formal alliance with the Mexican labor movement, and that he should urge the Wilson administration to recognize Carranza.[19]

Thus, by the spring of 1915, the stage had been set. The first contacts between the largest and most influential labor organizations in each country had been made, and both had agreed to the desirability of a closer relationship. Beyond this, however, there was little agreement and little that was clear on either side. It was clear that the Casa was interested in using Gompers and the AFL to help the Constitutionalist cause in the United States. It was also clear that Gompers and some of his advisers were interested in promoting closer relations with the Mexican labor movement. Beyond that, seeking to fathom the motivation behind AFL policy produces complexities.

On the one hand, Murray appears to have been motivated primarily by his old attachment to Mexico and the revolution. He saw in the revolution a chance to build a better life for the poor of Mexico, and naturally associated himself with it. As a socialist, he could hardly have been repelled by the increasingly left-wing path it appeared to be taking. With the rise of the Casa, he saw the chance to have the AFL help develop a strong socially oriented labor movement in Mexico. Perhaps he saw in the Casa an embodiment of what he himself had worked for in the United States—a labor union oriented not just toward helping its own members but toward fighting for the benefit of all the underprivileged of the community, in the political as well as the economic arena.

Santiago Iglesias, on the other hand, appears to have been inspired by a much broader vision, one encompassing all of Latin America. Like many others at the turn of the century, Iglesias was alarmed by the growing trend toward the "internationalization" of capital. This, of course, was a non-Leninist way of describing the prewar expansion of the investments of companies in the industrialized countries of Europe and North America into the underdeveloped countries of the world, often in the form of international cartels. In early 1915 this threat was magnified by the calling of the First Pan-American Financial Congress, a meeting of financial and industrial interests of the hemisphere, chosen by their governments, to outline plans for the development and regulation of the hemisphere's commerce. "Labor" was not represented, although it appeared obvious that decisions taken at the conference would affect labor in all of the countries of the hemisphere. Iglesias became convinced, and succeeded in convincing Gompers and the AFL Executive Council, that the only answer to this new Pan-American organization of capital was a Pan-American organization of labor. These arguments were incorporated in the report on Puerto Rico and Latin America given by Iglesias at the 1915 AFL convention and the report of the Executive Council at the same convention.[20]

There was a slight difference, however, in the recommendations of each report. Iglesias directly recommended the calling of a Pan-American Labor Conference, whereas the Executive Council merely asked for authorization to enter into correspondence to prepare for "action in concert" by the workers of the Americas for their mutual benefit. It did not specifically recommend the calling of an official labor conference.[21]

The Executive Council pointed out that a start had been made through the establishment of closer relations with the "Casa del Obrero Mundial, translated by one of its adherents as 'The Federation of Industrial Workers.' " [22] Apparently someone, either in the Casa or the Executive Council, was alert enough to realize that a literal translation of the Casa's name might arouse some consternation in the AFL.

The motives of Murray, Iglesias, and the Executive Council of the AFL were rather clear. Those of the man who would play the largest role in the affair, Gompers himself, were not at that time as clear and would come to light only with the passage of time.

In 1915 the first hesitant steps toward closer cooperation between the AFL and the Casa were taken through exchanges or correspondence.[23] Then in August 1915 a man claiming to be a representative of Mexican labor showed up at AFL headquarters. His name was Col. Edmundo Martínez, and he was to be more hindrance than help to the cause of Mexican-American labor unity. Although he was welcomed to AFL headquarters as the first authentic representative of Mexican labor to visit them, and indeed, he did have credentials proving his membership in a federation of unions called the Federación de Sindicatos Obreros de la República Mexicana, he was in reality acting more as one of Carranza's agents in the United States than as the representative of the union.

Martínez's first major request of Gompers was not particularly modest, but neither, for that matter, was Martínez. There were fears that President Woodrow Wilson again was about to send troops to Mexico, and Martínez asked that Gompers arrange an interview for him with President Wilson so that he, Martínez, could explain the Mexican situation to the President. Gompers immediately tried to comply. In a letter to

Wilson, he enclosed a copy of a pro-Carranza assessment of the situation in Mexico that Martínez had sent him and asked the President to grant Martínez an interview. Wilson replied that he had read the letter and given it serious thought, but that he could not grant Martínez an interview. This would mean opening the door to practically everybody who wished to see him about Mexico, and, in Wilson's words, their number was "Legion." [24]

Despite being denied a personal interview, Martínez was not easily deterred. Although Wilson had studied Martínez's analysis of the Mexican situation and said that he would consider it in his deliberations,[25] Martínez appears to have felt that what was needed was an assessment geared more toward what he believed were Wilson's own personal sensibilities. Thus, immediately upon receiving Wilson's refusal of an interview, he wrote a letter that he must have felt was sure to get to the President's soft spot—his well-known Presbyterianism. Martínez revealed another aspect of what was becoming a very multifaceted role. He now presented himself as a Protestant and a Mason. He wrote:

> Besides having been selected by the Mexican Federation of Labor as their spokesman in the United States, I was also sent by the Masons of that country to present the case as we think it really is. Also, I was entreated by the Evangelical (Protestant) Mexicans to try to secure for Mexico the same right other people have.

Carranza, he said, was fighting against the domination of Mexico by the Church of Rome. He was also fighting against the domination of Mexico by large corporations (Martínez had obviously heard of the Clayton Anti-Trust Act) and was the same to the Mexican people as Wilson was to the American people. Villa and Zapata he dismissed as "vile murderers." He ended with some praise of Gompers ("we think a good deal of him in Mexico") and returned to his original religious interpretation of the Mexican Revolution for what vaudevillians used to call the "big finish":

> If the people there think that we Evangelical people and Masons have been untrue to them, it will be years before we can build up our work again. . . . Let us have what we want, freedom of worship.[26]

Wilson appears to have been unmoved by this plea.

Gompers, however, was moved, or at least convinced that the United States should recognize the Carranza government. Whereas Gompers the year before had expressed this conviction merely in an AFL convention resolution, one among many, he was now becoming more involved in the Mexican question. He obtained the approval of the Executive Council of the AFL for a long personal letter to Wilson asking for recognition of Carranza. "Time has proved," he wrote, "that Carranza is really the representative of Mexican democracy—that he represents their efforts to establish a government of the people and for the people." [27] Wilson replied that the letter would "form a valuable part of [his] thought with regard to a very perplexing matter," and he hoped that they were near a solution of the difficulties with Mexico.[28] About three weeks later, the Wilson administration extended de facto recognition to the Carranza government.

How great a part Gompers's letter played in influencing Wilson to recognize Carranza is impossible to tell precisely. Wilson's most reliable biographer does not mention Gompers or his letter in his very detailed analysis of the tortuous process that Wilson went through in making the decision.[29] Even a cursory knowledge of Wilson's personal way of reaching foreign policy decisions would tend to make one agree that the omission of Gompers's role in influencing the decision was a justifiable one. Whether Wilson actually heeded Gompers's advice is uncertain. But the fact that he did recognize Carranza soon after Gompers had so recommended was, if nothing else, a fortunate coincidence, which Gompers subsequently exploited to great advantage in his relations with Mexican labor.

NOTES

1. Jesús Silva Herzog, *Breve história de la Revolución Mexicana* (Mexico: Fondo de Cultura Económica, 1960), II, p. 31; Howard F. Cline, *The United States and Mexico* (New York: Atheneum, 1963), p. 151.
2. AFL, *Proceedings,* 1913, p. 364.
3. Ibid.
4. Arthur S. Link, *Wilson: The New Freedom* (Princeton: Princeton University Press, 1956), pp. 365–377; Cline, *United States and Mexico,* pp. 149–150.
5. See Capt. S. G. Hopkins to Venustiano Carranza, May 18, 1913, in Isidro Fabela, ed., *Documentos históricos de la Revolución Mexicana: Revolución y régimen constitucionalista* (Mexico and Buenos Aires: Fondo de Cultura Económica, 1960–1962), I, p. 49.
6. Gompers to Zubaran, July 25, 1914, American Federation of Labor Collection, Files of the Office of the President, Samuel Gompers Papers, State Historical Society of Wisconsin (hereafter referred to as Gompers Papers, SHSW).
7. AFL, *Proceedings,* 1914, p. 364.
8. Rosendo Salazar, *La Casa del Obrero Mundial* (Mexico: Costa-Amic, 1962), passim; Marjorie R. Clark, *Organized Labor in Mexico* (Chapel Hill: University of North Carolina Press, 1934), pp. 23–28; Silva Herzog, *Breve história,* II, pp. 10–12; interview with Rosendo Salazar, former member of the Casa, Mexico City, Sept. 23, 1964.
9. Silva Herzog, *Breve historia,* II, pp. 138–139, 142–143; Clark, *Organized Labor,* pp. 26–30.
10. "Pacto celebrado entre la Revolución constitucionalista y la Casa del Obrero Mundial" in Silva Herzog, *Breve historia,* II, pp. 177–180.
11. Ibid., pp. 143–144; Clark, *Organized Labor,* p. 33.
12. Vicente Lombardo Toledano, *Teoría y Práctica del Movimiento Sindical* (Mexico: Editorial Magisterio, 1961), p. 53.
13. Interview with Rosendo Salazar, Mexico City, Sept. 23, 1964.
14. Salazar, *La Casa del Obrero Mundial,* p. 165.
15. Grace Stimson, *Rise of the Labor Movement in Los Angeles* (Berkeley: University of California Press, 1955), p. 226.
16. Mrs. Ethel B. Turner, unpublished sketch of her friend John Murray in Sinclair Snow, "The Pan-American Federation of Labor" (Ph.D. diss., University of Virginia, 1960), p. 7.

17. Interview with Rosendo Salazar, a host of Murray's on his trip, Mexico City, Sept. 23, 1964.

18. Ibid.; Salazar, *La Casa del Obrero Mundial,* p. 165.

19. Snow, "Pan-American Federation," pp. 10–12.

20. AFL, *Proceedings,* 1915, pp. 56–57, 187–188.

21. Ibid.

22. Ibid., p. 57.

23. Ibid.

24. Gompers to Wilson, Aug. 9, 1915, and Wilson to Gompers, Aug. 11, 1915, reproduced in Gompers to Carranza, March 18, 1916, copied letters of Samuel Gompers, confidential and official, AFL-CIO Head Office Building, Washington, D. C. (hereafter referred to as Gompers Confidential CB).

25. Gompers to Carranza, Mar. 18, 1916, Gompers Confidential CB.

26. Edmundo Martínez to Woodrow Wilson, Aug. 12, 1915, Gompers Papers, SHSW.

27. Gompers to Woodrow Wilson, Sept. 22, 1915, Gompers Confidential CB.

28. Wilson to Gompers, Sept. 24, 1915, Gompers Confidential CB.

29. Arthur Link, *Wilson: The Struggle for Neutrality 1914–1915* (Princeton: Princeton University Press, 1960), pp. 456–494, 629–644.

3

The Elaboration
of Motives

IF THE AFL's support of Carranza's Constitutionalists appeared
to be a wise move in late 1915, by early 1916 doubts as to its
wisdom were beginning to creep into AFL headquarters. Each
of the factions that had fought Díaz had included strong anti-
clerical elements, and the Constitutionalists were no exception. To a great extent, the Mexican Revolution had turned
into a revolution against the resurgence, under the Díaz dictatorship, of the social and economic power of the church, supposedly crushed forever by the Reform Laws of the 1860s. This
was aggravated by the church's active opposition to the revolution. As the conflict between the church and the Carranza
government became more violent, antirevolution newspapers in
the United States were quick to exploit it with stories of priests
massacred, nuns raped, and churches desecrated. A large part
of the Catholic church of North America rose in open wrath,
and the attacks upon Carranza increased in intensity and
stridency. As a public supporter of Carranza, the AFL came
under attack as well.

The rabid opposition of the Catholic church to one of the
AFL's policies was no mean fact for an organization with many

Catholic members. By March 1916, Gompers was sufficiently worried about the alarming reports from Mexico to go to Secretary of State Robert Lansing to request that the State Department acquiesce and, presumably, give financial aid to an AFL committee that would go to Mexico to find out exactly what was going on there. Lansing listened to Gompers but apparently refused State Department support.[1]

Gompers then wrote Carranza a long letter. In it, he made it clear that his support of the First Chief had not been entirely gratuitous, and that he felt it entitled him to a certain degree of influence in Mexico. He began with a long, nine-page recounting of his support of the revolution, complete with documentation. He recalled being shown the Casa-Carranza agreement and his subsequent support of Carranza. When, shortly thereafter, the U.S. government was contemplating armed intervention in Mexico, Colonel Martínez came to him as "possibly the last hope" that some influence could be exercised to dissuade Wilson from intervening. "All other avenues seemed to have been closed," wrote Gompers. He reproduced his letter to Wilson of August 9, requesting an interview for Martínez, and Wilson's reply refusing the interview but stating that he would take Martínez's letter into account. Then, in a neat little evasion of the rules of logic, Gompers concluded:

> I assume that it is not necessary for me to call attention to the fact that United States troops did not go into Mexico. Whether my communication had any relation to that fact is not necessary to state, or even to claim. You may draw your own conclusions as your judgment may direct.

He then pointed to his September letter to Wilson, urging recognition of Carranza, and Wilson's reply, stating that it would form a "valuable part of [his] thought." Again, he let Carranza draw his own conclusions.[2] The implications, of course, were obvious.

After thus demonstrating his right to demand an explanation of his policies from the President of Mexico, Gompers asked him to reply to the recent charges of Archbishop Cloutier of Quebec that Carranza and "the trio of bandits" [3] were "tyrannizing Mexico, pursuing the priests and martyrizing the sisters and causing death everywhere." He also asked Carranza to answer the charges frequently voiced in the United States that he was anti-American and that there was "anti-American feeling and propaganda" among his counselors. He urged that "if there be any basis of truth, however slight, for these statements and rumors it ought to be eliminated, frowned upon, and stamped out." [4]

If Gompers's letter smacked somewhat of presumption, it smacked even more of naïveté. It was one thing to imply that Carranza should do something about the killing of priests and nuns, for sometimes it was taking place with Carranza's approval, as when a group of antirevolutionary priests in Mexico City were impressed into the Carranzista forces and sent into battle. It was another thing to ask Carranza to stamp out anti-Americanism among his advisers. One of the major aims of the revolution had become the attempt to rid the country of foreign domination, and in this case, "foreign," above all, meant "American." Wilson's landing of troops in Veracruz, although originally intended as an anti-Huerta move, had not exactly been conducive to the development of "pro-American" feelings among the Constitutionalists, especially in view of the difficulties they experienced in getting Wilson to withdraw the troops. Neither could Gen. John J. Pershing's excursion into Mexico at the head of 6,000 U.S. troops in search of Pancho Villa be expected to quell any anti-American feeling among Carranza and his advisers. Pershing had crossed the border just twelve days before Gompers wrote his letter to Carranza. To ask Carranza to "stamp out" anti-Americanism from his cabinet was like asking him to "stamp out" his whole cabinet, including himself.

As Gompers awaited a reply from Carranza, pressure built up within the Executive Council itself. Frank Duffy, the head of the Carpenters' Union and an Irish Catholic, broke into open opposition against Gompers's Mexican policy. He began to barrage Gompers with letters on the subject. He forwarded a letter to him from a Rev. Francis Kelly, president of the Catholic Church Extension Society, which backed up Archbishop Cloutier's charges. Duffy had tried to mollify Kelly by saying that the choice had been one of Carranza or Villa, and that Carranza had been endorsed as the lesser of two evils, on the basis of reports that he was favorable to labor. However, he then wrote Gompers opposing the continued endorsement of Carranza. "Nothing that I know of," he said, "has stirred up such feelings generally against the American Federation of Labor as the action of the Council in endorsing Carranza as head of the Mexican government last year." He also pointed to the great harm the policy was doing to the AFL organizing campaign in Quebec, where Archbishop Martell was using the AFL's Mexican policy to prove to the faithful that it was anti-Catholic, atheistic, and anarchistic.[5]

While Duffy's charges poured in, Gompers was left with no ammunition to fire back in defense of Carranza. He was left waiting for a letter from Carranza. Finally, near the end of May, beginning to realize that it might never come, he turned elsewhere in the hope of getting some hard information. He wrote to Murray telling him that Carranza still hadn't answered the charges of anti-Catholicism and asked Murray and friends of his acquainted with the situation to write letters to him providing the information requested of Carranza.[6] The next day he wrote Martínez a similar letter.[7] Martínez happened to be going back to Mexico for a visit. Upon his return to Washington a month later, he delivered orally what he professed to be a reply from Carranza to the charges.

According to Martínez, Carranza said that he had never received Gompers's letter. However, after he, Martínez, had very forcefully presented the story of Gompers's achievements for Mexico, General Carranza "seemed visibly affected." He asked Martínez to take back a personal message of appreciation to Gompers and to tell him that

> if he had been surrounded by anti-American people in his cabinet he was unconscious of it, and just as soon as he became aware of any such persons around him they would be dismissed. So far as freedom of religion and toleration [were] concerned, he wanted Mr. Gompers to be sure that everything would be done to give perfect liberty in Mexico, equal rights and opportunities to all, but that there would be no special privileges given to any religion. Jews, Protestants and Catholics would all fare alike.[8]

The message, even if authentic, was not very useful to Gompers, but he was in no position to be choosy. He had Martínez write it out in the form of a letter to him. At least he would have something on paper. In the letter, Martínez embellished the message a bit and added a few details, saying that the Carranzistas were "Mexicans first, Catholics second" and that they were not anti-Catholic but were opposed to foreign priests and to the contravening by the church of the laws of the Reform of 1856–1857. He said they were not anti-American, but simply against foreigners who exploited them. They were not against "honest producers." [9] This was the closest Gompers ever came to receiving a reply to his letter from Carranza.

Gompers was becoming rapidly disillusioned with Carranza, but he had too much invested, in the form of the ill will the AFL had incurred by supporting him openly, to pull out now. The rough spring of 1916, however, had forced him to realize that the AFL was no longer dabbling in foreign charity work in Mexico. It now had a stake in the game, and Gompers was forced to think of what he hoped to win. The general outlines of his expectations emerged that spring and summer.

As Gompers waited for a reply from Carranza, the relationship between Carranza and his labor allies was rapidly deteriorating. The deterioration was caused by differences over the social and economic goals of the Revolution and the effects of uncontrolled inflation upon workers' wages. This had led in the spring of 1916 to a series of strikes that were forcibly suppressed by the Carranza government.[10] On May 22, 1916, the labor unions of the Federal District called a general strike to enforce their demands that they be paid in gold or its equivalent in paper money. The strike was immediately suppressed by the threat of military intervention.[11] The next day, Gompers sent a letter to the Casa asking for a conference in El Paso, Texas, between representatives of the AFL and representatives of the Casa and as many other Mexican labor organizations as possible. The official object of the meeting was described vaguely in terms of discussing matters affecting the mutual welfare of the labor organizations of the two countries and formulating plans for future cooperation.[12] However, in a letter sent simultaneously to Carranza informing him of the meeting, Gompers said that he felt that the meeting was desirable in view of information he had recently received about the course of events in Mexico.[13] The implication was obvious. The meeting would be an AFL expression of solidarity with the Mexican labor organizations in their developing struggle with Carranza. Implied was an AFL threat to repudiate Carranza.

By mid-June, Gompers appears to have lost most of his confidence in the Carranza government. The major question for the AFL in Washington had subtly changed from what was to be hoped for from the Mexican Revolution to what could be salvaged from it. The answer appeared obvious to Gompers: the labor movement. He had a conference on Mexico with John Murray and Judge Charles A. Douglas, a lawyer in close contact with Gompers about Mexico. Although he was Carranza's legal representative in Washington, Douglas was becoming increasingly exasperated with Carranza as well. Both Murray and Douglas agreed with Gompers that the labor movement was about the only worthwhile thing that had emerged from the revolution, and that it was the thing to be fostered.[14]

Once he had come around to this rather negative conclusion, Gompers was forced to start thinking in terms of the more positive gains he hoped for from the fledgling Mexican labor movement. He wrote an article for the *American Federationist* in which he discussed the benefits that the AFL would derive from the upcoming Mexican-American labor conference. In it he returned to Santiago Iglesias's plan for a Pan-American Federation of Labor, altering the objectives slightly. He wrote:

> And who knows, but out of that meeting may come a larger conference in which shall be represented the workers' organizations of all countries making up this great America of ours, a Pan-American Federation of Labor, that shall make not only this great power for internal and international right, justice and welfare, but shall help in the establishment of a broad international labor movement of the whole world, and that international parliament of man for which philosophers have dreamed and poets have sung, and which it is the mission of the workers to establish, shall be realized.

Although the international parliament of man did not become a primary objective of the AFL strategy from the conference, the Pan-American Federation of Labor did.

On a more practical level, and in more down-to-earth prose, Gompers pointed out the bread-and-butter benefits that would be derived from closer cooperation with Mexican labor:

> Those who know and understand the force of the industrial ties that unite Mexico and the United States know that there is no boundary line between the industrial problems of the workers of the two countries. This is not only because of the over-lapping of

the interests of the employers of the two countries but because of the intermingling and blending of the workers of the two countries.

He pointed to the two million Mexicans living in the United States and the many Mexican laborers and miners in the West and Southwest. They were notoriously hard to organize, and he needed only to allude to their existence to point to the possibility of help from Mexican unions in organizing them into AFL unions.[15]

Striking at one of the raw nerves of American unionists, Gompers also recalled some recent strikes in which employers brought in Mexican strikebreakers or threatened to do so. "There must be understanding and cooperation between the workers of Mexico and the United States," he wrote, "in order that neither may permit themselves to be used for the undoing of all." [16]

Thus Gompers had come up with a raison d'être for the conference that should have appealed to the sensibilities of all AFL members, from the most idealistic to the most practical. However, while Gompers was giving the above reasons for holding the conference to members of the AFL, his counterparts on the other side of the border were getting a completely different impression of its purposes. They believed that it was primarily to be a meeting to put pressure on their governments to head off a war between the two countries. To the Mexicans, it was clear which country was threatening to intervene militarily. U.S. troops were already encamped in Mexico and showed no signs of preparing for an early departure. Therefore, it was obvious to the Mexicans that the main purpose of the meeting would be to help the AFL pressure the Wilson administration into not invading Mexico and withdrawing Pershing and his troops.

They were given good grounds for believing this from the very first. Accompanying Gompers's invitation to the Casa to hold the conference was a letter from John Murray, which said:

If there is anything which can prevent war between our countries
it will be a frank declaration of the representatives of the workers'
organizations of these countries that they will not fight against
each other.[17]

Thus, when Dr. Atl, a Casa intellectual and editor of *Acción
Mundial,* the most influential Mexican labor newspaper, accepted Gompers's invitation to attend, he wrote that he en-
thusiastically accepted the offer of a conference to unify labor
in the two countries to prevent war.[18] Two days later the Casa
and the Confederación de Sindicatos Obreros del Distrito
Federal, a federation of most of the important trade unions
in the Federal District, which was closely tied to the Casa,
wired their acceptance of the invitation.[19]

When he issued the invitation, Gompers had not set a date
for the proposed conference. The course of outside events,
however, soon set the date by itself.

June was a month of crisis in Mexican-American relations.
Charles Evans Hughes, the Republican presidential nominee,
was attacking Wilson's Mexican policy, and Gompers and his
associates feared that this would drive Wilson into drastic,
bellicose action.[20] On June 15, an attack on a Texas town by
Mexican irregulars and an American threat of retaliation set
the war machinery going on both sides.[21] The Mexicans were
worried as well. Assuming that the labor conference was intended to stop the clash that seemed to be impending between
the two countries, four days after the labor organizations had
wired their acceptance of the idea of a conference, they wired
again that they wanted the conference to be held in Eagle Pass,
Texas, on June 25, just nine days later.[22] Given the vicissitudes
of train travel in Mexico in those days, this meant that their
delegates would be leaving almost immediately.

The Mexicans arrived at Eagle Pass on June 23, two days
after the El Carrizal skirmish between Pershing's forces and the
Carranzistas, in which twelve American soldiers were killed and

twenty-three were captured. War between the two countries seemed imminent. The week before, Wilson had called up the National Guard.[23] In Eagle Pass, the Mexicans found no AFL delegation waiting to meet them. Dr. Atl and Luis Morones wired Gompers in Washington asking for a conference as quickly as possible, in view of the imminent danger of war. Unfortunately, the Executive Council of the AFL was scheduled to meet in Washington the next day, and Gompers felt that he could not go to Texas. He spoke with Judge Douglas about the situation, and they decided that Gompers should invite the Mexicans to send a delegation to Washington, where they could also meet the members of the Executive Council. Douglas said that he would arrange for the Carranza government to pay their expenses and telegraphed them urging them to come.[24] Atl and Morones replied that they would send a sub-delegation to Washington to arrange for a time and place for a full-fledged conference.[25]

Meanwhile, if the Mexicans assumed that Gompers was in favor of the withdrawal of Pershing's "Punitive Expedition" and would back them strongly in this rather obvious means of reducing the tension between the two countries, they were wrong. As far as is known, Gompers had never publicly or privately opposed the expedition. When, on June 21, Judge Charles A. Douglas approached him with a plan for the withdrawal of Pershing's troops to the border and the formation there of a neutral zone, Gompers expressed doubt about the wisdom of the withdrawal. He feared that it might be interpreted by the Mexicans as an act of weakness on the part of the United States and "provoke aggression" on their part. It was a rather groundless fear, and Douglas finally succeeded in persuading him to present the plan to President Wilson.[26] Gompers arranged a meeting with Wilson for the next day, but that night the shooting at El Carrizal took place. The next day, before he went to see the President, Gompers met with Douglas, Murray, and two Mexican labor men who had just arrived

from Yucatán. Gompers and Douglas agreed that in view of
the events of the previous night they could not at once ask
Wilson to implement Douglas's plan for immediate withdrawal. They agreed that the only concrete proposal that could
be made at the time was that the whole matter be submitted
to arbitration by neutral countries or to a joint commission of
the representatives of two countries, as provided for in the
Treaty of Guadalupe-Hidalgo of 1848.[27]

In his conference with Wilson, Gompers made both suggestions, offering the first only for possible use in the future.
He said that he realized that it was inapplicable at that
moment. As for the suggestion of mediation of the dispute,
Gompers told Wilson that Douglas had telegraphed Carranza
suggesting that he ask for mediation. Wilson replied "That is
very good," and said that they could rest assured that if such
a message were received it would be given "most serious
consideration." [28]

With Wilson giving the impression of being very conciliatory, Douglas sent Carranza a message saying that any suggestion for arbitration of the matter would be received with favor
by Wilson.[29] Carranza replied that "every offer to adjust matters would be looked upon with favor by the people of Mexico,"
a reply which, more than anything else, indicated that he was
working through other, more regular, channels. The next day,
the Bolivian minister in Washington unofficially suggested
Pan-American mediation of the dispute, and the following day
this suggestion was accepted "in principle" by the Mexican
ambassador in Washington. Secretary of State Robert Lansing
immediately told reporters that the offer would not be accepted
even if made.[30] Lansing then received Wilson's approval of a
memorandum stating that the El Carrizal incident was not
a subject open to mediation of any kind.[31]

The day after Gompers's reassuring meeting with Wilson,
Secretary of Labor William Wilson assured Murray and
Martínez that the President would not be driven into any

impetuous action over the incident. Secretary of War Newton D. Baker gave Murray's friend the journalist Lincoln Steffens assurances of the same kind.[32] Thus a certain amount of calm confidence in the President's ardent desire to avoid war over the issue reigned in AFL headquarters. A few days later, Murray outlined the tack he planned to take with the Mexican labor delegation when it arrived: he would make it clear that the projected conference was to be, not a peace conference, but a labor conference.[33] Unbeknown to all concerned, Wilson the day before had begun to draft a bellicose message to Congress that amounted to withdrawal of recognition of the Carranza government. If delivered, it probably would have led to war.[34]

One of the main points of contention in the El Carrizal incident was that Carranza's forces were holding the twenty-three American soldiers taken prisoner in the battle. Their release would help to ease tensions, and Douglas persuaded Gompers to send Carranza a telegram asking him to free them.[35] Gompers did this, asking Carranza to release the men "in the name of common justice and humanity" and in the interest of understanding and peace between the two countries.[36] However, before the message could have reached Carranza, he had already ordered the release of the prisoners.[37] News of the release reached Washington that evening.[38] The next day, Carranza sent Gompers a telegram saying simply that he had ordered the release of the prisoners.[39] Coming as they did, the two telegrams together could be interpreted to mean that Carranza had released the prisoners at Gompers's behest. Gompers was not averse to interpreting the events in this fashion in the following years.

Carranza's release of the prisoners and the vast amount of mail that poured into the White House opposing war with Mexico succeeded in deflecting Wilson from his warlike path. Instead of the "war message" he had prepared to send to Congress, Wilson delivered a moving, conciliatory speech that made it clear that he would not go to war with Mexico.[40] By the time the Mexican labor delegates arrived in Washington early in the morning of July 1, the threat of war had passed, and Gompers, presumably unaware of Wilson's original message to Congress, drafted after their meeting, could rest assured that he had helped to abate the tension.

NOTES

1. Memorandum, Mar. 14, 1916, Gompers Papers, SHSW.
2. Gompers to Carranza, Mar. 18, 1916, Gompers Papers, SHSW.
3. Presumably a reference to Villa, Zapata,. and Carranza together.
4. Gompers to Carranza, Mar. 18, 1916, Gompers Papers, SHSW.
5. Kelly to Duffy, Apr. 10, 1916; Duffy to Kelly, Apr. 14, 1916; Duffy to Gompers, Apr. 14, 20, May 2, 1916: all Gompers Papers, SHSW.
6. Gompers to Murray, May 26, 1916, Gompers Papers, SHSW.
7. Gompers to Martínez, May 27, 1916, Gompers Papers, SHSW.
8. Florence C. Thorne (Gompers's secretary), memorandum, June 26, 1916, Gompers Papers, SHSW.
9. Martínez to Gompers, June 27, 1916, Gompers Papers, SHSW.
10. Jesús Silva Herzog, *Breve historia de la Revolución Mexicana* (Mexico: Fondo de Cultura Económica, 1960), II, pp. 197–198; Marjorie Clark, *Organized Labor in Mexico* (Chapel Hill: The University of North Carolina Press, 1934), pp. 37–41.
11. Clark, *Organized Labor*, p. 41.
12. Gompers to Casa, May 23, 1916, Gompers Papers, SHSW.
13. Gompers to Carranza, May 23, 1916; U.S., Department of State, *Papers Relating to Mexico: 1910–1929, Relations with the United States* (hereafter referred to as State Department Papers), 812.504/54.
14. Florence C. Thorne to Gompers, memorandum, June 16, 1916, Gompers Papers, SHSW.
15. This was one of the favorite ideas of John Murray, who was involved in the United Mine Workers' attempt to organize Mexican miners in the Southwest, and it is likely that Gompers picked this up from him. See Murray to Gompers, June 8, 1916, Gompers Papers, SHSW.
16. Samuel Gompers, "Liberty's Hope is in Thy Keeping, Organized Labor," *American Federationist* (July 1916): 575.
17. Rosendo Salazar, *La Casa del Obrero Mundial* (Mexico: Costa-Amic, 1962), p. 227.
18. Dr. Atl to Gompers, June 9, 1916, Gompers Papers, SHSW. Dr. Atl's real name was Gerard Murillo. He subsequently became one of Mexico's most famous painters, known especially for his paintings of live volcanoes, to one of which he eventually lost a leg.

19. Casa and Confederación de Sindicatos Obreros to Gompers, June 11, 1916, Gompers Papers, SHSW.

20. Florence C. Thorne, memorandum, June 12, 1916, Gompers Confidential CB.

21. Arthur S. Link, *Wilson* (Princeton: Princeton University Press, 1964), IV, p. 299.

22. Confederación de Sindicatos Obreros and Casa to Gompers, June 16, 1916, Gompers Confidential CB.

23. Link, *Wilson,* IV, p. 301.

24. Florence C. Thorne, memorandum, June 24, 1916, Gompers Papers, SHSW.

25. Thorne, memorandum, June 26, 1916.

26. Florence C. Thorne, memorandum, June 21, 1916, Gompers Papers, SHSW.

27. Ibid., June 22, 1916, Gompers Papers, SHSW.

28. Ibid.

29. Florence C. Thorne, memorandum, June 23, 1916, Gompers Papers, SHSW.

30. Link, *Wilson,* IV, p. 311.

31. Ibid.

32. John Murray, memorandum, June 24, 1916, Gompers Papers, SHSW.

33. Florence C. Thorne, memorandum, June 27, 1916, Gompers Papers, SHSW.

34. Link, *Wilson,* IV, pp. 312–314.

35. Florence C. Thorne, memorandum, June 28, 1916, Gompers Papers, SHSW.

36. Gompers to Carranza, June 28, 1916, in AFL, *Proceedings,* 1916, p. 68.

37. Link, *Wilson,* IV, p. 314; Charles William Toth, "The Pan-American Federation of Labor" (Master's thesis, University of Illinois, 1947), p. 37.

38. Link, *Wilson,* IV, p. 314.

39. Carranza to Gompers, June 29, 1916, Gompers Papers, SHSW.

40. Link, *Wilson,* IV, pp. 314–318.

4

The AFL Changes Course

THE TWENTY Mexican labor men in Eagle Pass had chosen Luis Morones and Salvador González García, both members of the Casa, as their delegates to Washington.[1] Dr. Atl came to Washington as well, but he was on a diplomatic assignment for the Carranza government and could not attend the labor conference. Gompers did not meet him until Lincoln Steffens brought him to Gompers's office some days after the labor conference had ended.[2] Upon their arrival in Washington, besides the ever-present Martínez, the delegates found Carlos Loveira and Baltasar Pages, two labor aides of Socialist Gov. Salvador Alvarado of Yucatán, awaiting them as well. Thus, a reasonable semblance of a joint conference could be held.

The letter of credentials with which Governor Alvarado had provided Loveira and Pages is illustrative of the importance that many Mexican left-wingers attached to the idea of international working-class support for their cause—not only as an ideal, but as something which would aid the Revolution. He said that the object of the excursion was twofold. First, it was to help in the formation of the proposed Pan-American Federation of Labor. At the same time, the trip was intended to move public opinion in favor of our cause, which, in the opinion of our laborers, and he who is signing this, is the cause of international Socialism.

It is certain that if the Mexican revolution does not receive the support that can be given it by the radical elements abroad, socialists, freethinkers, syndicalists, etc., it is because its true program and revolutionary character are not known.[3]

Thus Loveira and Pages had not only been sent to the United States, but they were to tour Latin America as well. In the United States, Gompers was not the only "representative of the working class" with whom they met. They also met with Eugene Debs, the leader of the Socialist party of America,[4] and it is likely that they were in contact with members of the IWW.[5]

The conference between the representatives of the labor movements of the two countries lasted for three days and could be considered a mixed success. Without fuller representation of the Mexicans, it was almost impossible to achieve anything in regard to the more practical, bread-and-butter objectives that Gompers had outlined for the conference, and these were abandoned. However, some progress was made by each side toward the achievement of its main objectives. A "joint declaration" was issued calling for the convocation of another conference, in which the workers of both countries would be more fully represented, to formulate plans for maintaining permanent relations between the labor movements of the two countries and for the establishment of a Pan-American Federation of Labor.

This appeared to satisfy the AFL's desires to start on the formation of the PAFL. However, citing the deplorable state of Mexican-American relations as the reason, the declaration judged such a conference to be untimely for the moment, and it was agreed that it should be deferred until later in the year. To satisfy the Mexicans, with their fear of imminent attack by the United States and their confidence in the ability of the labor movements of the two countries to do something about it, a joint committee, consisting of two representatives from each labor movement, was to stay in Washington. It had the power to convene the conference at any time to avert an international crisis.[6] As its one concrete recommendation for the solution of the differences between the two countries, the conference urged the establishment of a joint commission of "high-minded citizens, fully representative of our nations," to investigate the problems and make recommendations for their settlement.[7] It soon became obvious that, among the "high-minded" and "fully representative" citizens, Gompers expected there to be representatives of the labor movements of the two countries, or, at least, of the AFL. This was the seed of an idea that was subsequently to grow greatly in importance for Gompers.

The idea of labor representation on official and semiofficial government commissions emerged again shortly after the conference, when Gompers wrote a statement calling for the formation of the PAFL for Loveira and Pages to take with them on their trip to Latin America. Gompers pointed to the economic High Commission that had just toured Latin America to improve commercial relations and deplored the lack of labor representation on it. He urged the Latin American labor movements to press their governments for labor representation on it.[8] Until then, the AFL had merely accepted the absence of labor representation on these semiofficial commissions and had turned to the idea of a PAFL as a counterweight to them. Now the AFL, although still pressing for the creation of a PAFL, was trying to get representatives on the commissions as well. If Latin American countries appointed labor representatives to these commissions, the Wilson administration would find it difficult indeed to refuse to do the same.

Gompers sent Wilson a copy of the joint declaration of the labor conference, and Wilson's short reply perhaps reflected an awareness of what Gompers would be pressing for. Wilson said that he was pleased to see the workers of the two countries get together, but that he entirely agreed that it would not be wise to hold a general conference at that time.[9] He did not mention the suggestion of the declaration for a joint commission, even though at that moment he was working out plans for a mixed Mexican-American commission to settle the differences between the two countries.[10] Perhaps he knew Gompers well enough to know that mention of Gompers's suggestion would enable Gompers to claim some credit for the commission's formation and provide him with ammunition for a demand for labor representation on it.

Still, when news of the proposed joint commission leaked out a few days later, Gompers was not to be deterred. He immediately wrote to his main channel to the cabinet, Secretary of Labor William B. Wilson, a longtime AFL man, saying that, in view of the importance of organized labor in Mexico and the close ties between the two labor movements, labor should be represented on the commission.[11] Gompers sent the letter to the Secretary of Labor on the understanding that he would show it to the President. He also had his private secretary phone William B. Wilson and tell him that he, Gompers, was "under no circumstances . . . to be considered for the Commission, but, of course, would be pleased to be consulted in re-thereto." He told his other secretary that this meant that he "ought to be consulted about but not appointed on the Commission." [12] Gompers then came up with an idea that must have appeared clever at the time. Two days later, he wrote directly to President Wilson. He mentioned that he had already written urging that a joint commission with labor representation be set up to inquire into the causes of the friction.[13] He now urged that the representative of organized labor on the commission be William B. Wilson.[14]

The ploy was an obvious one. By appointing the Secretary of Labor to the commission, President Wilson would, on the surface, be merely appointing a cabinet member to it. From the way plans for the commission were shaping up, this would be perfectly normal.[15] However, because Gompers had specifically asked that the Secretary of Labor be appointed as the representative of organized labor, his appointment could be used by Gompers as a precedent for claiming the right to have labor representation on many government bodies that actually had much more to do with labor.

Woodrow Wilson must have seen what Gompers was aiming at. Secretary Wilson's qualifications were none too impressive, especially for a delicate mission in international affairs, and it was obvious that his appointment would be more the result of his ties with the AFL than of any of his more innate qualities. The President answered Gompers with a simple reply stating that unfortunately the proposed commission would be too small to be "representative." [16]

Gompers remained undeterred. Soon after he received Wilson's reply, Murray told Gompers of a rumor that the Mexican members of the Commission would be Luis Cabrera and two other conservative Carranzistas, and that the American commissioners "would also be of the reactionary type." He suggested that Gompers write to the President urging that the commission be enlarged.[17] Gompers, of course, was not averse to that idea. He again wrote Wilson and, emphasizing the importance of labor in both countries and their role in averting a crisis, suggested the enlargement of the commission, implying, obviously, that it should be enlarged with representatives of labor.[18] Wilson replied that he appreciated Gompers's point, but that at present the main obstacle was Carranza's refusal to grant the commission "sufficient scope and power to do any comprehensive work." (Carranza refused to have it discuss anything but the immediate withdrawal of Pershing's forces.) Gompers then telegraphed Carranza asking him to expand the scope of the commission, but there is no indication that a reply was ever received.[19]

The commission eventually got under way, in its original six-man form, without the benefit of labor representation. But this unsuccessful beginning was merely a start in Gompers's quest for a voice for labor in government commissions. With the passage of time, and with a deepening commitment on the part of Gompers to first the Wilson administration and then the war, Gompers's efforts eventually bore some fruit. In the meantime, he continued pressing the idea at every opportunity. He had found another use for his ties with Mexican labor. His special position with regard to Mexican labor and the importance of organized labor in Mexico were now being used by Gompers as a means of gaining entry for the AFL into the charmed circle of government in Washington.

It is somewhat ironic that at the same time Gompers was beginning to take the AFL along a more "political" path, he was continually advising the Mexicans to direct their unions along "economic" lines and, like the AFL, eschew political organizations and politicians.[20] In a letter to the Confederación de Sindicatos Obreros de la República Mexicana, Gompers gave a detailed outline of the way they should structure their union. It amounted to an exact replica of the organizational scheme of the AFL, even down to recommending that the unskilled be organized into trade unions (as opposed to industrial unions) and that politicians be excluded from city central labor unions.[21] When Gompers advocated "economic" rather than "political" organization for Mexican labor unions, the implication was that, like the AFL, the federation should devote itself to improving the lot of its workers and use the strike as a weapon in collective bargaining with employers for concessions, and not, like the IWW and the anarcho-syndicalists, use the strike as a weapon for changing the political-economic structure of the whole society.

Aside from the normal problems aroused by translation from one language to another, Gompers's suggestions must have appeared particularly strange to those Mexicans who bothered to examine them. To Mexicans, the terms "political" and "economic" applied to labor action were almost exactly opposite in meaning as they were to Gompers. As has been shown with regard to the Casa, to the Mexican labor men, "economic" organization meant anarcho-syndicalism, and "political" organization meant the reformist path they were now embarked upon.

Still, to the Mexicans, what was important was not what Gompers recommended *they* do but what *he* could do for them. Thus, upon the return of the Casa delegation from the United States, even many of the open IWW supporters in the Casa supported the idea of closer ties with the AFL. In the discussion that took place at the Casa upon the return of Morones, José Barragan Hernàndez reflected this attitude. He said:

> Gompers doesn't protect the purity of the ideals of the working class, he lives surrounded by economic comforts, but the old leader can be of use to us, so that Mexican *obrerismo* can open the way for the Industrial Workers of the World.[22]

If the Mexicans had any trouble understanding Gompers, he must have had much more trouble understanding them. His suggestions that they form replicas of the AFL and stay out of politics betray a great lack of understanding of the Mexican political and economic scene. For the fledgling Mexican unions, staying out of politics meant annihilation. It was only from politicians and the government that they could get aid in organizing workers. If they incurred the wrath of the government, there was nothing to stop their being closed down. They simply did not have the power to "go it alone." The tiny proportion of the population who were urban workers did not provide them with even a potentially large enough power base to allow them to think of trying to organize an independent locus of power capable of confronting and withstanding the power of the government. The Casa-Carranza agreement was an admission of this situation, and the subsequent history of Mexican unionism bore it out.

Adding to Gompers's difficulties in trying to understand what was happening in Mexico was the dearth of sources of concrete and true information. Colonel Martínez, who was a frequent visitor to Gompers's office and who was, until July 1916, the only Mexican with whom Gompers was in close contact, did not help matters. He prepared the ground for the July conference by describing the Casa as "anarchists, impossibilists, and the IWW of Mexico," vilifying Dr. Atl and Luis Morones and, for good measure, characterizing General Obregón as rash and impetuous.[23]

Soon after the conference was over, three men arrived at Gompers's office with a letter from Martínez introducing them as representatives of the Federación de Sindicatos Obreros de la República Mexicana, the organization that he was supposedly representing in Washington. While they were waiting outside Gompers's office, they were asked to prepare a list of all of the organizations that were affiliated with their federation. The list contained names of about 500 organizations. They stated that their organization contained affiliated unions with a total membership of about 500,000. They also claimed that their organization was the only national labor organization in Mexico.[24]

Gompers appears to have at least partially believed them. He wrote to Chester Wright saying that they "unquestionably represent a promising bona fide labor movement. They brought lists of over 500 labor organizations affiliated together in the Federación."[25] A little over a week later, in a letter to Frank Duffy, he said, "Authentic information is given me that not less than 250,000 trade unionists are already organized under the Confederación de Sindicatos Obreros de la República Mexicana."[26] Apparently even Gompers balked a bit at the figure 500,000. After all, the AFL at that time had less than 2 million members.

As for the real size and strength of the organization, it is difficult to tell from this vantage point, years after it had disappeared, along with many others, into the graveyard of revolutionary labor organizations. The confusion in AFL headquarters over the exact names of the many similar-sounding Mexican organizations adds to the difficulties. However, it is likely that Martínez's credentials were from an organization in the city of Veracruz, which, in spite of its ambitious title, not only did not succeed in expanding into the rest of the republic but never even succeeded in becoming the dominant organization in Veracruz itself.[27]

The three delegates, on the other hand, appear to have had credentials from an organization set up by a workers' congress held in Veracruz in March 1916 in an unsuccessful attempt to unify the labor movement. According to one of the most reliable historians of the labor movement of Mexico, the congress "was sterile of results," and the organization it created "never functioned in any way." [28] Murray and Florence Thorne, Gompers's secretary, later found out that the Mexican labor representatives who had gone to the border for the joint conference had rejected the credentials of the three men from Veracruz and that they had come to Washington on their own. They took the opportunity of their meeting with Gompers to denigrate the power of the Casa and describe it as anarchistic.[29]

Martínez was not the only one providing Gompers with a steady flow of misinformation and imposters. At times during the month of July, Gompers must have felt as if he were sitting in the midst of a three-ring circus. Near the end of the month, just as the real status of Martínez's three protégés was being cleared up, Arthur T. Flood, the AFL organizer in Chicago, arranged for Gompers to meet with a man named A. A. Ravola who claimed to be a representative of the organized workers of the state of Sonora. After expounding for a while on the childlike nature of Mexican workers, Ravola was pressed for information about the organized labor movement. It turned out that he really did not know much about the labor movement and actually was not a representative of the labor movement but a newspaperman.[30] Never one to admit defeat, at least in front of others, Gompers wrote Flood: "It was quite apparent that in addition to being a representative of organized labor, Ravallo was a government man. . . . However, this is but additional proof of the strength of the labor movement." [31]

The lack of a direct channel of responsible information about the labor movement of Mexico seriously hampered Gompers throughout the fall of 1916, when it appeared that Carranza was trying to crush the labor movement. Carranza had managed to suppress the threatened general strike over inflation in May, but the inflation continued over the summer. Finally, at the end of July, the Casa and the unions of the Federal District launched another, better organized, general strike to demand payment of wages in specie or its equivalent in paper money. The strike began on July 31 and for a short time was effective. Carranza responded by arresting the leaders, closing down the Casa and ejecting it from the building that the government had given it.[32]

The next day, he revived an obscure old antibandit law and decreed the death penalty for all those who attempted to foment or participate in a strike in any "factories or enterprises destined for public service." [33] By the following day, the strike had collapsed. With its headquarters closed and many of its leaders in prison, and having earned the open antipathy of the government, the Casa started a decline from which it never recovered.

Meanwhile, the ban on strikes continued in force, and Gompers tried to get it rescinded. He went to see the Mexican and American peace commissioners who were meeting in Atlantic City. Luis Cabrera, one of Carranza's top labor aides, was one of the Mexican commissioners, and Gompers took the opportunity to protest Carranza's no-strike decree to them. The Mexicans replied that Carranza was still prolabor, but that the strike was not over working conditions but for payment in specie—an impossibility—and was intended to overthrow the government. They pointed out, also, that only one labor leader had been sentenced to death. Gompers was not swayed by these persuasive arguments and stuck to his guns.[34]

Later, John Murray went to Atlantic City and spoke to Cabrera. Murray threatened that the matter would be brought up at the upcoming AFL convention in Baltimore. Cabrera tried to justify the decree on the ground that it was necessary for the public welfare. He said that it was really a form of martial law and would be withdrawn as soon as possible. He again reaffirmed Carranza's friendliness to labor.[35]

The matter was brought up at the AFL convention, but in a way that did not really put the Carranza government in a bad light. The report of the International Relations Committee noted that Gompers had protested to the Mexican representatives and gave a summary of their explanation, as follows:

> An order for a general strike had been issued by irresponsible, and at that time unknown, parties and demands made for conditions impossible to be conceded. . . . The government's representatives in Mexico sought in vain to have a conference with the persons who called the strike for the purpose of reaching an adjustment, but . . . no representative of any of the workers, organized or unorganized, responded.[36]

This latter statement was a lie. Not only did the members of the strike committee respond to Carranza's call for a meeting with him when the strike broke out, but at the meeting, when they refused to call off the strike, he had them all arrested.[37]

Still, despite the watered-down version presented to the convention, it was agreed that efforts to obtain the revocation or modification of the decree should continue.[38] Although there is no indication that the AFL did anything further about the matter, Carranza revoked the decree sometime later.

Again Gompers was hampered by the lack of direct information from Mexico. The AFL had that summer invited the Mexicans to send representatives to the Baltimore convention to give firsthand information about the labor situation in Mexico, but the invitations had never been answered. John Murray lamented that the convention's sole source of firsthand information about the situation had thus been cut off, and he suspected the Carranza government of doing it.[39] Given the deterioration of relations between Carranza and labor, he had every reason to suspect this. There is no indication in available Mexican sources that the invitations were ever even received.

Meanwhile, throughout the fall of 1916, Gompers had other, more pressing matters to deal with. The most important of these was the threat of United States involvement in the war in Europe and the AFL's policy towards this.

It was a presidential election year, and Wilson, although doubtful of his ability to keep the United States out of war, was forced by political reality to run on a "He Kept Us Out of War" platform. At the same time he had been pressing a "preparedness" campaign to put the nation on a more warlike footing. The issue of "preparedness" cut across party lines, and Wilson met with strong opposition on it from within his own party. Any influential support he could garner for it was greatly appreciated.

Until the outbreak of the war in Europe, Gompers had been a confirmed pacificist. Although in later years he claimed that the outbreak of the war itself caused him to immediately abandon pacifism, it appears more likely that, along with many other Americans, he became gradually convinced, in the ensuing year and a half, that American entry in the war was inevitable. In January 1916 he made his first public pronouncement in favor of "preparedness." Later in the year, when Wilson had Congress create a powerful Council of National Defense to put the economy on an efficient war footing, Gompers was appointed as the representative of "labor" on its Advisory Commission, the body that did most of the actual work.[40]

Gompers's acceptance of this important post represented a major public departure from his traditional emphasis on the separation of labor and government. However, it is easy to see how he was not at all reluctant to accept it. It gave the AFL a strong voice in shaping the wartime economy. This would be useful in two ways: it would protect AFL unions from harm in the reorganization of the economy and the distribution of government contracts, and it could serve as a base for the expansion of the AFL's power and membership. By joining the administration, Gompers put himself in an excellent position to use the power of the federal government to support the expansion of the AFL. In spite of his traditional protestations that the labor movement must remain independent of politics and government, Gompers was not loath to use the power of his new position to promote the expansion of the AFL. This he did with considerable success.[41] It is hard to recall Gompers's previous attempts to have the principle of labor representation on government commissions accepted without thinking that this must have been among his objectives all along. By throwing his support to Wilson on a crucial issue at a crucial time, Gompers succeeded in achieving his objective to an extent that must have been beyond even his greatest hopes a few months earlier.

Gompers had to pay a price for his newly acquired power. The price was the almost total submission of the AFL to the foreign policy of the Wilson administration. The AFL now willingly became another tool for the administration to use in constructing what started out as "defense" policy and soon became "war" policy. In international affairs, this meant that in its relations with foreign labor movements, the narrow interests of the AFL itself were now completely subordinate to the interests of the defense and war efforts. This became clear almost immediately with regard to relations with the Mexican labor movement.

Soon after Gompers joined the Council of National Defense, he asked for and received the approval of the AFL convention in Baltimore for the creation of a Pan-American Federation of Labor Conference Committee, which would try to arrange a Pan-American labor conference to create a hemispheric labor organization. Gompers was the chairman of the committee, John Murray was secretary, and Santiago Iglesias and Carlos Loveira represented the organized workers of Puerto Rico and Yucatán respectively.[42] The first meeting of the committee was held in the AFL building in Washington on January 31, 1917, with the above four present. A manifesto urging the labor movements of other Latin American countries to send delegates to be members of the committee was drawn up and sent out.[43] The results were disappointing. In August of that year, Edmundo Martínez joined the committee as the representative of his ephemeral organization.[44] By that time, however, he had been appointed Mexican consul in Chicago, and he could attend few of the Washington meetings.[45] Also, somewhere along the line, a Cuban and a Chilean had been dredged up to lend their names to the committee, but they contributed little more than that to it.[46]

In an article in the *American Federationist,* Gompers was quite explicit about the reasons for his revived interest in the PAFL. He wrote:

> The movement was not a matter of premeditation grown out of years of desire of the workers of this hemisphere to form a PAFL and a closer alliance of all Pan-American countries, but had its origin in the developments of the past two-and-a-half years as manifested in the European conflict.[47]

It is also interesting to note that one of the objectives of the

PAFL had now become to form a "closer alliance of all Pan-American *countries.*" Presumably, they were to be allied in support of U.S. foreign policy.

Gompers soon became occupied with other aspects of the war effort, and Santiago Iglesias had to return to Puerto Rico. This left the bulk of the committee's promotional work to John Murray and Carlos Loveira. In the summer of 1917, Murray had to go to Arizona because of a strike of Mexican miners there. This left Loveira alone in Washington. He worked on there until December 1917, when he was recalled to Yucatán.[48] When he left, the committee quietly expired.

The failure of the committee to drum up support in Latin America is not surprising. In the first place, with the exception of Mexico, organized labor in the Latin American countries amounted to almost nothing. In general, labor organizations south of Mexico usually consisted of small groups of intellectuals with no effective unions behind them, or of ephemeral organizations that would spring up to conduct a strike and disappear when the strike was broken. Also, most of the Latin American countries were still too overwhelmingly agricultural to have developed a significant class of urban workers. Those who tried to organize unions had to start with a very small potential base. Laborers in agriculture and the extractive industries were generally poor prospects for organization. They were too much at the mercy of their employers, who had the military power of the governments behind them. It was apparent from the start that any Pan-American Federation of Labor, in spite of its impressive title, would be essentially a Mexican-American labor organization.

Thus, for getting Latin American participation, everything depended upon the Mexicans. However, with the suppression of the Casa, there was no national organization that could claim to be at all representative of organized labor in Mexico. The Mexican labor movement now consisted of hundreds of local unions. There were some national organizations that stretched further than the bounds of one locality, such as the Railway Workers Union, and some local federations of labor that were capable of uniting different unions into common fronts, such as the federation in the Federal District, but there was nothing even faintly resembling a national federation of unions. Without one, it would be impossible for the AFL to enter into a meaningful official relationship with the Mexican labor movement. The bureaucratic obstacles alone would have proved insurmountable. The Mexican-American labor alliance would have to remain in abeyance until a real national federation of unions emerged in Mexico.

NOTES

1. Samuel Gompers, "The U.S.–Mexico–Labor—Their Relations," *American Federationist* (August 1916): 642.

2. Memorandum, July 7, 1916, Gompers Papers, SHSW.

3. John Murray, "Behind the Drums of Revolution," *Survey* 37 (Dec. 2, 1916): 239.

4. Ibid.

5. See Florence C. Thorne, memorandum, July 7, 1916, Gompers Papers, SHSW.

6. "Mexican-American Compact, July 3, 1916," in AFL, *Proceedings*, 1916, pp. 59–60.

7. Ibid.

8. Gompers to the Workers of All American Countries, July 6, 1916, Gompers Papers, SHSW.

9. Wilson to Gompers, July 6, 1916, Papers of Woodrow Wilson, Library of Congress (hereafter referred to as Wilson Papers), File IV, Box 142.

10. Howard F. Cline, *The United States and Mexico* (New York: Athenum, 1963), p. 182.

11. Gompers to William B. Wilson, June 10, 1916, Gompers Papers SHSW.

12. Gompers to Florence Thorne, June 12, 1916, and Gompers to R. Lee Guard, June 12, 1916, Gompers Papers, SHSW.

13. This was apparently a reference to the Joint Declaration of the Labor Conference, which had asked for a "fully representative" commission. Gompers's more recent letter had been addressed to the Secretary of Labor.

14. Gompers to Woodrow Wilson, July 14, 1916, Gompers Papers, SHSW.
15. Indeed, Secretary of War Baker was eventually appointed to it by Wilson.
16. Wilson to Gompers, July 19, 1916, Wilson Papers, File VI, Box 186.
17. Florence C. Thorne, memorandum, July 31, 1916, Gompers Papers, SHSW.
18. Gompers to Woodrow Wilson, July 23, 1916, Gompers Papers, SHSW.
19. Thorne, memorandum, July 31, 1916.
20. See Gompers to Governor Alvarado of Yucatán, July 18, 1916; Gompers to Confederación de Sindicatos Obreros de la República Mexicana, July 18, 1916, Gompers Papers SHSW.
21. Ibid.
22. Rosendo Salazar, *La Casa del Obrero Mundial* (Mexico: Costa-Amic, 1962), p. 229.
23. Florence C. Thorne, memoranda, June 24, 26, 1916, Gompers Papers, SHSW.
24. Thorne, memorandum, July 31, 1916.
25. Gompers to Chester Wright, July 21, 1916, Gompers Papers, SHSW.
26. Gompers to Frank Duffy, July 21, 1916, Gompers Papers, SHSW.
27. Marjorie Clark, *Organized Labor in Mexico* (Chapel Hill: The University of North Carolina Press, 1934), pp. 11–12.
28. Ibid., p. 56.
29. Thorne, memorandum, July 31, 1916.
30. Ibid.
31. Gompers to Flood, July 31, 1916, Gompers Confidential CB. The AFL people referred to him as Ravallo or Rovallo. Later, they learned his name was A. A. Ravola, an associate of General Adolfo de la Huerta in Sonora. A. A. Ravola to Gompers, Nov. 17, 1916, State Department Papers, 812.504/72.
32. The old Jockey Club, known as the House of Tiles, now a refuge for Americans as part of the Sanborn's chain of drugstore–restaurant–gift shops.
33. Clark, *Organized Labor,* pp. 41–42; Murray, "Drums of Revolution"; Rosendo Salazar y José G. Escobedo, *Las pugnas de la gleba, 1907–1922* (Mexico: Editorial Avante, 1923), pp. 205–207; Jesús Silva Herzog, *Breve história de la Revolución Mexicana* (Mexico: Fondo de Cultura Económica, 1960), pp. 204–205.
34. Samuel Gompers, memorandum, Oct. 12, 1916, Gompers Papers, SHSW.
35. John Murray, memorandum, Nov. 21, 1916, Gompers Papers, SHSW.
36. AFL, *Proceedings,* 1916, p. 64.
37. Clark, *Organized Labor,* pp. 41–42.
38. AFL, *Proceedings,* 1916, p. 64.
39. Murray, memorandum, Nov. 21, 1916.
40. Samuel Gompers, *Seventy Years of Life and Labor* (New York: E. P. Dutton & Co., 1925), pp. 322–352.

41. Leo Wolman, *Ebb and Flow in Trade Unionism* (New York: National Bureau of Economic Research, 1936), pp. 23–24.

42. "Manifesto of the Pan-American Federation of Labor Conference Committee," Feb. 9, 1917, Gompers Papers, SHSW.

43. AFL, *Proceedings,* 1917, p. 63.

44. Ibid., p. 64.

45. Gompers to Woodrow Wilson, July 16, 1917, Gompers Confidential CB.

46. Sinclair Snow, "The Pan-American Federation of Labor" (Ph.D. diss., University of Virginia, 1960), p. 46.

47. Samuel Gompers "To Pan-Americanize Labor," *American Federationist* 24 (Mar. 1917): 208–209.

48. Snow, "Pan-American Federation," p. 52.

5

The Revival
of the Mexican-American
Labor Alliance

THE HOPES FOR a Mexican-American labor alliance and a Pan-American Federation of Labor had been allowed to slumber during the latter part of 1917 and early 1918. However, in early 1918, events in the United States and Mexico soon reawakened and reinvigorated them. The major stimulant was the growing uneasiness in Washington over Mexico's neutrality in the war, the feeling that it was pro-German neutrality. At the same time, in Mexico, the semblance of a national labor organization seemed finally to be emerging.

Fear of pro-German influence in Mexico had been rife in the Wilson administration for some time before the United States officially entered the war. It had reached near-panic proportions in early 1917 with the publication of the Zimmerman note, a German proposal for a Mexican-German alliance in the event of American entry into the war. Less than two weeks after the United States entered the war, Secretary of State Robert Lansing told Wilson that he expected a Mexican ultimatum demanding the withdrawal of American ships from Tampico, the oil-production center, which would lead to war. He recommended that the United States occupy Tampico and the Atlantic-Pacific railroad across the Isthmus of Tehuantepec.[1]

The Germans saw Mexico as a weak spot in the defenses of the United States and flooded it with propaganda. They secretly bought newspapers in Mexico. The American propaganda agency, the Committee on Public Information, set up a branch in Mexico, but its efforts seemed paltry in comparison to those of the Germans. The Germans had a much easier job. They had inherent anti-Americanism to work with, and little anti-Germanism to work against. All of this, plus Carranza's attitude of stiff neutrality, caused jitters in Washington. Every innocuous sign of diplomatic courtesy shown to the Germans by Carranza was often interpreted in Washington as a sign that he was at least going to allow the Germans to set up bases in Mexico and at worst declare war on the United States. Thus when, in the spring of 1918, Carranza cabled greetings to the Kaiser on the occasion of his birthday, grave worries were aroused in Washington and among pro-Americans in Mexico.

Judge Charles A. Douglas went to Mexico City and had a talk with Carranza, telling him that it had been a grave error, that many of his friends thought that he was too friendly to the Germans. Douglas tried to get Carranza to abandon neutrality and enter the war on the side of the Allies, but to no avail.[2]

Upon his return to Washington, Douglas suggested to Gompers that the Pan-American Federation of Labor be created. He felt that it would be welcomed by Carranza. He also suggested that a commission of labor men be sent to Mexico to drum up support for such an organization.[3] Given the context, it is obvious that Douglas intended the commission be used as an instrument for persuading Mexico to enter the war on the side of the Allies.

When the matter was presented to him in this light, Gompers's interest in the PAFL quickly revived. Douglas wrote a complete report of his visit, and Gompers immediately sent it to Wilson. He wrote a covering letter pointing out the use that the PAFL could be with regard to the Mexican question and suggesting that the government underwrite a U.S.–Mexican labor meeting.[4] He also took immediate steps to prepare the proposed labor commission to Mexico. He appointed John Murray to head it and obtained letters of introduction for Murray from General Obregón, who was in Washington at that time, to friends of Obregón who would be sympathetic to the proposed alliance.[5]

Carranza could look upon the proposed alliance with a certain amount of equanimity, for he was in the process of sponsoring a national confederation of trade unions which he expected would be subservient to the government. At his behest, on March 22, the governor of Coahuila had invited all the labor organizations of the country to a congress, to be held in Saltillo, the capital, to form the long-awaited national confederation. Carranza hoped to form a confederation that would be resistant to the influence of the Casa and give him control over at least a part of the organized labor movement. He was doomed to failure. On May 1, 1918, the opening day of the congress, unionists representing every shade of radical opinion showed up, and, as is traditional with left-wing groups throughout the Western world, each ideological group aspired to control the congress. After the smoke had cleared and the usual walkouts had occurred, one thing was clear: the organization that emerged from the din was not controlled by Carranza.[6]

The new organization was called the Confederación Regional Obrera Mexicana (Mexican Regional Workers Confederation), which was subsequently known as CROM in Mexico and the Mexican Federation of Labor in the United States. The official title is significant. The unions that were members of the new organization represented wildly different ideologies, and the first program of the new confederation was somewhat of a left-wing mishmash. But the overall influence of anarcho-syndicalism still remained a potent force. The word "regional" in the name meant that the organized labor movement of Mexico was to be the Mexican section of the world labor movement, which to those at the congress still meant the anarchist movement. Also, the organization adopted as its official motto an old anarcho-syndicalist slogan, "Salud y Revolución Social" ("Health and Social Revolution," which sounds more like a toast than a revolutionary motto).[7]

However, in spite of the free use of anarchist jargon, the formation of the CROM actually meant the death of anarcho-syndicalism in Mexico. In place of the "direct action" of anarchism, it advocated "multiple action"—which meant the combined use of the strike, to obtain better working conditions from the employers, and direct political action, in the manner of the unions of Britain—to achieve a change in the whole socioeconomic system.[8] One year later, the political arm of the CROM was founded, and its title, the Partido Laborista de México, shows the influence of the Labour party of Britain.[9]

The man elected to head the Central Committee of CROM, Luis Morones, was a twenty-eight-year-old labor leader from the Federal District who would become the dominant figure in the Mexican labor movement in the 1920s and one of the most powerful men in Mexico. To Americans who were horrified by events in Mexico, he became the symbol of Mexican "bolshevism." To his opponents within Mexico, he became the symbol of the corruption of the new political élite that had grown out of the revolution. During the 1920s, when he became corpulent and rather degenerate-looking, with his fat fingers enlaced in diamond rings, when lurid rumors of the Nero-like debauches he held in his country home flashed through Mexico City, Morones fit the latter stereotype more than the former. However, in 1918, he was still young enough, and almost lean enough, to be thought of as a true, relatively incorruptible leader of the working classes.

Certainly, his working-class pedigree was rather impressive. Born in Tlalpan, a poor suburb of Mexico City at that time, of working-class parents, he attended primary school and then went to work in a local electrical company. He became a mechanic for the British-owned Mexican Light and Power Company and soon rose to foreman of the company's repair shop. When Madero began his agitation, Morones began to speak out for him and liberalism and soon achieved renown as an orator. When the Madero revolution erupted, he became a member of the Casa and began to work at organizing unions. He helped form the Union of Electricians and Workers of the Mexican Telephone Company and was elected its first secretary-general. In the first flush of the Carranza–Casa alliance, when Carranza took over Mexico City, Morones was made manager of the telephone company, but when the Casa rebelled against Carranza in 1916, he was one of the labor leaders imprisoned and sentenced to death by Carranza.

He and all but one of the other leaders were released from jail after sixteen days, but Morones was out of a job. Luckily, in late 1916, the small town of Pachuca elected an old friend of his as municipal president, and the friend appointed Morones secretary of the Municipal Council. From this base, over the next two years, he reestablished his contacts with labor leaders in the Federal District and formed a group called the Grupo Acción, gradually drawing other important labor leaders, such as Ricardo Treviño of the IWW of Tampico, into it. When the Workers Congress at Saltillo was announced, they decided that they would emerge from it with control of a national labor organization. This they succeeded in doing.[10]

The Federation of Unions of the Federal District had remained aloof from the congress because of its connections with the Carranza government, but some unionists from the Federal District, headed by Morones, had attended. When, with the election of Morones, it appeared that the unionists from the Federal District had gained control of the organization, the adhesion of the federation of the Federal District became just a matter of time, in spite of its recently adopted anarcho-syndicalist program abjuring all political action. Meanwhile, relations between CROM and the federation had grown close, and the American labor commissioners, soon to arrive in Mexico, would at least be able to deal with two major organizations that together could claim to represent a large proportion of the country's organized workers.

While preparations for the trip of the commissioners were being made, Gompers was awaiting the reaction of Wilson to the new plan. After a week of waiting, he wrote to the President's secretary, Joseph Tumulty, that although the President probably did not deem it necessary to reply, he would like a word from him as to his views on the subject. Wilson told Tumulty that he had not answered because he could not make up his mind about it.[11] Clearly, Wilson was not too anxious to have Gompers embark upon a new bout of labor diplomacy in Mexico, especially if the U.S. government was to be implicated in any way. Finally, on May 7, a week before the commission was to leave, Wilson wrote Gompers that he had decided against any official government participation in a U.S.-Mexican labor meeting.[12] Thus, the labor commission would have to go as just what it pretended to be, a delegation from the AFL alone. This had been intended all along, although Gompers had intimated that government financial help to defray the expenses of the trip would be welcome. As for the conference that the commissioners were supposed to promote, Wilson's letter ruled out overt government support, but as subsequent events would show, it did not rule out covert financial support.

The commission to Mexico was composed of Murray, Santiago Iglesias, and James Lord, the head of the AFL's mining department. Following a long tradition in diplomacy, it had two sets of aims: one public and one secret. The ostensible aims of the commissioners, as outlined in the credentials given the commissioners by Gompers, were of the usual general nature, with emphasis on achieving better understanding between the two countries, bettering working conditions, and forming the PAFL. As bait for the Mexicans, one of the objectives was to lay the groundwork for the negotiation of an agreement for the mutual acceptance of union cards.[13]

However, the real purpose of this mission was to use the Mexican labor movement to force Carranza to abandon neutrality.[14] That this was the real aim of the mission was evident from the start, in the circumstances that gave rise to its formation.

When Murray, Lord, and Iglesias arrived in Mexico City, they found the Mexican unionists well on their guard. Immediately upon their arrival, in one of the milder reactions to their visit, the left-wing newspaper *El Pueblo* said that it was not clear exactly what the intentions of the three were, but that Mexican workers should be on the alert not to be taken in by "false doctrines" and abandon neutrality in the war.[15] Murray later complained that they were continually attacked by the "pro-German" press, which charged that they were there to entice Mexico into the war on the Allied side. He said that only the one pro-Allied paper, *Excelsior,* gave an accurate account of their visit.[16]

The commissioners succeeded in arranging for two public meetings. The first, on May 29, was with delegates from the powerful Federación de Sindicatos Obreros del Distrito Federal at its headquarters. The second was a mass meeting held at the Teatro Ideal four days later.[17]

At the first meeting, with the room packed with representatives of the Federal District unions, the American delegates presented their official credentials and outlined their ostensible aims. Then Luis Morones rose and asked for permission to speak against the propositions of the Americans. He said that, in spite of the denials of the Americans, there was indeed a political purpose behind them. He charged that Lord and

Murray were active in a prowar organization called La Defensa Social de los Estados Unidos (he might have been referring to one of the subdivisions of the Councils of National Defense), the former as president and the latter as secretary. He said that he feared that the American workers were prevented from making a social pact with the workers of Mexico by the present world conflict, which was of no concern to the Mexican workers, who placed their hopes for improvement in the labor struggle.

Iglesias tried to refute Morones's charges. He said that as delegates of the AFL they did not have the authority or the right to interfere in the internal or external affairs of Mexico. "We are not in any way preaching war," he said, "because only the working masses of Mexico can do that." He pointed out that the proposals that the Americans had presented in no way affected Mexican government policy. He ended with the warning that, with the increased movement of capital from the United States to Mexico, it would be necessary for the Mexican labor movement to be able to count on the support of its comrades in the United States in its struggle to defend its rights. The meeting then adjourned, with the Mexicans promising to study the proposition and let their decision be known at a later date.[18]

The Mexican unionists were still discussing the propositions when the next mass meeting was held at the Teatro Ideal. This was an all-American show, and Iglesias was the main speaker. Again he reaffirmed the mission's completely nonpolitical nature and vehemently denied the rumors that had been circulating through the capital to the effect that the real intention of the mission was to swing the Mexican proletariat behind the Allied cause. "Our mission is very much more noble and much higher," he said. He spoke of the necessity for closer cooperation, which the proximity of the two countries imposed upon their workers, and the benefits that would ensue. Then, in a clever stroke, presumably to show that he was not a reactionary intent on selling out the workers, he said some good words about socialism. His emphasis was not upon the nationalization of industry but rather upon worker participation in politics and government. He used as his examples the gains made through participation in public affairs by the workers of Australia and Puerto Rico. According to *Excelsior,* the speech made a very good impression on the audience. It must have, for Iglesias disposed of the omnipresent question from the floor about the persecution of the IWW in the United States by saying that it was much too complicated to go into then and there, and that, anyway, it was a question that concerned only the United States.[19] That this answer did not lead to riot is proof that Iglesias must have made at least a half-decent impression.

The invitation of the AFL met with serious opposition within the CROM and the Federación of the Federal District. Aside from the usual complaints that the AFL was a reactionary union, which worked hand-in-hand with the American capitalists and supported the forcible suppression of the Wobblies by the U.S. government, protests were made against allying with an organization that supported the government of a country that treated the Mexicans within its borders as second-class citizens.[20] However, the issue of the maltreatment of Mexicans in the United States proved to be a two-edged sword, for it was argued that through establishing closer relations with the AFL the Mexican unionists might be able to do something for their compatriots north of the border. After all, many AFL unions in the West and Southwest, who refused to admit Mexicans to membership, were among the leading offenders. The same could be argued on the issue of the suppression of the IWW. Few Mexican unionists, sympathetic to the IWW or not, condoned this suppression, and many were quite aroused about it. Some, such as Morones, saw the possibility of using the AFL to do something about it, whereas others, such as the Tampico local of the IWW did not. These two issues—the maltreatment of Mexicans in the United States and the persecution of the IWW—became the major motives for those Mexicans who accepted the idea of a joint conference.

Five days after Iglesias's speech, the CROM and the Federación were ready with an answer to the American propositions. The two organizations gave essentially the same reply. They approved of the proposals for an interchange of union cards and protection of immigrant workers. But because of the present world situation and the fear of entering into relations in the international field that might "hinder their freedom of action in the political field," they were not inclined to enter into an official alliance at that moment. However, they would try to send observers to the upcoming St. Paul convention of the AFL to collect information and, if the circumstances permitted, would be prepared to attend an international conference held on the U.S.–Mexican frontier. The answers were very vague and even contradictory because they represented an amalgam of three different answers that had been presented at a meeting of the Federación three days earlier, all of which accepted the AFL proposals in principle but not for the present.[21] Still, to the Americans, the important thing was that they had been given a qualified green light for arranging a conference. They had only to beware of moving too fast. That the Mexican reply, in spite of its vagueness, was a green light was put into relief by the fact that it led to the withdrawal of the IWW local in Tampico from CROM.[22]

Within a month, CROM and the Federación had agreed to Laredo, Texas, as a proper site for the proposed conference. Gompers and his aides immediately began working on the arrangements. The first order of business appears to have been to get the U.S. government to covertly underwrite the expenses of the proposed conference. Gompers promptly invited three key men who could be of great use in obtaining government assistance to his office to hear the secret report that the American labor commissioners had prepared upon their return from

Mexico. The men were Felix Frankfurter, an important member of the War Industries Board who was acting as an official administration liaison officer with labor; George Creel, head of the Committee on Public Information, the government propaganda agency; and Secretary of Labor William B. Wilson.[23]

The three approved the idea of a joint conference. It was decided that Gompers should go directly to Wilson and ask for an appropriation of secret funds with which to carry it out. The question of funds was an important one, for by this time the idea of the conference had been expanded to include using it as a platform for prowar propaganda. Gompers now wanted to use the opportunity as an occasion for setting up a prowar Pan-American labor newspaper for distribution throughout Mexico. This explains Creel's presence at the meeting.[24]

Gompers made an appointment with President Wilson and presented his propositions. Wilson agreed to give the money to subsidize additional propaganda in Latin America but insisted that it be done openly.[25] At a cabinet meeting the next day, Wilson explained his reasons for this. In his diary, Secretary of the Navy Josephus Daniels noted these down:

> Cabinet. Gompers wanted to buy certain Mexican papers to help make favorable sentiment to Americans. WW No. [Woodrow Wilson said no.] Labor had helped Carranza and Carranza had turned on union labor. Instead of helping, a subsidized paper, making propaganda, reacted. Witness German use of money to buy papers and writers.[26]

The German use of money to buy papers had indeed backfired in many places, especially in the United States, but Wilson's insistence upon having the government openly support the conference and the newspaper with funds would have led to certain disaster. It is hard to see how the Mexicans would have even attended the conference if it had been openly paid for by the American government.

Within a week, Wilson was persuaded that the only way in which the paper could be aided was covertly. Creel's committee began to underwrite the costs of the proposed *Pan-American Labor Press*. In a letter of introduction to Bernard Baruch, the head of the War Industries Board, written for Murray and Chester Wright, who were to be the joint editors of the paper, Creel asked Baruch to aid them in every way possible, explaining that "money for the venture comes from the Government and in every respect it is a Government proposition."[27] The money was given to the editors through an organization called the American Alliance for Labor and Democracy.[28]

The American Alliance for Labor and Democracy was an organization set up by Gompers, prowar unionists, and defectors from the antiwar Socialist party of America to combat antiwar sentiment among American workers and Socialists. It was supposed to have been an independent organization sustained by contributions from its members. Indeed, it appears that at the beginning Gompers, who was the president of the alliance, and other members did contribute some money from their own pockets.[29] However, Gompers soon went to Creel and offered to place the organization at his disposal. Creel's committee would naturally also defray the expenses involved. Creel responded with alacrity, promising to support Gompers in his attempt to "Americanize" the labor movement on the condition that the campaign be run by organized labor itself. He suggested that the first objective of the campaign be the Lower East Side of New York City and that an office be secured there and a director hired.[30] From the time the alliance office was first set up, it was under the supervision and direction of George Creel, and the bulk of its budget was supplied by his committee.[31] Mainly for public appearances, a public appeal for funds was made, and Gompers himself contributed one hundred dollars.[32]

By July 1918, just before the alliance began to be used as the cover for the transmission of funds to the AFL for its

Mexican project, Congress had slashed the appropriation for Creel's committee. Creel was trying to shift the responsibility for subsidizing the alliance over to the Labor Department. He had written to Robert Maisel, director of the alliance, telling him that his August paycheck would be the last one from the CPI.[33] Wilson's promise to subsidize the Mexican–American labor conference appears to have come along just in time to keep the alliance under Creel's jurisdiction.[34] At the end of August, with the machinery for arranging the joint labor conference and the new newspaper in motion, Creel asked Wilson for, and immediately received, a secret appropriation of $50,000 from the President's special National Security and Defense Fund "for the use of the American Federation of Labor on the Mexican Border." [35] Creel appears to have given only $25,000 to the alliance for use by Murray and Chester Wright.[36] The rest of the money likely went to keep subsidizing the alliance, which was playing a supporting role in the efforts of Murray and Wright.

Gompers's success in appealing to Wilson was based upon powerful arguments, and was indeed significant, for it meant that Wilson was agreeing to extend to the field of foreign policy the same kind of government–labor cooperation that appeared to be working so well for both sides in the domestic field. Gompers made it clear that this was what he was proposing in a letter written to Wilson immediately after Wilson's initial rejection of the proposal for a covert subsidy for the joint conference and newspaper. He pointed out that the war had brought about "a departure from many old lines of thought and action" and that Wilson had been quick to recognize this in formulating his domestic labor policies. He continued:

> Exactly in line with the new policy of recognizing the organized labor movement and cooperating with it because it has a genuine function that can be served by no other agency, is the present proposal for the government to cooperate in a great international

movement by labor organizations to bring about better understanding between Mexico and the United States. . . . To me there is but one question: Can organized labor make friends for the United States where other agencies have failed?

He then pointed to the AFL's success in making friends in Mexico and asked for money to spread the good work to the rest of Latin America.[37] It is clear that Gompers's sights were on gaining a role for the AFL not only in Mexican–American relations but in the field of foreign relations as a whole. It is also clear that this role was to be played by the AFL in cooperation with, rather than independently of, the government. In the same way as the cooperation of the AFL had proved useful and indeed, at times, indispensable to the government in domestic labor relations, the utility and indispensability of the AFL in foreign affairs would now be shown as well. Gompers's trump card would be used again much later under a different Democratic President. As he phrased it with regard to Mexico, it was "the fact that the labor movement has nothing to gain that would act to the disadvantage of the people of Mexico."[38]

Wilson appears to have been swayed by Gompers's arguments. Within a week he appropriated $10,000 from his National Security and Defense Fund to pay the expenses of a proposed AFL mission to Europe.[39] In addition, Wilson gave Creel permission to start aiding the AFL with the arrangements for the Laredo conference.

NOTES

1. Lansing to Wilson, Apr. 18, 1917, 711.12/43A, State Department Papers; Wilson to Lansing, Apr. 19, 1917, 711.12/43–1/2, State Department Papers. Wilson recommended that they wait and see and explore the possibility, saying "There is absolutely no breach of the Monroe Doctrine

in allowing the British to exercise an influence there which anti-American sentiment for the time prevents our exercising." Ibid.

2. Judge Douglas, report, Apr. 16, 1918, Gompers Confidential CB.

3. Ibid.

4. Gompers to Wilson, Apr. 16, 1918, Wilson Papers, File VI, Box 147.

5. Sinclair Snow, "The Pan-American Federation of Labor" (Ph.D. diss., University of Virginia, 1960), p. 55.

6. Marjorie Clark, *Organized Labor in Mexico* (Chapel Hill: The University of North Carolina Press, 1934), pp. 59–61; Vicente Lombardo Toledano, *Teoría y práctica del movimiento sindical Mexicano* (Mexico: Editorial Magisterio, 1961), pp. 54–55.

7. Lombardo Toledano, *Teoría y práctica*, p. 54.

8. Ibid., p. 55.

9. "Laborista" is a very unusual word to use in the name of a Mexican workers' organization. "Labor" in Spanish is usually just used to connote "work." The normal words for "workers" and "laborers" are "trabajadores" and "obreros." Thus, a literal translation of the party's name would be something like "Workist party."

10. J. H. Retinger, *Morones de México,* (México, D.F.: Biblioteca del Grupo Acción, 1927), pp. 15–48.

11. Gompers to Tumulty, Apr. 24, 1918, and Wilson to Tumulty, Apr. 25, 1918, Wilson Papers, File VI, Box 187.

12. Wilson to Gompers, May 7, 1918, Wilson Papers, File VI, Box 147.

13. *Pan American Labor Press* (Aug. 28, 1918). The only available copy of this short-lived periodical appears to be that in the library in the AFL-CIO Building in Washington, D.C.

14. "Confidential Report of the AFL Commissioners to Mexico," by Murray, Iglesias and Lord (n.d.), in the possession of Mrs. Ethel B. Turner, Los Angeles, cited in Snow, "Pan-American Federation," p. 56.

15. *El Pueblo* (Mexico City), May 24, 1918.

16. Report of the Labor Commission to Mexico, *Pan-American Labor Press* (Aug. 28, 1918).

17. *Excelsior* (Mexico City), May 30, June 3, 1918.

18. Ibid., May 30, 1918.

19. Ibid., June 3, 1918.

20. Moises Poblete Troncoso, *El movimiento obrero latinoamericano* (Mexico: Fondo de Cultura Económica, 1946), p. 222.

21. *Excelsior,* June 5, 8, 1918.

22. Poblete Troncoso, *Movimiento obrero*, p. 222. However, its leader, Ricardo Treviño, remained in CROM, and continued as a powerful member of the Grupo Acción until the late 1930s.

23. Gompers to George Creel, July 10, 1918, Papers of the Committee on Public Information, National Archives, Washington, D.C. (hereafter referred to as CPI Papers), CP1-A1 (17).

24. Ibid.

25. Gompers to Woodrow Wilson, July 30, 1918, CPI Papers, CPI 1-A1 (17).

26. Josephus Daniels, *The Cabinet Diaries of Josephus Daniels 1917–1921*, ed. E. David Cronon (Lincoln: University of Nebraska Press, 1964), p. 324.

27. Creel to Bernard Baruch, Aug. 8, 1918, CPI Papers, CPI 1-A1 (46).

28. Robert Maisel to Gompers, May 12, 1919, Gompers Papers, SHSW.

29. Gompers to Creel, July 18, 1918, Gompers Papers, SHSW.

30. Creel to Gompers, July 26, 1917, CPI Papers, CPI 1-A1 (17). The reasons for the choice of this objective are obvious. The Lower East Side was the center of the nation's Jewish population and a stronghold of the Socialist party, both of which were generally opposed to the war. A municipal election was coming up. and Morris Hillquit, the Socialist candidate for mayor, appeared to have a good chance of winning, which would be interpreted as an indication that the nation's largest city was opposed to the war. Creel was apparently quite worried and promised the alliance an avalanche of support. He promised to give it foreign-language literature and speakers to explain "the real meaning of America" to the people of the Lower East Side in their own tongues. He said that no aid was to be expected from the Yiddish dailies but he felt certain that they could "appeal to a number of rich Jews and get them to start a daily that will serve our purposes." Ibid.

31. Gompers to Robert Maisel, July 31, 1917, and Gompers to Creel, Aug. 8, 1917, American Alliance for Labor and Democracy Copybooks, AFL-CIO Building, Washington, D.C. (hereafter referred to as AALD Papers).

32. Gompers to J. G. Phelps Stokes, Aug. 23, 1917, AALD Papers.

33. Creel to Roger Babson; Creel to Robert Maisel; Creel to Gompers: all July 17, 1918, CPI Papers, CPI 1-A1 (26).

34. The CPI continued to subsidize the alliance even after the war had ended. See Gompers to Maisel, Mar. 14, 1919, Gompers Papers, SHSW.

35. Creel to Wilson, August 28, 1918, Wilson Papers, File VI, Box 597, Folder 4674; notation under "George Creel," Aug. 28, 1918, Wilson Papers, File VI, Box 187.

36. Maisel to Gompers, May 12, 1919, Gompers Papers, SHSW.

37. Gompers to William Wilson, July 30, 1918, CPI Papers, CPI 1-A1 (17).

38. Ibid. This assumes, of course, that Mexican entry into the war would not have acted to the disadvantage of the people of Mexico.

39. Secretary of Labor William Wilson to President Wilson, memorandum, Aug. 7, 1918, Wilson Papers, File VI, Box 597, Folder 4674.

6

The Courtship
Consummated

WITH THE U.S. government now giving its complete support, the arrangements for the Laredo conference were made. Although the conference was supposed to be nonpolitical, concentrating on issues of interest to the two labor movements, Gompers issued invitations to speak to Presidents Wilson and Carranza and the governors of the border states of the United States and Mexico.[1]

Although it was originally intended as a conference between Mexican and American labor, with the proposed Pan-American Federation of Labor to be simply one of the points discussed, Chester Wright convinced Murray to invite delegates from other Latin American countries as well to discuss matters affecting Latin America as a whole.[2] Thus on the American side, the "Mexican-American Labor Conference" gradually metamorphosed into the "Pan-American Labor Conference," whose main aims were to drum up support for the U.S. war effort and organize the Pan-American Federation of Labor, an organization that would be useful for that purpose as well.

As the work of the upcoming conference was being expanded

on the northern side of the frontier, to the south it was under-
going the opposite transformation. The Mexican unionists
were making it explicitly clear that they would have nothing
to do with anything concerning the war, and that they were
intent mainly on improving the lot of Mexican workers in the
United States. The CROM and the Federación drew up a list
of seven proposals that they would advance at the conference.
The proposals were aimed at getting the "direct and decisive
cooperation" of the AFL in a campaign to remove the restrictions on Mexican workers going to the United States and on
those who were already there. Included were a proposal for
stationing unionists from both countries at border stations and
the demand that Mexicans in the United States be allowed to
enter AFL unions on an equal basis with Americans.[3] At the
suggestion of the Federación, an eighth proposal was added.
It mentioned the war in Europe, said that the Mexican delegation was opposed to the interference of either the United
States or Mexico in each other's affairs, and limited the questions to be discussed at the conference exclusively to labor
matters.[4]

Luckily for all concerned, the war in Europe came to an end
two days before the conference convened in Laredo on November 13, 1918. Still, as the delegates assembled for the opening sessions of the conference it soon became apparent that
there would be many points of conflict between the two movements. The Americans and Mexicans had come to the conference with completely different intentions. The Mexicans
intended it to be a labor conference in the narrowest sense,
discussing purely labor matters, with the chief aim that of
improving the lot of Mexican workers in the United States.
With the war officially over, the major aim of the Americans
still remained that of securing Mexican support for American
foreign policy. In place of securing Mexican support for President Wilson's war effort, Gompers was now intent on securing
their support for his peace terms. In the longer run, the AFL

now looked towards the establishment of a PAFL to provide an outlet for exercising AFL leadership for labor throughout Latin America, a labor counterpart of the Monroe Doctrine.

In his opening speech, Luis Morones made it clear that the Mexicans suspected what the AFL's intentions for the conference now were. He said that the Mexicans had crossed the border "not to render vassalage to a powerful labor organization" but to deal with the AFL as equals. Then, in an extraordinary step, he addressed his speech not to the assembled American delegates but to Mexican workers in the United States. He said that the Mexican representatives had come in order to allow the complaints of the Mexican workers in the United States to be felt "in the very heart of the United States," and appealed to them to step forward and express their grievances to the Mexican delegation.[5]

The CROM then put forth its concrete proposals for what the work of the conference should be. First, it proposed the appointment of one or two CROM delegates to reside in the United States, who in cooperation with the AFL would work at organizing and watching over Mexican workers in the United States.

Second, the AFL and CROM were to appoint permanent representatives in cities near the border and points of embarkation to ensure that workers going from one country to another "should be the object of the attention which they, undoubtedly, deserve." Also, Mexican workers in the United States were to be allowed to join AFL unions on an equal basis with American members.

The Mexicans then laid their bargaining counters on the table, proposing that the creation of a permanent PAFL be postponed until a delegation was sent to the other Central and South American countries that had expressed interest, and that, in the meantime, the present conference should be limited to implementing the above proposals. As an added fillip, they also proposed that an agreement be reached as to the best way to exert influence to secure the release of workers who were political prisoners in U.S. jails. They were, of course, referring to the IWWs who had been imprisoned.[6] The Mexicans were threatening to wreck the proposed PAFL and use the AFL's support of the persecution of the Wobblies as one of their justifications if the AFL did not cooperate in implementing their proposals.

The Mexican proposals threw the AFL into a quandary. The leaders of the AFL delegation felt that there was little they could do with regard to the problem they appeared most competent to deal with—that is, the status of Mexican workers vis à vis AFL unions. The AFL was a labor confederation that conceded a great deal of autonomy to its member unions. Indeed, that was one of the keys to its longevity. Whereas most national unions who were members of the AFL had clauses in their constitutions that allowed their executive committees to put recalcitrant local unions into a form of receivership, eject the leaders, and administer them directly, the Executive Council of the AFL had no such powers with regard to the national unions. About the only coercive measure the Executive Council could take against unions that failed to abide by its decisions and recommendations was to expel them from the federation. This was a drastic measure for a federation that sorely needed every member it had.

The dilemma of the AFL on the question of Mexican workers in the United States is illustrated in an exchange that took place in the Committee on Resolutions of the conference, to which the proposals had been submitted for consideration. A Mexican delegate from Arizona submitted three questions to the Americans.

(1): "Will American unions agree to admit Mexican workers into their ranks?" William Green replied that the AFL itself had no jurisdiction over this, that the international unions who compose it set their own standards regarding admission of foreigners, initiation fees, and the like. Morones apparently became somewhat heated over that answer and interjected that he wanted the establishment of an interchange of union cards immediately. Gompers reminded him that the AFL had no jurisdiction over this as well.

(2): "Will Mexican members have the same rights and privileges as the American members?" To this, Green had a less feeble-sounding reply. He said that all members of international unions were guaranteed the same rights and privileges regardless of race, creed, color, or nationality. This might have been true in theory, but as everyone there must have known, it was certainly not true in practice. AFL unions had devised many forms of second-class membership to deprive those Mexicans who were allowed in of a voice in union affairs.

(3): "Will the antagonism of races continue within the organization?" Green answered that the object of the PAFL was to eliminate race antagonism in all the Pan-American countries.

In spite of Gompers's previous protestations that it was powerless to do so, the AFL soon agreed that the committee recommend that some system of international transfer cards and the exchange of union cards be established at the conference. This recommendation was accepted by the conference as a whole. However, in view of the AFL's previous disclaimers of its ability to do anything about this, the resolution turned out to be rather meaningless, and nothing was accomplished along this line.[7]

The AFL was forced into making some concessions to the Mexicans by the Mexican threat of not cooperating in the formation of the PAFL unless something were done for their compatriots north of the border. When the whole question reached the floor of the conference the CROM and the Federación introduced a resolution that amounted to another thinly veiled threat of noncooperation. It declared that discrimination against Mexican workers in the United States presented a major obstacle to the unification of the labor movements of the two countries. This extensive discrimination, "fully verified and well known by the labor organizations of this country, provoke protests and give rise to distrust. It is unquestionable that unification is impossible where there is lack of trust." They added that the AFL could do something about these abuses and were sure that it would give its most careful attention to doing so.

Green, seeking to mollify the Mexicans, immediately recommended that the part of the resolution concerning abuses by American border authorities be referred to the Executive Council of the AFL for investigation and action. Finally, however, he became exasperated with the continued concentration on the embarrassing subject of discrimination against Mexicans (his union, the United Mine Workers, was one of the major offenders in the Southwest). He berated the conference for becoming a "clearing-house for grievances" rather than getting on with what he thought should be its main business, that of organizing a Pan-American Federation of Labor.[8]

In the end, the resolution calling for the appointment of permanent representatives in border towns and the one that Mexican workers should be allowed to join American unions on an equal basis with American members were adopted by the conference, but there is no indication that much more was done about the matter.[9]

The discussions of the Mexican proposals with regard to their compatriots in the United States led to some acrimonious debate, but their proposal that the AFL work to secure the release of political prisoners who had been unjustly imprisoned raised the temperature of the conference to the boiling point.

The IWW question had always been a sore point with the AFL. With America's entry into the war, Wilson and various state governors took the opportunity to have many Wobblies imprisoned on various charges of impeding the war effort and sedition, and Gompers was in no mood to intervene on their behalf. With the war over and the IWW virtually crushed, he was still in no mood to see them released. The IWW could become a great nuisance to the AFL, and Gompers and the other leaders of the AFL did not see why they should work for the release of subversives who declared themselves to be hereditary enemies of the AFL. Also, the question of the IWWs became particularly touchy when raised by Mexican unionists, for underlying all of the AFL's dealings with Mexican labor was the fear of IWW influence in Mexico.

In the 1910s there were considerable grounds for these fears, for there were many IWW locals in Mexico. If the IWW, or people closely allied to it, ever achieved control of the Mexican labor movement, they could pose great problems for AFL unionists, especially those in the West and Southwest. Gompers and those involved in Mexican affairs for the AFL were extremely sensitive about the whole question, and any suggestion of including the IWW in the formal relations being established between the two labor movements sent them into a dither.[10] The Mexicans knew this, and when the representatives of one labor group wanted to vilify another to Gompers they would almost invariably call it "the IWW of Mexico," even though there were official IWW locals in Mexico.

On the Mexican side, there were few authentic IWWs among the representatives of the CROM and the Federación at the conference in Laredo. In fact, with the Federación now on the verge of officially joining CROM, they were both now embarked upon a course that was almost the antithesis of that advocated by the IWW. However, an ideology does not die easily in peoples' minds. People often retain an emotional tie to it long after they have ceased to follow its precepts. If the Mexicans were no longer following anarcho-syndicalist principles, it did not mean that they had lost their sympathy for their former comrades-in-ideology. Indeed, it is not unlikely that many Mexican unionists rationalized their departure from anarcho-syndicalism as a temporary measure, forced upon them

by the exigencies of the moment. In their vehement defense of
the IWWs in the United States, they sought to prove to themselves that they had not really abandoned the old faith. It is
always easier to be a radical with regard to someone else's
country.

When the Mexican proposal that the AFL work to secure the
release of "political prisoners unjustly imprisoned in the
United States" finally came up for open discussion, Gompers
at first tried to evade the issue by playing ignorant. He pressed
the Mexicans for the exact meaning of the resolution, asking
if it meant that the AFL should try to obtain freedom for all
people who were unjustly imprisoned. If not, he asked them
to furnish him with specific names of prisoners and the charges
against them. The Mexicans were not prepared to do this, and
Morones at first demurred. Then Rafael Quintero, representing the Casa, declared that the prisoners to which the resolution referred were not, as Gompers had implied, all prisoners
unjustly imprisoned but specifically those members of the
IWW who had been propagandizing against the war. With the
issue no longer couched in vague terms, the debate now began
in earnest.

The AFL delegates' defenses consisted mainly of the traditional AFL attacks on the IWW as "wreckers" of the labor
movement. Daniel Tobin, head of the Teamsters Union, called
it "the greatest barrier recently in the progress towards union
movement, especially in the extreme Western States, than any
other institution or movement we have had to contend with
in recent years." He was not too clear in explaining how this
justified putting them behind bars.

It was a delegate of the Mexican IWW who struck the
common note of the Mexican arguments and perhaps summed
them up best. He appealed to the idea of the universal fraternity of workers and pointed to the necessity for toleration
of different ideas on organization and methods within the labor

movement. He asked the AFL to tolerate the IWW, saying, "It is a contradiction to proclaim liberty on the one hand, and on the other hand gag the right of free speech." [11]

After yet another Mexican appeal to the fraternity of the workers of the world, no matter what their race or organizational affiliation, Gompers finally exploded. He rose to his feet, determined to show the conference once and for all who exactly was running the show. He began:

> At the outset, let me say that there is a peculiar notion prevailing among some of the delegates, who seem to think that it is a gracious act on their part to accept the invitation to and attend this conference. The invitation to participate in this conference is the result of years of work of the American Federation of Labor to assist the Mexican people.

He then launched into his standard enumeration of the many things the AFL had done for Mexico, adding that, by taking a strong stand against Carranza's no-strike decree, the AFL had compelled the adoption into the Mexican Constitution of 1917 a clause guaranteeing the right to strike. In the United States, Gompers said, the AFL had managed to accomplish all that it had done for American labor and had acquired the power and influence that it had only because it was the only labor movement in the country. "The IWWs in the United States," he said, "are exactly what the Bolsheviki are in Russia, and we have seen what the IWW Bolsheviki in Russia have done for the working people of Russia, where the people have no peace, no security, no land, and no bread." He proceeded to lay his cards on the table. The AFL, he said, had come to the conference to offer a helping hand to the Mexicans and had found themselves consistently put on the defensive. If the Mexicans persisted in pursuing this course, the helping hand would be withdrawn.

It was now Gompers who was threatening to break up the

conference. Morones's bluff was called, and he was quick to capitulate. He rose and delivered a conciliatory speech. He pointed out that the Mexican delegates had been the objects of strong criticism in Mexico for dealing with the AFL. The real intent of the resolution regarding the IWW was to silence those critics in Mexico who were circulating rumors that the AFL was permitting the jailing of workers, especially those who belonged to the IWW. By giving the criticisms a chance to be aired and denied, the conference had laid the criticisms to rest. Adding a note of finality to the discussion of the question, he ended:

> I congratulate myself and ourselves as well that this question was brought forth, because in the future it will save us many disasters and similar discussions.

The conference soon agreed to pigeonhole the resolution by referring it to the Executive Council of the AFL for investigation and any action that it deemed necessary.[12]

It was now clear who held the upper hand in the conference. Gompers then tried to get the Mexican delegation to support his Wilsonian proposals for the peace to be imposed on Germany and the world. Officially, the proposals were those of an Inter-Allied Labor and Socialist Conference held in 1918. However, their similarity to Wilson's Fourteen Points made endorsement of them tantamount to endorsement of the Fourteen Points and Wilson's position at the upcoming Peace Conference.

At first, Gompers ran into a minor roadblock when the Mexican delegates reminded the AFL that, only the day before, the Resolutions Committee, headed by William Green, had, over the objections of the Mexicans, turned down a Mexican resolution that the conference should not "meddle in the internal affairs of the two republics, and especially in their international problems, when these problems can be settled without resort to arms." Green had argued for rejecting the resolution on the ground that the conference had been called to consider labor questions only. In the ensuing debate, when Gompers submitted the peace proposals for the approval of the conference, the Mexicans tried to rely on Green's argument, which had been their point of view all along. Morones and Torres declared that they themselves agreed with the principles enunciated in the resolution, but they were not empowered to vote on the parts that did not deal directly with labor. However, it soon became clear that the real reason they refused to vote for the resolution was that it would expose them to the charge of being tools of American foreign policy. They continually hinted at this through references to the inability of the mass of Mexican workers to understand the real meaning of the resolutions and by pointing to the very real prejudices against the United States that existed south of the Rio Grande.

Santiago Iglesias then attacked Morones and Torres for not working to educate the Mexican masses by voting for the resolutions and teaching them their true meaning. He said that the working people of Mexico were peculiar in their prejudices (implying that they were prejudiced against the United States on racial grounds), but that it was the task of the Mexican labor leaders to work to eliminate this prejudice and not succumb to it. This aroused Morones and Torres, who heatedly denied that they were racially prejudiced. Though they favored those parts of the resolution that endorsed liberty, they could not vote for the rest. The key sections they opposed were those that proposed a League of Nations and opposed economic nationalism.

Gompers then offered to separate the sections of the resolution that the Mexicans found objectionable from the rest, challenging the Mexicans to vote against them and justify their position to the people of Mexico. This again placed the Mexicans in a dilemma, for in reality they did not want to vote for anything having to do with U.S. foreign policy. Voting for some parts of the resolution and against others probably would have been the worst thing they could have done because it would expose them to attacks from all sides. Morones again tried to outline the problems the Mexicans faced in dealing with foreign policy with the AFL. "The peoples of Mexico and Central and South America," he said, "do not understand the aspirations of the American Federation of Labor, nor do they understand the people of the United States. All the knowledge they have of the people of the United States is through soldiers' bayonets." The Latin American delegates, he continued, had come to the conference to gather information about the true spirit of the AFL and tell the people of their countries that it was not what they had imagined it to be. But this could not be achieved in one day, and he pleaded for patience on the part of the AFL. He concluded by saying, "We cannot agree with the proposal that we vote separately on these propositions in regard to these important problems." Gompers shouted, "Yes, sir; you will."

Gompers was aroused, and in the face of his intransigence Morones was forced to compromise. He said that each Mexican delegate would sign his name to the resolution, but as an individual, and that this act would be subject to the ratification of his co-workers in Mexico. Gompers at first refused to accept this, but after meeting with the Mexican leaders that night on the matter, he declared it acceptable to the AFL.[13]

In spite of the difficulty in reaching compromises on some issues, the joint labor conference was quite successful from the AFL point of view. The armistice had deprived the conference of the chance to be used for its original main purpose, that of putting pressure on the Mexican government to enter the war, but the upcoming Peace Conference, and the chance to proclaim the support of working men of Pan-America for Wilson's peace aims provided it with a substitute *raison d'être* as far as its short-term achievements were concerned. In the longer run, in spite of threats of noncooperation by the Mexicans, arrangements for the speedy formation of the Pan-American Federation of Labor were made.

The founding convention of the PAFL met in New York City on July 7, 1919. Twenty-five delegates, representing labor groups in the United States, Mexico, Guatemala, El Salvador, Honduras, Peru, Ecuador, the Dominican Republic, Costa Rica, Chile, and Argentina, duly created the PAFL, with Gompers as president.[14] Although the list of countries represented looked fairly impressive, in reality Mexico and the United States were the only two that had sizable labor movements worthy of note. From its foundation to its demise, the PAFL was never much more than a Mexican-American organization.

From the start, Gompers viewed the PAFL as a means of implementing a "Monroe Doctrine" for labor. Through the PAFL the AFL would be able to protect the rights of the labor movements of Latin America in the same way as the U.S. government presumably was protecting the governments of Latin America against foreign intervention. Two months before its founding convention, he wrote an article making it clear that this was his concept of what the PAFL should be.

> The Monroe Doctrine, which has just received a new consecration by being written into the League of Nations Covenant, and which safeguards the political integrity of all the Pan-American nations and secures them against foreign intervention, must and will be supplemented by the Pan-American Federation of Labor doctrine that the rights of the wage-earners to freedom, justice, and democracy must be safeguarded at all hazards and secured against infringement of any kind from any source.[15]

By 1919, then, with the new opportunities being presented by the new world order that the Peace Conference at Versailles was supposed to construct, Gompers was expanding his vision of what should be the role of "labor" in the United States into one which would encompass the whole world. He was anxious to have "labor" play an integral role in the new League of Nations and had a campaign mounted to recommend him as one of the official U.S. peace commissioners.[16]

President Wilson would go just so far on the question of labor representation on official commissions. The idea of conceding it on the all-important commission that was to help decide the fate of the postwar world seemed to him to be pushing the concept too far. He was adamant in his refusal to have Gompers as one of his official commissioners. Even if Gompers were appointed as a private citizen, the move would be interpreted as the appointment of a special labor representative.[17]

Although he failed to have Wilson appoint him a commissioner to the main Peace Conference, Gompers did enlist Wilson's support for the idea of having a separate labor conference meet in Paris alongside the Peace Conference to draw up a charter of the rights of labor and to form an international labor organization that would be part of the proposed League of Nations. Gompers became the chairman of the conference and spent much of the year 1919 in Paris.

Thus, in 1919, it must have seemed to Gompers, along with many others, that a new world order was dawning for the labor organizations of the world as well as for its governments. The PAFL was to be but a part of this new labor order. In the same way as the United States was assured at Versailles that it would continue to retain its paramount influence in Latin America, the formation of the PAFL, supplementing the League's International Labor Organization and the new international labor organization being created in Amsterdam, would ensure the dominant role of the AFL in the international labor relations of the Western Hemisphere. That there really was not much for the AFL to dominate at that moment did not appear to be too important. Gompers expected that, with the aid of the increasingly powerful AFL, strong labor movements would soon develop in many Latin American countries. In the meantime, Gompers could derive increased weight for his influence in international labor relations by assuming the role of sole spokesman for Pan-American labor at international labor meetings. One of the actions of the first convention of the PAFL was to authorize Gompers to represent the labor movements of the various Latin American countries at the meeting of the International Federation of Trade Unions (known as the "Amsterdam International") later that month.[18]

Throughout 1919, although Gompers was very occupied with the Peace Conference, bolshevism, and the wave of organization and strikes that swept the United States along with the postwar inflation, the AFL continued to keep a watchful eye on developments in Mexico and strengthened its ties with the Mexican labor movement. Early in the year, when some U.S. senators renewed their periodic demands for U.S. intervention in Mexico, Murray made the rounds of New York editors in an attempt to stimulate anti-intervention editorials. He secured the cooperation of the editors of the *New York Tribune*, the *New Republic*, the *Nation*, and *Survey*, who, he said, "promised, with an enthusiasm rather unusual to New York editors, that they would support the work of the Pan-American Federation of Labor, especially in its desire to prevent intervention in Mexico." [19] Later in the year, when it appeared to the AFL that the Carranza government, in proposing constitutional amendments that would divest the nation of its ownership of all hydrocarbons, was also trying to limit the right to strike, Gompers sent letters of protest to Carranza and the secretaries of the Mexican Chamber of Deputies and Senate.[20] It is likely that this interpretation of Carranza's proposed constitutional changes was given to Gompers by CROM, which opposed them. In the course of the year, Morones visited the United States twice, and on his second visit he was seated as the delegate of CROM to the AFL convention in Atlantic City and given one symbolic vote.[21]

Thus, in the immediate postwar period, after a somewhat shaky start, the Mexican–American labor alliance seemed to be looking forward to fruitful prospects. Both the AFL and CROM were experiencing booms in membership figures, and the influence of the AFL and the labor movements of the world in international affairs appeared to be rapidly rising. The tide soon turned.

NOTES

1. Gompers to Hon. John Barrett, Aug. 27, 1918, Gompers Papers, SHSW.
2. Murray to Chester Wright, Oct. 19, 1918, and Murray to Representatives of Labor Organizations of Latin America, Oct. 19, 1918, Gompers Papers, SHSW.
3. *Pan-American Labor Press* (Sept. 18, 1918).
4. Ibid. (Dec. 4, 1918).
5. Ibid.
6. Ibid.
7. Ibid.
8. Ibid.
9. Ibid.
10. For example, see memorandum, July 7, 1916, Gompers Papers, SHSW.
11. *Pan-American Labor Press* (Dec. 4, 1918).
12. Ibid.
13. Ibid.
14. Gompers to Grover H. Whelan, July 7, 1919, and Gompers to Robert Lansing, Sept. 4, 1919, Gompers Papers, SHSW.
15. Samuel Gompers, "Labor's Menace in Mexico," *American Federationist* 26 (May 1919): 404.
16. See Frank Morrison to W. G. Lee, Nov. 21, 1918, and John Morrison to Gompers, Nov. 22, 1918, Gompers Papers, SHSW, and the many copies of letters to President Wilson in support of Gompers in the same collection.
17. Wilson to Frank Morrison, Nov. 22, 1918; Morrison to Wilson, Nov. 26, 1918; Wilson to Morrison, Nov. 27, 1918: all Gompers Papers, SHSW.
18. Gompers to Latin American ambassadors, Sept. 3, 1919, Gompers Papers, SHSW.
19. Murray to Gompers, Feb. 21, 1919, Gompers Papers, SHSW.
20. Gompers, "Labor's Menace in Mexico," p. 404.
21. Murray to Gompers, Feb. 21, 1919; AFL, *Proceedings*, 1919, p. 360.

7

Gompers's Last Years

GOMPERS'S POLICY of cooperation with the U.S. government in international affairs benefited the AFL during the war, but the policy had its inherent weaknesses. Had there been a national consensus on foreign policy, and had the prospect of a new administration not meant the prospect of a changed foreign policy, it might have been more successful. However, this was not so in the immediate postwar years. Even before the details of the proposed Covenant of the League of Nations were officially made public, a great debate raged about it. The complete identification of the foreign policy of the AFL with the policy of Woodrow Wilson certainly did nothing to ensure the AFL a privileged position in the corridors of government power if a Republican administration were elected. The custom of granting labor representation on some government bodies had not been going long enough or consistently enough for it to be considered a tradition that Wilson's successors were at all bound to follow. It had been based on little more than the special relationship that existed between Gompers and Wilson and, more importantly, the unusually strong bargaining position in which the war had placed the AFL.

94

With the signing of the Armistice, any administration had much less to gain in return for concessions to Gompers's desires for a greater voice in government for "labor" and special treatment for the AFL. Even if the Senate had approved the League Covenant, and an internationalist Democrat had been elected in 1920, it is likely that Gompers's importance in foreign affairs would have been severely restricted. With the failure of Wilson's campaign to secure ratification of the League Covenant, his stroke and incapacitation for the rest of his term, and the election of a Republican president in 1920, Gompers's influence on foreign policy was reduced to almost nothing. At the same time, the failure of a wave of inflation-induced strikes in late 1919 and early 1920 led to the beginning of a decline in AFL membership from which the organization would not begin to recover until the 1930s.

The failure of Gompers's grand design for labor's role in international affairs did not mean the abandonment of the special relationship that the Mexican and American labor movements were developing. After all, there still remained some practical benefits that both the AFL and the CROM hoped to gain from it. What it did mean was a radical shift in emphasis. The topics that came up for serious discussion and negotiation between the AFL and CROM changed from wide-ranging issues such as freedom for IWWs, the war, and the peace to more practical matters, such as Mexican immigration to the United States—which CROM had wanted to emphasize all along. Now the AFL turned slowly to these matters, and as the 1920s wore on, its interest in them rose in almost inverse proportion to its declining interests in broader topics. In contrast, CROM, which had started out intent mainly on extracting concessions from the AFL with regard to such matters as the plight of Mexican workers in the United States, gradually lost much of its interest in negotiations over the practical, "labor" aspects of its relations with the AFL.

On the surface, as long as Gompers was alive, this was not

readily apparent. Thanks to his sense of showmanship, the real nature of the relations between the two labor movements often became obscured behind a cloud of hoopla and symbolic gestures that gave the impression of an ever-strengthening alliance being created.

The issue that was to become the major object of attention in the 1920s was the desire of the AFL to have Mexican immigration to the United States drastically restricted. Although this did not come to the foreground until after Gompers's death, it had concerned him and many AFL members since the war. The wartime emergency had caused the U.S. government to drop its literacy requirements for immigrants from Mexico and to encourage the importation of Mexican contract labor to man labor-short war industries. Gompers and most American unionists feared that after the war, with the labor shortage over, these Mexican workers and others who might join them in the United States would accept lower wages than their American counterparts and provide a ready-made pool of strikebreakers. These fears were soon borne out. In the steel strike of 1919, large numbers of Mexicans were transported from the Southwest by firms in the Chicago area to man the great steel mills that the AFL men were refusing to work.

During the 1920s, immigration from Mexico accelerated rapidly. Because of the huge number of illegal entries (usually estimated at about half the total),[1] no one will ever know exactly how many Mexicans crossed the border to live and work in the United States during those years. Carey McWilliams's study of place of birth in the census figures for Arizona, California, New Mexico, and Texas indicates that over one million Mexicans emigrated to these four states from 1900 to 1930, with over 750,000 of them coming in the 1920s.[2] In some industries of the Southwest, such as mining and railways, they came to compose 60 to 70 percent of the common labor force.[3]

In addition, Northern steel plants and other companies, pleased with their experiments with Mexican labor during the war and the great steel strike, embarked on policies of having trainloads of Mexicans shipped up for them by recruiting agents in the Southwest. In 1926, for example, the superintendent of employment at the Pittsburgh Plate Glass Company factory in Ford City, Pennsylvania, recalled having them sent up in "shipments" of sixty or thirty from San Antonio in 1923.[4] In the same year, the National Tube Company, an affiliate of U.S. Steel, imported 1,300 Mexicans from Texas to work in its Lorain (Ohio) plant, and Bethlehem Steel imported about 1,000 to work in its plants in Bethlehem, Pennsylvania.[5] By 1926, over one-fourth of the 8,000 workers at the Inland Steel Company's East Chicago plant were Mexicans. According to company officials, Rumanians were tried first, but they were too lazy. The Mexicans, the officials said, were generally not very strong, but they were good workers.[6]

The influx of Mexicans posed great problems for AFL unions in the industries affected. In general, they were regarded as notoriously hard to organize. There was considerable justice in this sentiment, for Mexicans, like many immigrants, came from a country with a markedly lower standard of living and were willing, at first, to work for lower wages than native American workers. Many Mexicans, even after residing in the United States for many years, still regarded their stay as only temporary and nursed the dream of saving enough money to one day return to the *patria* to live the "good life." Many earlier immigrants from Europe had cherished the same dream, but for Mexicans, with simply a short train ride instead of a long ocean voyage separating them from the homeland, it was a much more attainable, and therefore a more persistent, hope. Thus, they were frequently loath to jeopardize their chances at making a quick "fortune" by participating in strikes and other union activities.

If Mexicans were notoriously hard to organize, AFL unions in the Southwest were equally notorious for discriminating against them. The AFL unions tended to reflect the pattern

of discrimination against Mexicans that prevailed in the Southwest. Even where they were accepted into union locals, various
forms of second-class membership were often designed for them.
Mexicans and AFL unionism in the Southwest tended to mix
like oil and water.

Soon after the war had ended, Gompers wrote to Secretary
of Labor Wilson asking what the government's plans were with
regard to Mexican immigration. He made it clear that he
wanted the prewar restrictions reimposed. Wilson assured him
that this would be done.[7] Although some people, such as John
Murray, saw part of the solution to the problem in the recruitment of Mexicans into the AFL,[8] from then on the major part
of the AFL's efforts were aimed at restricting Mexican immigration into the United States—first through more restrictive legislation, later through cooperation with CROM. Some years
later, Lewis Warfield, an American transportation engineer
who had worked for Porfirio Díaz, had been friendly with
Madero, and had unofficially advised the Wilson administration on Mexican policy, recalled a conversation he had with
Gompers and Murray in Gompers's office in 1918. They told
him, said Warfield, that "they had no interest in Mexican
labor other than to keep them from coming here to compete
with our labor after the war." [9] Although either Warfield or
Gompers must have been exaggerating, it is doubtful whether
the story was completely fabricated. But it does indicate an
early concern with the problem on the part of Gompers.

In 1919, at the instigation of John L. Lewis of the United
Mine Workers Union, the AFL convention went on record as
opposed to immigration from Mexico as well as from Europe
and the Orient. In his speech to the convention, Lewis justified
the proposal by pointing to the "disposition on the part of
certain mining interests of this country to import Mexican
labor to displace American labor in certain producing terri-
tory." He added that the question also was of concern to the
metalliferous miners and railroad maintenance-of-way men.[10]

Mexico thus was added to the list of countries upon which the AFL wanted the government to place restrictive immigration quotas. In the succeeding years, Gompers and the AFL's lobbyists in Congress worked hard to have Mexico included in the proposed immigration restriction bills.

The climax of the AFL's legislative efforts came late in 1923, when it was apparent that Congress was going to pass some sort of bill restricting immigration. The questions that arose were: what kind of bill would be passed, and what countries would be subject to its restrictions? At a conference with Secretary of Labor J. J. Davis in September 1923, Gompers got Davis to agree on the desirability of putting immigration from Mexico on the quota system, giving it a quota of two percent.[11] The quota system itself had been imposed in an immigration act of 1921. The earlier act had restricted immigration from various countries to a certain percentage of the number of persons residing in the United States who had been born in those countries as of the census of 1910. The new act was going to push the base year back to 1890, which would more effectively curtail immigration from all but the Anglo-Saxon and northern European countries. One of the major objections to placing Mexico on the quota system was that it would deeply offend Mexico to be placed under it while Canada, the northern neighbor of the United States, was exempt from it. Gompers therefore suggested that, to avoid the charge of discrimination against Mexico, the two percent quota should apply to Canada as well.[12]

On December 3, 1923, Davis assembled a conference of labor leaders in Washington and read them a number of clauses in the immigration bill that the administration was going to put before Congress. It provided that both Mexico and Canada should come under the two percent quota. However, Davis's bill, which was introduced in the Senate, was not the only one before Congress. In the House, Congressman Albert Johnson, the powerful chairman of the House Immigration Committee, was guiding a bill through his committee that would not subject Mexico and Canada to the quota. Gompers met with Johnson in March 1924 but failed to persuade him to add the two countries to the list. Johnson said that, if they were included, the bill would not pass in the House. Gompers's AFL lobbyists continued to press for the inclusion of Canada and Mexico in the House bill, but to no avail.[13] In the final bill that emerged from the House-Senate joint conference, Mexico and Canada remained exempt from the quota system. The problem of Mexican immigration remained to plague Gompers's successor.

Until his death in late 1924, Gompers kept the AFL's campaign to restrict Mexican immigration aimed at Congress. His stand on the subject was only a minor embarrassment with regard to the AFL's relations with CROM, but the issue provided enough potential explosive power to deter him from trying to enlist the aid of CROM in the campaign. On the practical level, the AFL's major interest in Mexico was to see the development of a strong labor movement there. This was not the product of sheer altruism; it would help to head off maneuvers by American businessmen that could wreak serious harm on AFL unions. In 1919, when Carranza appeared to be endangering the right to strike in Mexico, Gompers pointed out the very real danger this presented to American unionists.

This latest development in Mexican Labor affairs presents a serious condition which menaces the interests of American workingmen as it does the rights and liberties and hopes of the Mexican wage-earners. That American financiers are deeply involved in this latest attack on the rights of Mexican workers is not seriously questioned. It is estimated that the investments owned and controlled by American capitalists in Mexico exceed $2,000,000,000. Outlaw the right to strike in Mexico, deny the workers of Mexico the opportunity of a fair and just wage and the mines, mills and oil wells of America can well be closed while Mexican products of peon labor may be freely dumped into the markets of the United States.[14]

This fear provided a strong basis for Gompers's continued support of CROM and was a recurring theme in his justifications of the necessity for close relations between the two movements.

On the Mexican side, as CROM's membership, power, and ties to the Mexican government grew, its interest in maintaining close relations with the AFL drifted back to the original purpose for which they were established—that of using the AFL to intervene on behalf of the Mexican government in its recurring crises with Washington. Also, the AFL was the only major foreign labor organization that was interested in establishing closer relations with CROM. From 1918 to 1921, CROM repeatedly sent delegations to Europe in an attempt to establish closer relations with the European labor movements and the Amsterdam International, only to be greeted with supreme indifference and condescension by the Europeans, who could not bring themselves to believe that a real labor movement could emerge from Mexico, a country of revolutions, bandits, and peons.[15]

The CROM needed little help from the AFL in strengthening its position within Mexico, for with the overthrow of Carranza in 1920 it entered into a new era in its relationship with the Mexican government. General Obregón had always cultivated close relations with the labor movement; when he and Gen. Plutarco Elias Calles overthrew Carranza, the CROM supported him. Relations between CROM and Carranza at best had always been tenuous, and when he showed signs of planning to perpetuate himself in office after his constitutional term had expired, the CROM was not unhappy to see him dispatched. And dispatched he was—gunned down by unknown persons as he fled the victorious forces in the hills. The AFL had been informed by CROM, through their representatives on the border, of the impending revolution, and Gompers was prepared to offer its full support as soon as it was accomplished.[16] When news of the revolution reached the United States, Gompers immediately issued a press release praising the new regime.[17]

Shortly after Obregón took power, with the Wilson administration witholding U.S. recognition from his government, Obregón sent Morones to Washington as his special representative to deliver an oral message to President Wilson. Morones went first to Gompers, who arranged interviews for him with Wilson and Secretary of State Bainbridge Colby.[18] Morones's task was to assure Wilson that Obregón did not intend to harm American financial interests in Mexico. But Obregón's pride and nationalism would not allow him to put this in writing before recognition was granted. The demand of the U.S. government that he do so became the major stumbling block in the three years of negotiations over recognition that ensued. Morones's role, however, was not to negotiate recognition; another man had been sent secretly to do this.[19]

Morones also brought a letter from Obregón to Gompers asking Gompers to lend Morones any possible assistance in his mission. Morones explained the present situation in Mexico and the nature of his mission and succeeded in quashing any qualms that Gompers might have developed over the assassination of Carranza. Gompers appears to have been satisfied by Morones's explanations. He wrote to Obregón: "There is every appearance that the leaders of the revolution have been entirely blameless for this awful deed." [20]

Aside from the usual importance that recognition by the U.S. government had for Latin American countries, it was especially important for the Mexican revolutionary governments to achieve it. The United States was the major source of arms for the government, and as long as recognition was withheld, an embargo was placed on legal arms shipments to Mexico. Also, if it did not recognize the new regime, the United States was not obliged to try to stop a new anti-Obregón revolution from being organized within its bounds. Through CROM, the enthusiastic support of Gompers was enlisted for the new regime. Whether it was as influential in furthering the recognition of the Obregón government as Obregón and Morones hoped it would be, is moot. However, in the United States of the 1920s any significant support the Mexican government could garner for itself was not to be shrugged off. The fact that Morones could secure support for the Obregón government from the man who claimed to speak for American labor certainly did no harm to Morones's claims for a privileged position within the Mexican power structure.

In June 1920, soon after Morones returned to Mexico, Gompers publicly denounced the recommendation of Senator Albert Fall's subcommittee that the United States send a "police force" across the border unless Mexico altered her constitution to give added protection to American mineral and agricultural holdings there. He said that this would lead to war. He also labeled the recommendation of the subcommittee that financial aid be extended to Mexico if it agreed to the terms of the report as a "Prussian proposition." [21] Later in the year, the AFL convention condemned the Fall subcommittee and the propaganda being spread by "oil, mining, and other interests" about Mexico. It commended President Wilson's policy of "non-intervention and non-interference, not only in the past, but for the future." [22]

In January 1921, the PAFL convention was held in Mexico City. This provided Gompers an opportunity to show his support of the new Mexican leaders and enabled them to meet him and impress him. Gompers held extended private conferences with Generals Obregón, de la Huerta, Calles, and Antonio I. Villareal, the most powerful generals in the new government, who convinced him to try to persuade the State Department to extend recognition.[23] Gompers kept his promise. Later in the year, when Robert Haberman, an American living in Mexico who was one of the leaders in CROM, was sent by the Mexican government on a mission to the United States, he brought a letter from Calles to Gompers, in which Calles said that he had been informed of Gompers's efforts with the State Department and was greatly pleased by them.[24]

Meanwhile, Gompers kept up his public praise and support of the Obregón regime. In a speech to a group of Mexican workers, he took the rather unusual step of telling strangers what their political stand in their own country should be.

> I urge you to stand by the men in your government, as repre-
> sented by your great President, Obregón, and by your Ministers
> Calles, de la Huerta, and Villareal, and see to it that there is no
> reactionary revolution that shall place the power of your republic
> in the hands of reactionaries again.[25]

The next year, the AFL convention passed a resolution urging the U.S. government to extend immediate recognition to the Obregón regime.[26]

In 1923, when the Mexican and American governments agreed to hold a joint conference in Mexico City to try to settle their differences, Gompers tried to get labor representation on the American side. When this failed, James Lord was sent to Mexico City to act as an observer for the PAFL at the conference, which was held on Bucareli Street and soon became known as the Bucareli Conference. Although the meetings were closed, he did manage to meet with both the U.S. and Mexican commissioners to present to them the pro-Obregón viewpoint of the AFL.[27] When the Harding administration finally reached a settlement with the Mexican government, and recognition was extended, Gompers telegraphed congratulations to Obregón and CROM and received expressions of gratitude for his efforts from them.[28]

There were other external signs of strengthening ties between CROM and the AFL. In October 1920, Gompers finally appealed to Wilson to declare an amnesty for political prisoners jailed for antiwar activities.[29] A few months later, he asked the President to grant a pardon to Eugene Debs, who remained imprisoned on similar charges.[30] It is not unlikely that CROM's sensibilities on the question played a part in changing his attitude. Also, the practice of CROM and the AFL of sending delegates to each other's conventions became a common one. This proved useful in July 1921, when the AFL delegates at the CROM convention warned Gompers that two U.S. cruisers sent to Tampico supposedly to protect American lives and property there during an oil-workers' strike might intervene against the strikers. Gompers forced Secretary of State Charles Evans Hughes to state on record that this was not so.[31]

In November 1921, when the Mexican government became aroused over its exclusion from the planned Washington Conference on Disarmament, Morones, in the name of the Mexican Labor party and CROM (which he claimed had 450,000 members, a vastly inflated figure), sent Gompers a long statement of protest. He asked Gompers to give it the widest possible publicity and "appropriate comments." [32] He also sent identical letters to key AFL leaders.[33] Gompers was a member of the advisory committee to the American delegation to the conference and used this official position to gain an interview with President Harding on the matter. He presented Harding with Morones's protest and used the opportunity to press for American recognition of Mexico. He tried to explain the Mexican viewpoint, as told to him by President Obregón in Mexico City that January, but Harding held firm. When Gompers said that President Obregón did not think that it was right that Mexico should be obligated to enter into and sign a treaty promising to do things which she was morally obligated to do and wanted to do, Harding replied: "We think she ought to, and that's how the matter now stands." [34]

Gompers was unsuccessful in changing the President's position of both questions. Morones's protest was received with the traditional promise to give it careful consideration. Things had indeed changed considerably from wartime, when Gompers could at least expect to be misled into thinking that the President was going to heed his advice.

If his work for the Mexican government did not have much effect on U.S. government policy, it does appear to have had a great effect on Gompers. Having met and aided the leaders of the country, he began to feel as if he were intimately acquainted with the politics of Mexico and in a position to give sound advice to CROM as to what its political position should be. When a dispute over the successor to Obregón broke out between General Calles, whom Obregón supported, and Gen. Adolfo de la Huerta, who had strong support in Congress, he invited the leaders of CROM to a conference in El Paso with himself, Chester Wright, and Canuto Vargas representing the PAFL. In an extraordinary step, he told CROM representatives that if he were a Mexican he would support Calles as the successor to Obregón. He urged CROM to give its complete support to Calles but at the same time preserve its own political identity. He also suggested that CROM and the AFL hold their 1924 conventions in Ciudad Juarez and El Paso, across the river from each other, at the same time.[35] Gompers need not have been concerned about whom CROM was going to support, for at that time Calles's election was viewed in Mexico as a certainty. Robert Haberman, representing CROM, dismissed Gompers's suggestion with this fact. He suggested that since Calles's election was a foregone conclusion, the site of the fourth congress of the PAFL should be shifted from Guatemala to Mexico City so that it could be held in conjunction with the festivities celebrating the inauguration of Calles on December 1, 1924. The conference agreed to all of the above suggestions.[36]

Later, in a public speech at a dinner in Juarez, Gompers repeated his endorsement of Calles and urged his audience to do so. When news of this reached Mexico City, de la Huerta's partisans became greatly aroused and mounted fierce attacks on Gompers and the followers of Calles, accusing the latter of planning a mass assassination of de la Huertista deputies in the Chamber of Deputies.[37] In November 1923, *Excelsior* published an angry editorial accusing Gompers of meddling in Mexico's internal affairs. It said that at the El Paso meeting Gompers had offered his aid to General Calles and had also threatened to provide American aid for a new revolution if Calles lost. "We know," continued the editorial, "that Gompers boasts of having helped to overthrow the Governments of Porfirio Díaz and Victoriano Huerta, but never before has he openly threatened us with American intervention if we fail to heed his demands in affairs that are ours only to decide." [38] Gompers stood firm against the protests from Mexico and said that he had no desire to change his Juarez declarations "except to strengthen them, if possible." [39]

Haberman was right about Calles's election being a foregone conclusion, but he had assumed that an election of sorts would be held with the present government still in power. This was put in doubt when de la Huerta chose the option of armed revolt. On December 5, 1923, the governors of five states rose in support of de la Huerta, and an armed rebellion was mounted, which seriously threatened the Obregón government. Even though a good case could be made for de la Huerta's sympathies for labor,[40] Gompers knew which side he was on from the beginning. CROM was supporting Calles and Obregón, and so was Gompers.

In the case of the de la Huerta revolt, Gompers was able to lend to his friends in Mexico assistance that went beyond the usual public declarations of support. When the U.S. government said that it would enforce the laws against illegal arms shipments from the United States, Gompers asked all AFL representatives and members who were connected with transport work to "assist" the government in detecting any smuggling of arms into Mexico for the use of de la Huerta's forces.[41] This was done in response to appeals for practical aid from

CROM.[42] Gompers also took the opportunity to denounce de la Huerta as a "tool of reaction," whose purpose was to "crush the labor movement, enforce compulsory labor by denying the right of workmen to leave their work, give back the land to great concessionaires, and set Mexico back a decade or so."[43]

De la Huerta was justifiably concerned about Gompers's opposition to him. After all, the only real issue that divided his followers from those of Calles was the age-old one of who was to control power. Ideological and political lines were completely muddled, and each side continually attacked the other as "reactionary" and "Bolshevik" at the same time. De la Huerta invited Gompers to visit him in his headquarters in Veracruz to see for himself that his charges were untrue. Gompers declined the offer.[44]

When the de la Huerta revolt collapsed, CROM and the AFL found themselves in an extremely favorable position with regard to power in Mexico. They had backed a winner and earned a claim to some of the spoils. CROM's support of Calles had proved very valuable, and Morones and its other leaders were assured of a position of privilege and power in the new hierarchy. Morones became Secretary of Industry and Commerce in the new government headed by Calles. The use of government power to help CROM organize and enforce CROM strikes, a practice that had been relatively common before the de la Huerta revolt, now became standard procedure. CROM became by far the most powerful labor organization in the country, and Morones became one of the most powerful men in the country, thanks to his dual role of labor leader and politician. On the AFL side, the aid that Gompers had extended to CROM's candidate placed CROM in debt to the AFL. Gompers did not live long enough to have the chance to call in some of this debt, but his successor, William Green, soon tried. Meanwhile, the relationship between CROM and the AFL reached a virtual state of euphoria, climaxed by the love-feast joint convention in El Paso and Juarez in November 1924.

On Monday, November 17, both conventions were officially inaugurated in the respective border cities. On the afternoon of the opening day, the delegates to the CROM convention, led by a Mexican army band playing martial music, marched en masse across the river to meet the AFL convention. Morones had been seriously wounded by an unsuccessful assassin in Mexico City, so the CROM procession was led by Juan Rico and other members of the Grupo Acción, the group that controlled CROM. When they entered the hall where the AFL was holding its convention, the AFL delegates rose, applauded, and the El Paso municipal band broke into "The Star Spangled Banner" and "El Grito de Guerra." Gompers greeted them, and Juan Rico and Ricardo Treviño made speeches thanking Gompers and the AFL for the help rendered to the workers of Mexico. Treviño, who had started his career as a labor leader in the IWW, came the closest to saying anything even vaguely suggesting radicalism. He said that the efforts of the organized labor movements of the two countries were against the same group of men, "the group of capitalists that reside in the United States who are now the strongest financial force in the world. It is not a struggle of Mexicans or a struggle of Americans, or even a struggle of only the Pan-American countries. It is a struggle of the workers of the world." [45] But these were mere words. The monstrous force was soon forgotten, and the joyous scene was repeated the next day, when the AFL convention marched across the river to meet their brothers in CROM. Gompers gave the major address.[46] The fact that Mexico was untainted by the curse of national Prohibition made the walk across the border even more worthwhile for the stoutly anti-Prohibitionist AFL delegates. The 1924 convention assumed a paramount position in the legends of hard-drinking AFL conventions, which is still recalled by survivors today.

As the conventions drew to a close, the AFL delegates prepared for what certainly must have been the highlight of the whole affair: an all-expense paid trip to Mexico City to attend the inauguration of Calles. On the last day of the AFL convention, Robert Haberman made the official invitation in the name of CROM. He said that CROM was paying for a special train of Pullmans, hotel accommodations, and as many of the other expenses as possible to enable the AFL delegates to witness the inauguration of "the first chief executive of a nation on this continent elected by organized labor, and only organized labor." [47] Things were indeed looking up for CROM.

The trip, however, was marred by tragedy. Gompers had been in failing health throughout 1924. He had taken ill in March, had spent six weeks in the hospital, and had been under a doctor's supervision and the constant care of a nurse ever since. He had rallied sufficiently to go to El Paso and Mexico City, but in Mexico City he was stricken again, this time fatally. He died in El Paso, while he was being returned to Washington, on December 13, 1924. [48]

At his death, Gompers appeared to have left Mexican-American labor relations in an optimum state, at least as far as CROM and the AFL were concerned. After the war and the defeat of Wilson, he had returned to his old role of protector and defender of the Mexican Revolution in the United States, and there can be no doubt that he enjoyed the role immensely. Gompers, especially in his later years, was not immune to vanity, as even a casual glance through his papers shows. His self-made role of elder-statesman adviser to the Mexicans appealed to him, and he assumed it often. Most of the Mexicans with whom he dealt appear to have realized this, and they took care to inundate him with flattery, which went beyond the bounds of traditional Latin courtesy and politeness. He, in turn, usually assumed an air of benign paternalism when dealing with Mexican unionists, attempting to give them the benefit of his years of experience as a labor leader in a more advanced country. That the Mexican Revolution and the success of CROM did wonders for his ego cannot be doubted. That this was one of the constants behind his continuing interest in Mexico is also apparent.

In the 1920s the AFL was practically excluded from a role near the real centers of power in Washington. Gompers, however, had whetted his appetite for national and international power during World War I, and he was pleased to play the role of one of the fathers of the Mexican Revolution and the Mexican labor movement. As he succumbed to old age, his interest in securing his chosen image in history—that of "labor statesman"—increased. This became one of the overriding considerations in his dealings with Mexico. He was most concerned with developing close relations with CROM and the Mexican government and was not overly concerned about the practical gains that the AFL might secure from them. He seems almost deliberately to have avoided raising issues, such as Mexican immigration and the interchange of union cards, which might threaten to shatter the cordial relations between the two movements. This was fine with CROM, which, with its increasingly close connection with the Obregón-Calles government, was mainly concerned with what Gompers could do for Mexico in Washington.

Thus, at the time of his death, Gompers left Mexican-American labor relations in a quite shaky state despite its surface glimmer. Much of the closeness between the AFL and CROM revolved around his own personality rather than around the direct interests of the two labor organizations. This was true especially of the AFL, which, since the war, had benefited very little from its relationship with CROM.

Ironically, CROM would continue to achieve the benefits it was seeking from the relationship only as long as relations between the U.S. and Mexican governments continued to move, as they had been moving for almost fifteen years, from crisis to crisis. CROM's links with the AFL were primarily of value to it because they appeared to be of value to the Mexican government.[49] The fact that CROM could be of use to the Mexican government in its relations with the United States played no mean part in the privileged position CROM achieved in Mexico. Indeed, it might be said that Morones took a leaf out of Gompers's book and achieved in Mexico almost exactly what Gompers had been aiming at in the United States during World War I.

In spite of the downgrading they received in Gompers's last years, there still were practical benefits the AFL could hope to achieve from its relationship with CROM. His successors recognized this, and as long as the possibility of achieving them existed, they worked to reinforce the ties that the AFL had created with CROM.

NOTES

1. George Edson, "Mexican Labor in the North Central States" [1927] typescript manuscript, Paul Taylor Collection (hereafter referred to as Taylor Papers), Bancroft Library, University of California, Berkeley.

2. Carey McWilliams, *North from Mexico* (Philadelphia: J. B. Lippincott, 1949), p. 163.

3. Ibid., pp. 168, 186.

4. George Edson, "Mexican Labor in the Pittsburgh, Pa., District" [1926], Taylor Papers.

5. McWilliams, *North from Mexico*, p. 184.

6. George Edson, "Mexicans in Indiana Harbor" [1926], Taylor Papers. This was a frequently repeated sentiment. See various reports by Edson, passim, Taylor Papers. From 1920 to 1930, the number of Mexicans living in the north central states jumped from around 3,800 to almost 200,000. McWilliams, *North from Mexico*, p. 184.

7. Gompers to William B. Wilson, Dec. 17, 1918, and Wilson to Gompers, Dec. 18, 1920, Gompers Papers, SHSW.

8. Murray wanted to make the atmosphere of the AFL more congenial to them, and possibly head off the problem of clashes over the restrictions against Mexicans in many AFL locals, by organizing separate Spanish-speaking locals where the situation warranted it. He recommended this to the AFL Executive Council just before the Laredo Conference in No-

vember 1918, but there is no indication that anything was done to implement this. *Pan-American Labor Press* (Nov. 13, 1918).

9. Lewis Warfield to Sen. William Borah, Jan. 17, 1926, William Borah Papers, Library of Congress, Box 268.

10. AFL, *Proceedings,* 1919, pp. 367–378.

11. Gompers to John L. Lewis, Mar. 27, 1924, Gompers Papers, SHSW.

12. Ibid.

13. Ibid.

14. Samuel Gompers, "Labor's Menace in Mexico," *American Federationist* 26 (May 1919): 404.

15. J. H. Rettinger, *Morones de México* (Mexico: Biblioteca de Grupo Acción), pp. 71–74.

16. AFL, *Proceedings,* 1920, p. 124.

17. *New York Times,* Feb. 7, 1920.

18. R. Lee Guard, memoranda, May 24, 25, 1920, Gompers Papers, SHSW.

19. Ambassador in Mexico to State Department, May 20, 1920, State Department Papers, 812.00/24044.

20. Gompers to Obregón, May 25, 1920, Gompers Papers, SHSW.

21. *New York Times,* June 4, 1920. Gompers appears to have forgotten that just two years earlier he had helped to present a plan to settle the difference between Wilson and Carranza that, in essence, amounted to the same thing. See E. H. Greenwood to Gompers, July 7, 1918; memorandum, July 17, 1918; Greenwood, memoranda, July 17, 18, 1918; J. R. Phillips to Greenwood, July 26, 1918; J. R. Phillips, "Memorandum for President Wilson," Aug. 1, 1918: all Gompers Papers, SHSW. See also J. R. Phillips to Woodrow Wilson, May 7, 1918, State Department Papers, 711.12/85.

22. AFL, *Proceedings,* 1920, p. 304.

23. Ibid., 1921, pp. 85–86.

24. Calles to Gompers, July 14, 1921, Gompers Papers, SHSW.

25. AFL, *Proceedings,* 1921, pp. 88–89.

26. Ibid., 1922, pp. 191, 221, 490–493.

27. AFL, *Proceedings,* 1923, p. 113; Pan American Federation of Labor, *Proceedings of the Convention,* 1924, p. 27 (hereafter referred to as PAFL, *Proceedings*).

28. Gompers to Obregón, Sept. 1, 1923; Gompers to CROM, Sept. 1, 1923; CROM to Gompers, Sept. 1, 1923; Obregón to Gompers, Sept. 7, 1923: all Gompers Papers, SHSW. AFL, *Proceedings,* 1923, pp. 364–365.

29. Gompers to Wilson, Oct. 15, 1920, Wilson Papers, File VI, Box 187.

30. Ibid., Dec. 15, 1920, Gompers Papers, SHSW.

31. Sinclair Snow, "The Pan-American Federation of Labor" (Ph.D. diss., University of Virginia, 1960), pp. 168–169.

32. Morones to Gompers, Nov. 15, 1921, Gompers Papers, SHSW.

33. See Morones to William Johnston, Nov. 15, 1921, Gompers Papers, SHSW.

34. Gompers to Morones, Dec. 22, 1921, Gompers Papers, SHSW.

35. Minutes de las conferencias celebradas en el Hotel Paso del Norte, El Paso, Texas, los días 25, 26 y 27 de octubre de 1923, Santiago Iglesias Papers, San Juan, P. R., cited in Snow, "Pan-American Federation," pp. 180–182.

36. Ibid.

37. *New York Times,* Dec. 16, 1923.

38. *Excelsior,* Nov. 7, 1923.

39. *New York Times,* Nov. 9, 1923. Calles telegraphed his thanks to Gompers. Calles to Gompers, Nov. 11, 1923, Gompers Papers, SHSW.

40. Indeed, when de la Huerta was Provisional President of Mexico after the overthrow of Carranza, he had helped the Arizona State Federation of Labor, an AFL organization, to combat the use of Mexicans to break a strike in the cotton fields. William Green to Morones, Sept. 9, 1925, Copied Letters of William Green, AFL-CIO Building, Washington, D.C. (hereafter referred to as Green Copybooks).

41. *New York Times,* Dec. 22, 1923.

42. PAFL, *Proceedings,* 1924, p. 34.

43. *New York Times,* Dec. 22, 1923.

44. Ibid., Jan. 31, 1923.

45. AFL, *Proceedings,* 1924, pp. 100–103.

46. R. Lee Guard to John Macrae, Nov. 26, 1924, Gompers Papers, SHSW.

47. AFL, *Proceedings,* 1924, pp. 166–167.

48. R. Lee Guard to Louis LeBosse, Jan. 28, 1925, Gompers Papers, SHSW.

49. A major factor that must be borne in mind was the consistent over-rating on the part of the Mexicans of the influence of Gompers and the AFL on American foreign policy.

8

An Experiment
in Labor Diplomacy

GOMPERS'S SUCCESSOR as president of the AFL, William Green
of the United Mine Workers, was a man of much different
temperament and personality. Much more retiring than
Gompers, he was the epitome of the old-style AFL "business
unionist." Whereas Gompers was flamboyant and showy and
had an arresting personality, Green could only be described as
bland and innocuous. While the change in leadership did
nothing to pull the AFL out of its slump in membership and
effectiveness, it did have important effects on the AFL's relations with CROM. Green did not value the relationship for
the opportunities it gave him to bask in the limelight, as had
Gompers in his later years. He was much more interested in the
practical benefits the AFL could derive from its connection
with Mexican labor. Under Green, many of the more formal
functions in maintaining the appearance of good relations were
left to Frank Morrison, secretary-treasurer of the AFL. To
many outsiders it began to appear that Morrison was the key
man in the AFL's relations with Mexico.[1] The real difference
was that, under Gompers, the AFL's relations with CROM had

been conducted practically as a one-man show, whereas under Green, the Executive Council of the AFL played a much greater role in formulating Mexican policy.

The difference in style between Green and Gompers is illustrated in an incident that occurred soon after Green took over. Green had intervened with the Governor of Texas to obtain the release of some Mexicans who had been imprisoned for their activities during the Mexican Revolution.[2] When the Governor ordered their release, the Mexican Foreign Office suggested that Clarence Idar, the AFL organizer in Texas who had played a major role in bringing pressure to bear on the Governor, accompany the released men to Mexico. The Foreign Office felt that this would dramatize the role played by the AFL in obtaining the release. Green vetoed the idea. He was sure that CROM and the Mexican government knew of the AFL's sympathy for the prisoners and its goodwill toward the Mexican labor movement; therefore, he did not think that Idar's accompanying the men to Mexico would add to this.[3] In a similar situation, Gompers would likely have sent an AFL brass band to accompany the men.

If he was less aware than Gompers of the value of publicity, Green was also more concerned about getting something out of the relationship that was to be publicized. Soon after taking office, Green changed the tactics of the AFL regarding the problem of Mexican immigration. Virtually abandoning hope of having immigration from Mexico cut off through legislation by the U.S. Congress, the AFL now tried to have it restricted from the other side of the border—by CROM and the government of Mexico.

In the spring of 1925, Green was forced to search for a solution to the problems that the continued immigration of Mexicans created for the AFL. The AFL was planning a major organization drive in the Southwest, particularly among the miners of Arizona and New Mexico. Clarence Idar, who was to help direct the drive, wrote to Green that continued immigration from Mexico presented a major obstacle and made the success of the plans doubtful.[4]

In his reply to Idar, Green outlined the AFL's predicament with regard to Mexican immigration. Government policy, he said, did not permit discrimination for or against any nation. If Mexico were placed under the quota and Canada were not, "the Mexican government could rightfully protest and would undoubtedly do so." The AFL was thus convinced that the quota could not be applied to Mexico without also being applied to Canada. Unstated was that in this form the quota could never pass Congress. As yet, said Green, the AFL had made no decision on what its policy should be, but the Executive Council intended to arrive at some conclusions and formulate a policy within the next few months.[5]

Green had attended Calles's inauguration and was much impressed by "how controlling was the influence of the Mexican Federation of Labor" in Mexico.[6] He soon determined to use the influence of CROM to help solve the problem. By early May 1925, he was seriously considering the advisability of calling an AFL–CROM conference to deal with the question.[7] A few days later, when another report of the adverse effects of Mexican immigration came in from an AFL organizer in Arizona, Green definitely decided to call a meeting with CROM to work out a long-term solution to the problem.[8] Meanwhile, as an immediate measure, he had asked CROM to obtain the cooperation of the Mexican consuls in the United States for the AFL organizing campaign in the Southwest. This the CROM did promptly, and Eduardo Moneda, the secretary-general of CROM, sent Green several letters containing promises of cooperation from the various consuls.[9]

At the next AFL Executive Council meeting, Green proposed an AFL–CROM conference on immigration, but the Executive Council deferred a decision. It recommended that Green investigate the matter further. Green devoted much time and thought to the problem and finally decided that the only solution lay in working through CROM.[10] He invited Eduardo Moneda, Secretary-General of CROM, and his associates— notably Luis Morones—to Washington on July 23 or July 24 to discuss Mexican immigation.[11] Two days later Secretary of State Frank Kellogg gave added impetus to the conference by precipitating a crisis in Mexican-American relations. Kellogg threatened that the United States would raise the arms embargo on Mexico (thus aiding anti–Calles plotters) unless the Mexican government complied with its demands. These demands included the immediate restoration of land "illegally" taken from Americans in Mexico in the course of enforcing the agrarian reform decrees and the indemnification of the Americans for their losses.[12]

Green telegraphed Moneda immediately urging that, because of the importance of the immigration problem and "recent developments of vital interest to both American and Mexican labor," CROM send a delegation of at least three representatives to the conference.[13] Then, in a press release, Green said that, although the conference had been proposed to consider immigration problems, Kellogg's statement had "created additional reason for an exchange of views between representatives of labor of Mexico and the United States." [14] After vigorous protests from the AFL and other anti-interventionist groups, Kellogg modified his statement, and the storm subsided. Luis Morones then took ill, and the conference was postponed until late August so that he could attend.[15]

The conference finally convened in Washington on August 27. The four Mexican delegates were led by Morones and Eduardo Moneda. The AFL delegation was headed by Green and Matthew Woll.[16] At the conference, it soon became clear that the Mexicans were also concerned about the problems caused by Mexican immigration to the United States, but from a vantage point different from that of the Americans. They were concerned about the economic and social plight of the Mexican immigrants, and the discrimination they met in the

United States, often by AFL unions. The Mexicans were intent on securing what they had tried to secure at the 1919 Laredo Conference: guarantees from the AFL that Mexicans in the United States would receive the same treatment from AFL unions as native-born Americans. To help achieve equal treatment, they saw two things the labor organizations could do. First, they could establish a system of "international union cards," which would guarantee the holder membership with full rights in the counterpart to his union if he crossed the border. Second, they could make an effort to organize people before they left their native lands.[17]

Green and the AFL, on the other hand, were determined to deal with the problems caused by Mexican immigration by cutting it off at its source. To achieve this, they proposed the principle of "voluntary self-restraint." This meant, in effect, that CROM was to press the Mexican government into severely restricting emigration to the United States.[18] The AFL obviously thought that Morones, the Secretary of Labor, Industry, and Commerce, presumed to be the strong man behind Calles, would certainly be able to accomplish this.

There emerged from the conference a compromise agreement, which embodied both the AFL and CROM views and thus pleased both sides. Each was able to read victory into the part of the agreement that contained its proposals and to ignore the section that embodied the proposals of the other. The AFL succeeded in having the final declaration open with a long statement calling for the two organizations to press their respective governments for the "adoption *and enforcement* of this new principle of voluntary restraint." [19] The agreement did admit, however, that lack of information prevented recommendations for specific legislation at that moment. Thus, the statement recommended that a joint committee, consisting of two members of each organization, be set up to study the problem and suggest specific action.[20]

At the conference, the CROM representatives had admitted

that Mexican immigrants often took jobs at lower wages than their American counterparts, but they claimed that this was for self-preservation. Because the immigrants were denied living conditions equal to those of American workers, they were forced to take the first jobs offered to them. Mexican immigrants, according to the CROM delegates, were also hamstrung because they were denied facilities to organize themselves or to join AFL unions. To satisfy these arguments, a statement affirming that immigrants should be guaranteed equal opportunity to join unions and equal status within them was written into the final agreement. However, there was no agreement to establish the most important means of facilitating this—the international union card. The new committee was to examine this possibility as well.[21]

Green was highly pleased by the outcome of the conference, and he apparently took the principle of "voluntary restraint" to mean that Morones indeed would have the Mexican government restrict emigration.[22] Morones, however, upon his return to Mexico, made it clear that he in no way interpreted the agreement to favor restriction of Mexican emigration. He emphasized the importance of securing equal rights for Mexicans in the United States and said that the conference had achieved much along these lines. He interpreted the section on equality of rights to mean that American workers in Mexico should not receive higher wages and better working conditions than their Mexican counterparts. The closest he came to mentioning "voluntary self-restraint" was to say that CROM had always advised Mexican workers not to leave the country and would continue to do so. Those who elected to leave, however, should be instructed not to depress the wage levels of the United States.[23]

Immediately upon the return of the delegates, the official magazine of CROM took pains to point out that CROM in no way favored restrictions on Mexican emigration to the United States. The only restrictions the CROM favored were those designed to curb the nefarious activities of the *engancha-dores*, the men who hired Mexican labor under false pretenses. "The delegates of Mexico and the United States worked hard and nobly," wrote *CROM*, "but for their labor to be crowned with definite success, many suns and many moons must pass, an indispensable interregnum for the Anglo-Saxons to convince themselves that they are not the superior beings they suppose they are." It would be a long time, the editorial concluded, before the fruits of the labors of the Mexican delegation would be gathered.[24]

While the Mexicans were emphasizing what could be called the civil rights section of the agreement, the AFL was playing it down. The Executive Council reported to the 1925 AFL convention that, as an immediate means of dealing with the problem, it urged workers to join the union of their trade in the country to which they go. The council pledged to bring about observance of this principle by its affiliates, but there is no indication that it made any major effort to persuade AFL unions to abandon discriminatory actions against Mexicans.[25]

By December 1925, Green was beginning to doubt CROM's desire to fulfill the part of the agreement concerning voluntary restriction of emigration. Reports of some of Morones's statements on the subject were filtering back to the United States. Clarence Idar wrote him concerning reports of an interview that Morones gave upon his return to Mexico, in which it appeared that CROM was interpreting the nature of the agreement differently from the AFL. Green expressed great interest in this and asked for a copy of a translation of the interview as soon as possible. He reaffirmed his faith in Morones to Idar, but it was apparent that his confidence had been shaken.[26] CROM had been trying to carry out the part of the agreement dealing with the organization of Mexicans residing in the United States. Immediately upon the ending of the conference Idar was appointed chief CROM organizer in the United States to assist in this,[27] but there is no indication that Morones was doing anything to have the Mexican government adopt a restrictive immigration policy.

The AFL sent representatives to the CROM convention in March 1926, and they spent much of their time lobbying for enforcement of voluntary restriction. They were assured that the Mexican government had no desire to see a large number of nationals leave the country, and it was intimated that something would be done after the joint AFL-CROM committee came up with some specific recommendations.[28]

For some reason, it took over a year to appoint the committee. Morones had appointed the two CROM members of the committee, but Green had delayed, possibly awaiting either a favorable turn of events in Congress or a good reason to have it meet in Washington. (The AFL could thereby save some sorely needed funds, and Green would have direct contact with the AFL negotiators.) Finally, in February 1927, an opportunity came with the decision to hold the Fifth Congress of the nearly defunct Pan-American Federation of Labor in Washington later in the year. Green appointed Matthew Woll and Edward F. McGrady, the chief AFL congressional lobbyist, as the AFL representatives on the joint committee and suggested to the Mexicans that the committee meet in Washington concurrently with the PAFL Congress. This was agreed to by CROM.[29]

The joint committee assembled in Washington in early August at the AFL head office. The AFL emerged flushed with success. According to Green, he had instructed the AFL representatives to say to the Mexicans: "Unless you meet the issues, unless you stop this influx of immigration into the United States, if you do not do this voluntarily, then we serve notice on you that the quota provisions of the immigration law will be applied to Mexico." [30] Green was bluffing. The complications that would ensue with Mexico and Canada, if one or both were placed under the quota, remained, and Congress was still in no mood to risk them. But either the bluff worked or the Mexican delegates signed agreements that CROM had no intention of carrying out, for the AFL emerged from the meeting with a CROM agreement to a detailed plan of voluntary restriction of immigration. The agreement outlined political and economic methods for dealing with immigration problems. The political steps could be undertaken by governments; the economic steps could be achieved directly by the labor organizations themselves.

In the political part of the agreement, CROM agreed to press the Mexican government to restrict Oriental and other "unsuitable" immigration into Mexico,[31] to enact restrictive emigration legislation, "which, in substance [would] conform to the Immigration Law requirements of the United States," and adopt a method of regulating emigration that would enable the enforcement of the above policy. In return, the AFL promised not to press for the inclusion of Mexico under the official quota.

The economic methods outlined in the agreement provided more substantial concessions to Mexican demands, but none of major proportions. The two organizations agreed to keep each other informed of labor conditions in their countries that might tempt employers to recruit cheap foreign labor, and the CROM was to make every effort to discourage emigration by Mexican workers to the United States and Canada. When it did take place, they would encourage the Mexican workers to join the relevant American unions, warning them that failure to do this would result in loss of their Mexican union cards. In return, the AFL agreed to make every effort to ensure Mexican workers free access to and equal membership in its affiliated unions. The two organizations also agreed to set up a bureau of emigration and immigration, to which workers and unions could apply for information on labor conditions and related subjects in the two countries.[32] There was no agreement on inaugurating the main goal of CROM—the international union card. The AFL had obviously won a major "diplomatic" victory—on paper, at least.

Green had high hopes for the agreement, for he was banking on the power of CROM in Mexico. In justifying the agreement to the AFL Convention in October 1927, Green said:

> We are trying to get results, and if my information is correct, coming as it does from many sources, the Mexican Federation of Labor wields a tremendous influence in the governmental affairs of Mexico. Particularly does it exercise a tremendous influence in this administration.
>
> Some have said there is an inseparable relationship between the Mexican Federation of Labor and the Calles Government; some have said that the Mexican Federation of Labor dictates the policies of the Mexican government. No man can go to Mexico without coming from there with a deep impression that the Mexican Federation of Labor exercises a tremendous influence in the legislative and governmental affairs of Mexico.[33]

If somewhat exaggerated, Green's information was substantially correct. Unfortunately for the AFL-CROM agreement, however, events in Mexico soon brought about the downfall of CROM from its position of high influence and power. The fall of CROM highlighted the importance which the AFL had placed on CROM's ability to have the Mexican government pass restrictive emigration legislation. At the next convention, the Executive Council reported that every effort had been made, by both the AFL and CROM, to carry out the August 1927 agreement, but "political changes in Mexico . . . make it impossible to carry out the voluntary agreement." Therefore, the Executive Council recommended the endorsement of an amendment to the immigration act making the quota system applicable to Mexico and Central and South America.[34] The idea of "voluntary self-restraint" had died a quick, certain death.

CROM was not unduly disturbed by the return of the AFL

to backing the inclusion of Mexico under the quota, for by this time they were well aware that the possibility of its becoming law was extremely unlikely. Relations between the governments of the United States and Mexico had improved perceptibly, thanks to the new ambassador in Mexico, Dwight Morrow, and the new conservative course of the Mexican government, and there was considerable reason for the U.S. government to avoid antagonizing Mexico. In late 1929, *CROM* correspondent F. L. Bustamante reported from the United States that although labor organizations were putting pressure on Capitol Hill to place Mexico under the quota, far greater pressure was coming from businessmen and chambers of commerce against doing so. In addition, the reluctance of the administration to allow a bill to pass that would antagonize Latin American countries unduly meant that there was little possibility of obtaining the legislation desired by the AFL.[35] The AFL Executive Council admitted as much when, in its report to the 1929 convention, it pointed to the great obstacles faced by the measure. In the cabinet, the secretaries of State, Agriculture, and Interior were actively opposed to it. Only the Secretary of Labor favored it.[36] Though the AFL continued to press for the inclusion of Mexico in the quota, its efforts in this direction were futile. When Green mentioned them to the secretary-general of CROM in 1931, the latter probably in all honesty replied that Green could be assured that the efforts would in no way affect the cordial relations between the AFL and CROM.[37]

In any event, the Great Depression soon accomplished what the AFL had worked for throughout the 1920s. Mexican immigration came to virtual standstill in 1930. In the subsequent years, during the depression, the flow was partially reversed. About 65,000 Mexican immigrants returned to their homeland, some voluntarily, some with the aid of the Mexican government. Others were summarily shipped back to Mexico by welfare agencies in the United States.[38]

NOTES

1. See Chief of the Division of Mexican Affairs to Ambassador Grew, Mar. 31, 1925, State Department Papers, 812.504/613.
2. Green to Gov. Ferguson, June 20, 1925; Idar to Green, June 30, 1925; Green to Idar, July 9, 20, 1925: all Green Copybooks.
3. Green to Idar, July 28, 1925, Green Copybooks.
4. Green to Idar, Apr. 23, 1925 (two letters), Green Copybooks.
5. Ibid.
6. AFL, *Proceedings*, 1927, p. 331.
7. Green to Idar, May 13, 1925, Green Copybooks.
8. Green to C. H. Moyer, May 22, 1925, Green Copybooks; W. C. Roberts, "Memo for Mr. Green," May 21, 1925, AFL Papers, Files of the Office of President, Papers of William Green, State Historical Society of Wisconsin, Madison, Wisconsin (hereafter cited as Green Papers, SHSW).
9. Green to Moneda, June 4, 1925, Green Copybooks; *CROM*, Year 1, no. 6 (May 15, 1925): 57.
10. Green to Matthew Woll, June 16, 1925, and Green to Iglesias, June 16, 1925, Green Copybooks.
11. Green to Moneda, June 12, 1925, Green Copybooks.
12. *New York Times,* June 15, 1925.
13. Green to Moneda, June 15, 1925, Green Copybooks.
14. Press release, June 17, 1925, Green Papers, SHSW, File B.
15. Green to Idar, July 11, 1925, Green Copybooks.
16. AFL, *Proceedings*, 1925, p. 86.
17. *CROM,* Year 1, no. 15 (Oct. 1, 1925): 1.
18. AFL, *Proceedings*, 1925, p. 87.
19. Ibid.
20. Ibid.
21. *CROM,* Year 1, no. 15, p. 3.
22. Green to Morones, Oct. 23, 1925, and Green to Moneda, Oct. 23, 1925, Green Copybooks. Indeed, the four members of the joint committee were not named for a year and a half, probably in anticipation of action by Morones which would preclude the necessity of the committee.
23. *CROM,* Year 1, no. 15, pp. 4–7.
24. *CROM,* Year 1, no. 13 (Sept. 1, 1925): 1. This became the usual interpretation which CROM people gave to the agreement, subject to variations injected to suit the audience. For example, see George Edson, "Memo on Conference of Home Mission Council, Dec. 21, 1926," Taylor Papers.
25. AFL, *Proceedings*, 1925, pp. 87–88.
26. Green to Idar, Dec. 1, 1925, Green Copybooks.
27. *CROM,* Year 1, no. 13, p. 3.
28. Clipping from *Fresno Labor News,* n.d. [March 1926?], Green Papers, SHSW.
29. "Informe del Consejo Ejecutivo de la Confederación Obrera Pan-

Americana cubriendo el periodo desde enero 1 de 1925 hasta junio 30 de 1927," *CROM*, Year 3, no. 16 (Aug. 15, 1927): 47–48.

30. AFL, *Proceedings*, 1927, p. 331.

31. Chinese and Japanese were emigrating to Mexico, obtaining Mexican citizenship, and then emigrating to the United States as Mexicans, unhampered by quotas.

32. AFL, *Proceedings*, 1927, pp. 95–98.

33. Ibid., p. 330.

34. Ibid., 1928, p. 95.

35. *CROM*, Year 4, no. 22 (Nov. 15, 1929): 37.

36. AFL, *Proceedings*, 1929, pp. 80–81.

37. Torres to Green, Sept. 18, 1931, Green Papers, SHSW, File B.

38. Carey McWilliams, *North from Mexico* (Philadelphia and New York: J. B. Lippincott, 1949), p. 185.

9

The Life
and Death of
the AFL-CROM Alliance

ALTHOUGH GREEN'S main interest in Mexico was curbing Mexican immigration, he continued the Gompers tradition of defending CROM and the Mexican government against attacks in the United States. This was CROM's major objective in maintaining good relations with the AFL. From the time he assumed the office of president of the AFL until CROM's fall from power in 1928, Green was involved with Mexican affairs. Only on the surface does it appear that he was less active in this respect than Gompers had been.

The surface belies the reality for various reasons. In the first place, the decline in AFL membership and importance during the 1920s meant a decline in Green's ability to influence American government policy. Also, Green never achieved the public stature that Gompers had secured for himself. Anything Green said seemed pale and weak compared to Gompers's pronunciamentos. Furthermore, although relations between the United States and Mexico continued in their deplorable state until 1928, there were fewer real crises, such as uprisings in Mexico, on which Green could take public stands. Compounding the AFL's difficulties was its dire financial condition, which lasted until well into the 1930s. This limited the organization's ability to send people to Mexico and even to comply with the agreements it made with CROM.[1]

Still, Green continued to do what he could in Washington for CROM, all the while pressing CROM for action on immigration in return. In early March 1925, at the behest of one of its affiliates, the Central Committee of CROM asked Green to communicate their protest of the death sentence against Sacco and Vanzetti to the United States government. CROM regarded the sentence as a case of capitalist vengeance against labor.[2] Green replied that, in accordance with an AFL convention resolution, he had asked the President and the governor of Massachusetts that a new trial be granted.[3] This smacked of mere formality, but CROM appeared satisfied with the reply.

In June 1925, Secretary of State Kellogg, after conferring with the American ambassador in Mexico, the President, and leaders of Congress, issued a statement intended to stir the Mexican government into halting the expropriation of American property in carrying out its program of agrarian reform. Kellogg strongly implied that unless the Mexican government restored property it had taken "illegally" from Americans and indemnified them for their losses, the United States would lift its embargo on arms shipments to Mexico. This would be of great aid to any opponents of Calles who planned armed uprisings. It warned that the Calles government could expect the American government to continue to prevent revolutions from being mounted on United States soil "only as long as it protect[ed] American lives and rights" and complied with its international obligations.[4]

Kellogg's statement aroused a storm of protest among anti-interventionists in the United States. When Calles refused to back down, Eugene Debs wrote Calles a public letter in which he applauded his standing up to "the servile lawyer who occupies, thanks to the 'interests' to whom he has dedicated his life, the post of Secretary of State in the present Wall Street Administration." [5] The day after Kellogg's statement, Green issued a press release deploring the secretary's attitude and defending the Mexican government. Green apparently was at a loss to figure out just what had occasioned the secretary's belligerent statement. The next day, he went to see the Mexican ambassador in Washington to see if he knew the reason. The ambassador also claimed to be unaware of the reasons for the Kellogg statement.[6] Kellogg had demanded also that the Mexican government act to restore the property confiscated by the government "on account of the unreasonable demands of labor." [7] The ambassador said that all he could think of that might have a bearing on the question was a minor incident on May 1 concerning U.S. Ambassador James Sheffield and his chauffeur, or the strike at the Jalapa Electric Company. There the workers had struck the American-owned company, and the owners had simply locked up the place and gone home, leaving the town without light, heat, and water. The authorities had reopened the utility, he said, offering to return it to anyone who identified himself as the owner upon his arrival.[8]

Green was concerned, but he was unsure of the ground on which he stood. He wrote in protest to Kellogg and demanded an explanation. He said that he was "seriously concerned that there should even be the implication that our government would lend aid and support to a movement against the constitutional government of Mexico." [9] Kellogg called Green to his office, telling him that he had confidential information that he did not wish to put in writing. At the meeting, Kellogg assured Green that the government had no intention of bringing about a revolution in Mexico or of endangering the stability of the Mexican government in any manner.[10]

Green either was not particularly impressed by Kellogg's assurances or he felt that he must still make a ritual protest for the sake of preserving the AFL relationship with CROM.

The same day, Green received a telegram from Eduardo Moneda, secretary-general of CROM, denying and protesting Kellogg's charges and asking Green to issue a statement on the situation.[11] Green complied and, in a press release announcing the upcoming AFL–CROM meeting on immigration, expressed his concern over Kellogg's threats.[12] He telegraphed Moneda expressing his apprehension and assured him of the full support of the AFL for the workers of Mexico and President Calles. The next day, he issued another press release, this time denying the charges, most prominently voiced in the *Washington Post* and the *Wall Street Journal,* that CROM and Morones were communistic.[13]

Whatever their effect in Washington, Green's protests made a good impression in Mexico. The magazine *CROM* was highly pleased. It quoted an Argentinian senator, who said: "I don't think that the Government of the United States, in its policy towards Mexico, worries about the liberty and welfare of that people. This view is so dominant that the Buenos Aires dailies are printing the declarations of the AFL and those of the American Government in parallel columns." [14]

The AFL continued to remain alert to any threat to the Calles government. In early 1927, when rumors again swept Washington that the government planned to lift the embargo against the sale of arms to Mexican revolutionaries, Green sent the AFL chief legislative lobbyist, Edward McGrady, to participate in a meeting of representatives of sixty national organizations at which an anti-intervention campaign was to be mapped out. McGrady was appointed to the committee that was to run the campaign.[15]

Throughout the 1920s, Mexico continued to bear the brunt of violent attacks from Catholic groups, big business groups, and conservatives in general, for its official anticlericalism and social revolutionary goals. The charges generally fell into three major categories: that Mexico was persecuting priests and nuns, that its agrarian laws and labor policies were confiscatory and

Bolshevik, and that the government itself was communist. Also, the CROM frequently was charged with being a communist organization, which either dominated, or was dominated by, the government. The AFL as a major defender of CROM and the Mexican government, was forced to deal with all of these charges.

In early 1926, an uproar arose in the United States over the introduction of a law in the Mexican Congress that would implement, in part, the agrarian reform promised in the constitution of 1917 and restrict the right of foreigners to own land. Green sent Santiago Iglesias to Mexico to investigate. Iglesias returned with a favorable report, and Green issued a statement defending the Mexican government's right to resolve its own problems. He pointed out that many American states had agrarian laws, and that in some of them foreigners were prohibited from inheriting land.[16]

Later in the year, Green and the Executive Council were faced with the problem of defending the Mexican government on the Catholic issue. In essence, the policies of the Calles government and many of the state governments toward the church were indefensible in American terms. The American public was not particularly aware of the unique role played by the Catholic church in Latin America. That churches were being closed down and priests subjected to various forms of intimidation was undeniable. After some correspondence with CROM on the matter, the Executive Council decided that the best way to handle the issue was to ignore it, declaring that it was a purely domestic matter in which the AFL had no right to intervene. In its report to the 1926 AFL convention, at which its Mexican policy came under fire from Catholic members, the Executive Council stated that it had not "tried in any way whatsoever to intervene in this matter and has made absolutely no effort to influence the decisions of the Mexican Federation of Labor." [17]

The International Relations Committee of the convention

heartily approved of this course, but it did recommend that the Executive Council make an investigation into the relationship alleged to exist between CROM and the Mexican government. The delegate who seconded this recommendation, a Catholic from Connecticut, tried to inject the religious issue. He said that he was confident that the Executive Council in their investigation would see that they had been deceived and that the Mexican government and its "kept woman"—CROM—were Communists intent on destroying religion in the first step toward turning Mexico into another Russia. He was denounced by Matthew Woll and Daniel Tobin, both Catholics and members of the Executive Council, who warned that injecting the religious issue into debates would have dangerous divisive effects on the AFL itself.[18]

Woll was assigned to investigate the charges that an unsavory connection existed between CROM and the Mexican government. Actually, the call for an investigation had probably been instigated by the Executive Council, which had a great interest in determining just how influential CROM could be in having the Mexican government restrict immigration. Woll went to an unlikely source for unbiased information on the subject—the State Department. He asked Kellogg for all the data he could furnish on the subject. Kellogg asked Ambassador Sheffield in Mexico to prepare a memorandum on the subject. Sheffield's memorandum was so biased and anti-CROM that Robert F. Kelley of the eastern European desk (the department's expert on "bolshevism") decided that it could not be sent to Woll in its present form. Instead of sending Sheffield's memorandum to Woll, he said, the State Department should invite Woll to examine other, less offensive, memoranda on the subject.[19]

Woll prepared a long official report absolving CROM of the charge that it was in the pay of the government. He portrayed it as an independent labor movement, whose members were active in government, which supported government when government supported it.[20] This indeed was the way things appeared to be on the surface. The difficulty was that Woll failed to see the importance that government support played in CROM's role as Mexico's dominant labor confederation. There is no doubt, however, that Woll and the Executive Council were greatly impressed by CROM's influence in the government.

CROM was consistently charged, in the American press and Congress, with being a "Bolshevik" organization, and the AFL consistently defended it against the charges. The charges, of course, were absurd. Although CROM was indeed to the left of the AFL politically, by the mid-1920s it had become as anti-Communist as the AFL. It definitely was not espousing the revolutionary unionism of the Third International in the 1920s. However, it had not taken the hard line of the AFL against the Russian Revolution, and there was much sympathy for the Soviets within CROM.

After a brief flirtation with the Russians in the early 1920s, CROM was forced to make a choice between cultivating close relations with them or with the AFL. It was obvious that the AFL could not regard as an ally an organization that had close relations with the Russian unions. The Russian unions, on the other hand, were unwilling to have much to do with an organization that considered itself an ally of the AFL. Matters reached a head in 1925. Morones declared that CROM would never affiliate with the Russians so long as the AFL held aloof.[21] This, of course, meant that CROM would never affiliate with the Russians. Then, Morones used an incident involving alleged snooping by the Russians on Eulalio Martínez, the Mexican labor attaché in Moscow, as an excuse to sever relations with the Soviets.

Martínez was withdrawn, and the next CROM convention was asked to officially suspend relations with the Soviet labor movement.[22] The convention also charged the Russian ambassador in Mexico with giving financial aid to radical groups that opposed CROM and the government.[23] The former charge was likely true, and, given the militant policy of the Third International, the latter charge was most likely true. However, a major reason for the break was also the attitude of the Third International toward the AFL. Martínez emphasized this point in his speech to the convention.[24]

Green had not instigated the break with Russia, but he did approve of it. He wrote Morones that he was gratified at his refusal to affiliate with the Russians.[25] When the CROM protested the activities of the Soviet ambassador, Secretary-General Ricardo Treviño sent a copy of the protest to Green, asking that the AFL give it publicity.[26] Treviño undoubtedly wished to confirm CROM's antibolshevism to Green as well as to the American public. As an added confirmation, he refused to have anything to do with any left-wing organization in the United States without prior AFL approval.[27]

Thus, when charges were raised in Congress that Morones and Haberman were "Bolsheviks," the AFL was ready to defend them in all honesty. Santiago Iglesias drafted a public statement, issued in the name of the Executive Committee of the PAFL, headed by Green, which said that not only were Morones and Haberman not Bolsheviks, but that they and CROM were staunch defenders against bolshevism. The statement declared that CROM had cooperated to the fullest extent with the AFL in combating "bolshevist" propaganda in North America.[28]

It was comforting for the AFL to be able sincerely to defend CROM against the charges of being a revolutionary union. This not only made it easier to establish close relations with CROM and negotiate on immigration; it saved the AFL from the prospect of having to face a revolutionary union at its back door. Santiago Iglesias made this clear in an article on the PAFL in the *American Federationist*. He wrote that the PAFL stood

on a declaration of policy squarely in harmony with the policies of the American Federation of Labor. It is the instrumentality through which constructive trade unionism can gain the ascendancy in Latin America, thus saving the American trade union movement from a continuing battle at its back door with a most destructive and revolutionary labor movement.[29]

The American critics of CROM, however, remained unconvinced by the anti-Soviet statements of Morones and Treviño and the AFL's clean bill of health for CROM. This is understandable, for the critics were mainly concerned with the threat that CROM posed to American investors in Mexico. This becomes apparent in the references to the subject in the dispatches of Ambassador Sheffield to the State Department. After CROM's break with the Soviets in 1925, Sheffield readily acknowledged the probable sincerity of CROM's anti-Soviet stand. However, he was always quick to point out that, in practice, this still did nothing to make them distinguishable from Communists. He was not as concerned about the spread of Soviet influence in Mexico as he was about the dangers that CROM's government-backed strikes posed to American corporations in Mexico. Indeed, when, in 1927, an anti-CROM union in the government-owned railway network accepted a gift of $25,000 from a Russian union to help continue a strike, Morones raised a hue and cry, but Sheffield remained unperturbed. He saw nothing to choose between the two unions; in practice, one was as bad as the other.[30]

As Green and the AFL defended CROM in the United States and tried to come to an agreement with it, CROM appeared to be prospering greatly in Mexico. By 1925, it was claiming a membership of 1.5 million.[31] Although Mexican unions' claims on membership figures were often exaggerated, CROM was by far the largest confederation of unions in the country and the most powerful. Its size and power had one main foundation—the support it received from the government.

The key to CROM's favored position in the government lay in its support of Calles and Obregón during the de la Huerta revolt of 1923. Then it had proved its loyalty, dependability, and usefulness to the Obregón-Calles machine. Also, together with the generals in the army, many of whom could claim the personal loyalty of their troops, and the Agrarian party, led in the 1920s by Zapata's former aide Diaz Soto y Gama, Morones's Partido Laborista, with its socialist allies in the Southeast, was one of the few organized groups in the country that could claim any kind of mass political support. In 1924, a rather bitter U.S. consul-general in Mexico recalled:

> It is well remembered that syndicalism [CROM] secured a new lease of power and influence by its open vociferous support of the government against the De la Huerta revolution of 1923, when all other political influences were either neutral, lukewarm, or hostile. Observers in the capital city during the crisis will remember the depth of passion with which the Mexican Regional Workers Confederation preached assassination of the government's enemies as the only means of maintaining labor supremacy. They also remember how the aforesaid Confederation boldly asserted that its constituency, seconded by the agrarians, stood alone in support of the government, and promised that steadfast allegiance would be rewarded.[32]

Calles had not confined his recruiting of labor support to the Federal District. When the revolt broke out, he travelled north to San Luis Potosí, near a center of rebel strength, and, possibly recalling the glorious days of the "Red Battalions" of 1915, distributed arms to labor unions and organized labor battalions.[33]

Government support for CROM took many forms. One of the most common techniques, and certainly one of the most effective, was the threat of nationalization or confiscation if owners did not recognize a CROM union as the bargaining agent for their workers. This could be done in a completely constitutional manner. Although no law outlining the procedures to be followed in implementing it had yet been passed, Article 123 of the Mexican Constitution stated that management had to recognize and bargain with a union if a majority of its workers belonged to it. When a union recognized as a bargaining agent by the government declared a factory on strike, the government could call the strike a legitimate one and enforce the closure of the factory, without the union having to mount picket lines.

Needless to say, this gave the President, who could do all of the above by decree, tremendous power to help his friends in the labor movement and hinder his enemies. Obregón had used these and other official powers to help CROM organize, but Calles, to many observers, seemed to be going overboard. The following episode exemplifies the lengths to which Calles went to help CROM, especially when it was trying to organize foreign-owned companies. In 1925 a CROM union struck the British-owned Mexico City tramway company. The Canadian manager, G. R. Conway, refused to admit that the union represented a majority of his workers, and a protracted strike ensued. Calles threatened to have Conway deported unless he gave in. When Conway persisted, Calles told him that, if he did not recognize the CROM union, not only would he be ejected from the country, but the government would also take possession of both the tramway company and its much more profitable parent, the Mexican Light and Power Company. Needless to say, Conway gave in.[34]

In 1926 the constitutional powers granted the government and labor were made even more effective by the passage of a federal labor law setting up legal institutional forms for the declaration and enforcement of strikes.

The Obregón-Calles government was content to continue its relation with CROM as long as it served to consolidate the government's power and did not hinder the government in any way. During Calles's left-wing phase, in 1925 and 1926, CROM was a useful body to have supporting him against the attacks of the conservative elements of Mexico and the United States. However, by 1927 he was beginning to mellow. He began to heed the vociferous opposition of American and Mexican landed interests to continued agrarian reform. The threats that American financial interests, allied with the U.S. government, could force Mexico into economic and social chaos appeared more apparent. Gradually, Calles slackened the pace of agrarian reform and slowly abandoned the antichurch drive. This paved the way for Ambassador Dwight Morrow's mission to Mexico, which finally reconciled the U.S. government and Wall Street to the revolutionary regime. It was obvious that, in this new atmosphere, the government's ties to CROM were becoming an embarrassment. Thus the way was slowly being prepared for their severance.

Calles himself could not do it, for publicly he was too committed to CROM to desert it too suddenly and openly. However, his colleague, General Obregón, was preparing to return to the presidency, and it was known that he would be the one to do the job. As early as the fall of 1927, when Obregón was conducting his campaign for the presidency, the former chief of the diplomatic department of the Mexican Foreign Office, who had resigned to work in Obregón's campaign, assured Ambassador Sheffield that it looked like Morones would suffer a complete loss of influence in the labor world if Obregón were elected, even though Morones had recently contracted to throw CROM support behind Obregón.[35] Obregón's election was a certainty, and the downfall of CROM appeared to be a near-certainty, at least as long as Morones and the Grupo Acción remained in control of it.

On July 17, 1928, after his election but before his inauguration, Obregón was assassinated by a young man who claimed to be a fervent Catholic and had done it for religious reasons. Nevertheless, Obregón's supporters and Morones's enemies accused Morones of being in some way responsible for the assassination. In the Mexico of the 1920s, where assassination was not an uncommon weapon in a politician's armory, this accusation was not as farfetched as it might seem. The rumors were given some credence when Morones disappeared from public view. The flames were fed even more with the publication, six days after the assassination, of a letter that Obregón had written four days before his death to the leader of an anti-CROM independent union in Nayarit who had been experiencing government opposition in his attempts to organize. In an obvious reference to the uses to which Morones put his post as Secretary of Industry, Commerce and Labor, he deplored the fact that there were government officials who were acting "in such a violent manner against the cause of labor." He asked the anti-CROM leader to continue his organizing work in spite of the government opposition he was encountering and assured him of his "full and frank" support.[36]

Calles had an official investigation conducted by friends of Obregón to determine the veracity of the rumors of Morones's culpability for the assassination. Morones was absolved of responsibility.[37] But still the rumors persisted. Soon Morones and other CROM men in the government were forced to resign their government posts. Obregón achieved by his death what he had planned to achieve while alive.

With charges that he was at least the "intellectual author" of the crime still circulating throughout Mexico, Morones was in deep trouble. He had wired Santiago Iglesias on July 2, before Obregón's death, asking him to come to Mexico.[38] When news of Obregón's assassination and Morones's troubles reached the outside world, Iglesias went to Washington to confer with Green. They decided that he should go to Mexico to investigate the charges and to see if he could be of assistance to CROM.[39]

As Iglesias left for Mexico, the Mexican police announced that they had broken the Obregón case and had captured some of the twelve accomplices in the plot, many of whom had confessed, and were searching for the remaining few at large. They all were Catholic fanatics, and the ringleader of the operation was a Catholic nun. None had any connection with CROM.[40]

In spite of the apparent capture of the real culprits, rumors of Morones's involvement continued to circulate and were used as part of the pretext for the exclusion, by Obregonistas and Agrarians, of members of the Partido Laborista who had been elected to the special Congress called to choose a provisional president.

Iglesias arrived in Mexico City on August 31 and was met at the station by CROM representatives, who sped him to the place where Morones was hiding out—his house. There he found Morones and almost all of the top leaders of CROM anxiously awaiting him. Morones explained that their lives were in danger, and that they had had to take extraordinary measures to guard themselves. He said that the sinister purpose of the charges against him and other CROM leaders was to create a public clamor large enough to justify new assassination attempts against them. (Morones had already been seriously wounded a few years back by an assassination attempt and could clearly be excused if he felt a little paranoid in this situation.)

Morones, by that time, appears to have abandoned his hopes of achieving government power again and was concentrating on retaining for himself and his associates control of CROM. He explained that he and other CROM members had resigned from the government in fulfillment of a pledge they would do so if their positions ever diminished the effectiveness of CROM.[41] He also said that "they" could do what they wanted with the public and political posts, that he and his colleagues would leave that field to others, but that never would they abandon their rights as citizens with regard to their labor organization.

In the next ten days, Iglesias spoke to many people throughout the political spectrum, including Calles, and he too came to the conclusion that the assassination was the work of a young religious fanatic who thought that he was saving his religion.

He dismissed the charges against Morones and the leaders of CROM as groundless and politically motivated. He noted that Calles had told him that he had personally talked with the young assassin and was convinced that he was a religious fanatic.[42] The fact was, however, that whatever Calles might have felt about Morones's personal culpability for the crime, Morones was now politically dead, and neither Calles nor the successors he chose showed any intention of wanting to resurrect him. Having lost the political power that enabled them to construct CROM and hold it together, Morones and his associates began to lose control of it, and its member unions began to desert. As its member unions began to defect from CROM, so did the AFL.

As we have seen, the major interest of Green and the Executive Council in retaining close relations with CROM lay in what it could do with regard to immigration. The AFL's hopes for success were pinned on CROM's ability and willingness to influence the Mexican government on its behalf. With CROM's influence on the Mexican government dead, the AFL's interest in retaining close connections died quickly as well.

Upon his return from Mexico, Iglesias was publicly optimistic about the future of CROM.[43] The AFL Executive Council presented a similar public face. Showing an ability to detect a silver lining in a dark cloud that would undoubtedly have made Samuel Gompers proud had he been there to observe, the council reported to the 1928 AFL convention that the CROM now had "the strategic advantage of not being responsible for administration of the government and hence is free to focus on economic problems and advancement." [44] However, in the same convention they recommended that, in view of the changed political situation in Mexico, efforts be renewed to have Congress place Mexico under the immigration quota. This shows that they were not unaware of the real import of the fall of CROM on the AFL-CROM relationship.

James Lord was sent to represent the AFL at CROM's convention, and he too was publicly optimistic. Perhaps he was also trying to help CROM get back into the good graces of Calles, who clearly was going to be the power behind the throne in the next administration, when, in his major address to the CROM convention, he said: "I have known Lloyd George, Viviani, Brandes, Briand, and Vandervelde, but I think that Calles stands above all of them as a statesman." [45] Or perhaps he was damning Calles with faint praise. In any case, by the time he left Mexico City, it must have been obvious to Lord that Calles envisaged no role for CROM in the political party he was constructing to preserve his control of the government.

There now was little that AFL or CROM could gain from retaining close relations with each other, and contacts between the two movements rapidly dwindled to the occasional ritualistic appearance of delegates at each other's conventions. To all intents, the AFL-CROM alliance died a quick death in 1928.

NOTES

1. For example, in 1925, Green had to abandon plans to send AFL organizers to Latin American countries to help the fledgling movements there organize "for the very good reason that the financial position of the American Federation of Labor [could] not permit." Green to Iglesias, Nov. 7, 1925, Green Copybooks. During the month of October, the AFL had to lay off most of its organizers in the United States because it could not meet their salaries.

2. *CROM*, Year 1, no. 4 (Apr. 23, 1925): 23.

3. Green to Moneda, Mar. 18, 1925, Green Copybooks.

4. *New York Times*, June 13, 1925.

5. Debs to Calles, July 7, 1925, in *CROM*, Year 1, no. 11 (Aug. 1, 1925): 19.

6. Memorandum, n.d. [June 1925], Green Papers, SHSW.

7. *New York Times*, July 13, 1925.

8. Memorandum, n.d. [June 1925].

9. Green to Kellogg, June 15, 1925, Green Copybooks.

10. Memorandum, n.d. [June 1925].

11. Ibid.

12. Press release, June 17, 1925, Green Papers, SHSW.

13. Memorandum, n.d. [June 1925].

14. *CROM,* Year 1, no. 17 (Nov. 1, 1925): 45.

15. McGrady to Green, Dec. 20, 1926, Jan. 19,1927, Green Papers, SHSW.

16. Statement quoted in "Informe del Consejo Ejecutivo de la Confederación Obrera Pan Americana cubriendo el periodo desde enero 1 de 1925 hasta junio 30 de 1927," *CROM,* Year 3, no. 16 (Aug. 15, 1927): 46.

17. AFL, *Proceedings,* 1926, p. 61.

18. Ibid., p. 361.

19. Woll to Kellogg, May 6, 1927, and Kellogg to Sheffield, May 11, 1927, State Department Papers, 912.504/853. Sheffield to Kellogg, May 16, 1927; Kelley to Gunther, May 27, 1927; Gunther to Kelley, June 14, 1927; Gunther to Woll, June 29, 1927; Woll to Gunther, Aug. 11, 1927: all State Department Papers, 812.504/858.

20. AFL, *Proceedings,* 1927, pp. 264–282.

21. Green to Morones, Nov. 19, 1925, Green Copybooks.

22. *New York Times,* Mar. 9, 1926.

23. Ibid.

24. *Fresno Labor News,* clipping, n.d., Green Papers, SHSW, File B.

25. Green to Morones, Nov. 19, 1925.

26. Iglesias to Green, n.d. [Apr. 1926?], and Treviño to Minister of Russia in Mexico, Mar. 26, 1926, Green Papers, SHSW, File B.

27. For example, see Treviño to Iglesias, Apr. 10, 1926, and Treviño to Anti-Imperialist League of America, Apr. 10, 1926, Green Papers, SHSW.

28. Iglesias, memorandum, n.d. [Mar. 1926?], Green Papers, SHSW, File B.

29. Santiago Iglesias, "The Child of the AFL," *American Federationist* 32 (1925): 929.

30. Sheffield to Secretary of State, Apr. 18, 1927, State Department Papers, 810.504/847.

31. Moises Poblete Troncoso, *El movimiento obrero latinoamericano* (Mexico: Fondo de Cultura Económica, 1946), p. 228.

32. Dawson to Secretary of State, Apr. 7, 1924, State Department Papers, 812.504/558.

33. Boyle to Dawson, Mar. 15, 1924, State Department Papers, 812.504/557.

34. Sheffield to Secretary of State, Mar. 14, 17, 1925, State Department Papers, 812.504/612, 812.504/613.

35. Sheffield to Secretary of State, Sept. 17, 1927, State Department Papers, 812.504/888.

36. Obregón to Bernardo E. de Leon, July 13, 1928, in *El Universal* (Mexico City), July 23, 1928.

37. *Excelsior,* Aug. 3, 1928.

38. This is according to the Spanish transcript of Iglesias's trip printed in *CROM*. Sinclair Snow, "The Pan-American Federation of Labor" (Ph.D. diss., University of Virginia, 1960), p. 126, cites the English translation of

the original Spanish report in Iglesias's papers as saying that Morones telegraphed on Aug. 8, after the assassination. I did not see the English translation, which is in Puerto Rico, and thus am going by the Spanish version.

39. Santiago Iglesias, "Informe sobre mi viaje extraordinario a México, desde agosto 23 a septiembre 21 de 1928," *CROM*, Year 4, no. 21 (Nov. 1, 1928): 27.

40. Their complete confessions began to be published in the Mexico City dailies the day that Iglesias left for Mexico. *Excelsior*, Aug. 22, 23, 1928.

41. For example, see *Excelsior*, Aug. 23, 1928.

42. Santiago Iglesias, "Informe sobre," *CROM*, Year 4, no. 21 (Nov. 1, 1928): 29–32.

43. "La organización de los trabajadores americanos ha resistido los ataques sin resentirse su estructura," *CROM*, Year 4, no. 21, p. 24.

44. AFL, *Proceedings*, 1928, p. 95.

45. "Es de transcendental importancia la novena Convención de la CROM. Crónica de los interesantes debates," *CROM*, Year 4, no. 24 (Dec. 15, 1928): p. 38.

10

The CTM
and the CIO

CROM BEGAN TO disintegrate almost as soon as it lost the support of the Mexican government, but Luis Morones and a reduced group of his cohorts continued to control the dwindling remnants. At its Ninth Congress in December 1928—at which James Lord lavished praise on Calles—CROM officially proclaimed its opposition to the government. It was a hollow act, for the government, still dominated by Calles, already had unofficially abandoned CROM. Three weeks later, many member unions left CROM. They were soon followed by others in a steady stream of defections.[1]

Within those unions that remained in CROM, a left-wing opposition to the conservative leadership of Morones was slowly coalescing around the figure of Vicente Lombardo Toledano, a leader in the teachers union and a member of the Central Committee of CROM. Lombardo, who came from a wealthy, upper-middle-class family, was not cast in the typical mold of Latin labor leaders. Well-educated, intellectual, and sensitive, he lacked Morones's brand of crude machismo, the overt flaunting of masculine strength, which endowed

146

Morones and his type with a certain degree of charisma. Whereas Morones was a fiery public speaker, Lombardo tended to be dry and pedantic. Morones, the poor boy who had made good, surrounded himself with opulence and women, while Lombardo, the rich boy turned leader of the working classes, wore the same blue-serge suit on all occasions. (His enemies used to charge that he had many blue serge suits, all identical.) Morones was fat and corrupt; Lombardo, lean and incorruptible. By any standards, Morones was much more successful at establishing himself as a true leader of the organized workers, a *caudillo* of labor, than was Lombardo. Lombardo could communicate to and influence the government and the intellectuals. Morones could communicate to the masses. Fortunately for Lombardo, "the masses" played a minor role in deciding national labor policy. He became the most powerful labor leader of the 1930s. Ironically, in view of his painfully obvious lack of mass appeal, he was often portrayed in the American press as the fiery, wild-eyed, Communist demagogue of Mexico.

Lombardo had been moving steadily leftward of CROM's rather conservative position throughout the 1920s, and by 1932 he considered himself a full-fledged Marxist. In 1932 he was elected secretary-general of the Federación of the Federal District. He then believed that he had enough support to directly challenge Morones for control of CROM. In late July 1932, he delivered a speech, "The Road is to the Left," advocating the renewal and intensification of the class struggle. Shortly thereafter, at a public meeting, Morones attacked Lombardo for propagating "exotic doctrines" among the masses. The next day, Lombardo resigned from CROM, taking a large number of CROM unions with him. They claimed to constitute a majority of CROM and convoked a special convention at which they called themselves "CROM Depurada" (purified CROM) and elected Lombardo as secretary-general.[2]

The next year, CROM Depurada joined with some other independent unions to form the Confederación General de

Obreros y Campesinos de México (CGOCM). The new organization proclaimed that it stood on three main principles: the class struggle, union democracy, and the independence of the labor movement from the state.[3] The latter principle, however, did not imply abstaining from supporting governments it liked.

In December 1934, Gen. Lázaro Cárdenas became President. Calles had picked him because he thought that he would make a pliable puppet, but Cárdenas soon turned against Calles. He began to cultivate the support of the CGOCM in preparation for a showdown with Calles. The CGOCM unions fomented a wave of strikes, boycotts, and demonstrations in favor of Cárdenas. On June 15, 1935, Calles publicly denounced the wave of strikes and threatened to dispose of Cárdenas if he continued his leftward course. Lombardo's big chance had come. He quickly organized a National Committee of Proletarian Defense, consisting of the CGOCM and other pro-Cárdenas labor organizations. The committee mounted a massive demonstration in support of Cárdenas in the main square of Mexico City, in front of the National Palace, and made it clear that any attempt by Calles to overthrow Cárdenas would involve grave risks. It was the first demonstration of organized support for Cárdenas and an important one. Calles, accompanied by his old colleague Morones, soon found himself on a plane bound for exile in the United States. In the same way as Calles had been indebted to Morones for his support against de la Huerta, so Cárdenas was now indebted to Lombardo for his support against Calles. The committee became the jumping-off point for the formation of yet another, broader, national labor confederation. In February 1936, the Confederación de Trabajadores de México (CTM) was formed.[4] It was obvious that the new confederation was enjoying and would enjoy the support of the Cárdenas government.

Officially, the CTM was a socialist union. Its declaration of principles was a left-wing program proclaiming that it would struggle for the abolition of the capitalist system. However, it declared that in order to achieve this goal, Mexico had first to free itself from the orbit of imperialism.[5] Thus, Cárdenas, who definitely was not trying to abolish the capitalist system, must still be supported. He was leading Mexico into the necessary precondition—political and economic independence. The ideological position of the CTM was quite similar to that of Communist parties in many underdeveloped parts of the world today—support for "bourgeois" leaders in movements for "national liberation."

Lombardo was a Marxist and quite enamored of the Soviet Union, but he was never a member of the Communist party. There were Communists in the CTM at its founding, and they had three seats on its Executive Committee. The era of the "Popular Front" had arrived, and the CTM appeared to the Communists to be a worthwhile alliance of progressive forces. However, within a year after its founding, the Communists made a bid for control of the organization. When they failed, they withdrew the unions they controlled from the CTM. After a few months of negotiations, in which Earl Browder, leader of the Communist party of the United States, intervened as a conciliator, the Communists returned to the CTM. Their defection proved costly to them, for upon their return they failed to regain the three seats they had previously controlled on the CTM Executive Committee. They were replaced by more "moderate" people, and the CTM's increasingly reformist policy was reinforced.[6]

The full support of the Cárdenas government paid handsome dividends to the CTM. To an even greater extent than in the Calles–CROM relationship, strikes by the CTM carried with them the threat of nationalization. Under Cárdenas, this was by no means an idle threat. For example, in 1936 and 1937, a strike against the Atlas hard-fiber factory in San Luis Potosí ended with its being delivered over to a workers' cooperative to run. A CTM-organized strike of agricultural workers in the rich La Laguna area led to the government's invoking the Agrarian Code and distributing the land to the peasants in the form of *ejidos,* Mexican communal farms. A strike against the national railroads of Mexico led to its nationalization.[7] The most spectacular nationalization of all, that of the entire oil industry, took place in 1938 after the foreign oil companies refused to carry out a government-imposed settlement of a CTM strike in the oil fields.

With strong government backing, unionism, and especially the CTM, flourished under the Cárdenas administration. By 1940 the percentage of the labor force that was unionized had reached 15 percent, a figure never attained again.[8] By 1940 a conservative estimate put total union membership at 878,000. A large majority of these people were in the CTM.[9]

Lombardo appears to have recognized that government support carried with it dangers as well as benefits. There was, however, little he could do to avoid the dangers. He continually tried to affirm the independence of the CTM from the government, and he and other high CTM officials did not repeat the practice of CROM and take high posts in the government. When President Cárdenas came to the First Congress of the CTM, Lombardo went out of his way to publicly affirm the independence of the CTM to the President. In welcoming Cárdenas to the congress, Lombardo said:

> We are an organization independent of the government. . . . You would not want a proletariat subjected to government direction and we would not want a head of government who would not be subjected to the will of the people of Mexico.[10]

After the meeting, in a private talk with Cárdenas, Lombardo again emphasized this point. He told Cárdenas that, although the interests of the CTM and the government were now identical, this did not mean that they would always be so. In the long run, said Lombardo, their interests would be different.

When this happened, the interests of the workers would not be subordinated to those of the government.[11] This was brave talk. Unfortunately, Lombardo's hopes did not correspond to the realities of the power structure of Mexico.

The reality was displayed graphically in the wave of strikes by CGOCM and CTM unions in 1935 and 1936. The Lombardistas had taken up the old cry of "direct action," claiming that they would force the employers to grant wage increases through the use of the strike alone, without recourse to the government or its Board of Conciliation and Arbitration. As Ricardo Treviño, the CROM leader, pointed out in a May Day speech in 1936, "direct action" failed in a whole series of bitter strikes. Although some strikes had lasted for many months, they all ended with the unions' bringing the disputes to either the Conciliation Board, the Department of Labor, or the President for settlement. Not one major conflict had been settled without government intervention.[12] The CTM, like CROM before it, needed government support if it was to be the dominant labor confederation in Mexico.

Lombardo, in his chat with Cárdenas, misread the lessons of the past. He assumed that the CTM was developing a different relationship with the government than that of CROM and Calles. He believed that he and the CTM now constituted a power bloc that could, if it wanted to, function independently of, and contrary to the wishes of, the President. He was wrong. The CTM's position depended on continuing government support, and Lombardo's personal position as leader of the CTM was dependent on continued support from the President.

From the start, Lombardo and the CTM, working from a Marxist theoretical basis, took a deep interest in international affairs. Thus, the CTM's first declaration of principles promised to promote international labor solidarity and "the international unity of the proletariat." [13] One of the first steps of the CTM was to begin work on something that had been on

Lombardo's mind since the 1920s—the creation of a "Latin American" (as opposed to "Pan-American," which implies including the English-speaking countries of the hemisphere) confederation of labor.

Lombardo had first proposed the creation of a Latin American confederation of labor in 1926, while he was a member of CROM.[14] A furor was raging over the Calles administration's new petroleum law, and Lombardo believed that the AFL, supporting as it did the capitalist system, would never intervene with the government of the United States against the interests of that government.[15] Lombardo had the CROM Depurada and the CGOCM back the idea, but nothing substantial was achieved. When the CTM was formed, it agreed to formally convoke a congress to create the confederation.[16]

In September 1936, Lombardo called for a Latin American labor congress of labor organizations in all the Latin American countries. In the argot of the day, he said that the solidarity and cooperation of the working class of Latin America was essential to ward off the imminent dangers of war and fascism and to afford mutual protection from foreign imperialists and internal reactionary oppression.[17] Two years later, a congress finally met in Mexico City to organize the Confederación de Trabajadores de América Latina (CTAL). Besides the Latin American delegates, there were "fraternal delegations" from Spain, France, and India and from the Congress of Industrial Organizations (CIO) of the United States.

Although he wanted to create a hemispheric labor organization that would exclude U.S. unions, Lombardo was not opposed to having close relations with American unionists. Indeed, from the very beginning, he set out to cultivate ties with the CIO, which was still in the process of separating from the AFL. Soon after its founding, in 1937, the CTM sent a large delegation on a tour of the United States to meet American unionists and explain the nature of the new labor organization.[18] In the same year, Lombardo himself went to the

United Mine Workers Union convention to meet with John L. Lewis, head of the CIO. Lombardo believed that the CTM could work with the CIO. Years later, he said that he never thought that the CIO was even potentially socialist, but he did think of it as being "progressive" with regard to labor organization and in favor of the New Deal. This was enough to persuade Lombardo to seek closer contacts.[19] That the CIO was emerging as the great rival to the AFL, and the AFL still officially supported Luis Morones and CROM, also influenced Lombardo.[20]

Lombardo was greatly impressed with Lewis. He had met Gompers in 1924 and was distinctly unimpressed with his intellectual capabilities, but Lewis struck him as the most striking and forceful American labor leader he had ever met.[21] Still, although he hoped to establish close relations with the CIO, he was wary of formalizing them in any way. Lewis and the CIO were too preoccupied with their domestic problems to have much interest in having formal relations with the CTM. Lombardo and the CTM concentrated on giving Lewis and the CIO the impression that they were the Mexican counterpart to the CIO and that Cárdenas was the Mexican counterpart to Franklin Delano Roosevelt. When Roosevelt was reelected in 1936, they sent Lewis a telegram hailing the reelection as a blow against fascism and reaction.[22] The CTM looked upon Roosevelt's reelection as an augury of continued good relations between Mexico and the United States and a continuation of the American government's "hands off" policy toward Mexico.[23]

The CTM's efforts to cultivate good relations with American labor and a favorable image for the Cárdenas government in the United States were not confined to interchanges of delegates and telegrams of congratulations. Soon after its founding, at the suggestion of the delegation it had sent to the United States, the CTM set up a thrice-monthly English information bulletin, called the *Mexican Labor News,* aimed at labor leaders and radicals in the United States. Its purpose was to counteract the attempts being made by Calles and Morones in the United States to label as "Bolshevik" the Cárdenas government and the CTM.[24] The tack generally taken by the *Mexican Labor News* was to emphasize the similarities between the CTM and CIO, Cárdenas and Roosevelt, and the AFL and CROM, the latter two being portrayed as the inveterate enemies of all that the former four stood for. It also continually emphasized the common interest of American and Mexican labor in fighting domestic and foreign fascism.[25] The delegation that had proposed the idea had returned from the United States with a list of 75 unionists who had expressed interest in receiving such a publication.[26] After a year in operation, the periodical had 1,700 subscribers, mostly in the United States. Six months later, its circulation had risen to 3,000.[27]

The CTM also embarked upon an active campaign to recruit American liberals and unionists to attend special summer courses given in English at the Workers' University in Mexico City, an institution subsidized by the CTM and the government and presided over by Lombardo Toledano.[28]

The CTM was quick to demonstrate its sympathy with American labor, and especially the CIO, by supporting CIO strikes whenever possible and trying to smooth over the organizational problems that Mexican workers in the United States presented to American unions. When CIO seamen struck on the West Coast, Lombardo ordered CTM dockworkers on Mexico's Pacific Coast to refuse to unload American ships docking there.[29] Early in 1937, two members of the CTM National Committee were sent to Texas to confer with labor leaders over discrimination against Mexican workers and to establish a modus operandi that would help to eliminate discrimination and improve the working conditions of Mexican workers in Texas.[30] Later in the year, spurred by the desperate condition of Mexican workers there, the CTM ordered its affiliates in all border points to work closely with the authorities to prevent Mexicans from crossing the border. It also worked with Texas labor organizations to repatriate destitute Mexican workers in Texas.[31] West Coast and Southwest locals of the CIO became aware of the aid the CTM could give them and sometimes called upon the CTM to help organize Mexican workers in the United States.[32]

All of these efforts to cultivate close relations with the CIO paid off rather handsomely for Lombardo and the CTM in 1938, when Mexican-American relations careened toward a new crisis with the refusal of American- and British-owned oil companies to submit to a strike settlement imposed by a government arbitration board. In response to Lombardo's appeal for support from the world's labor organizations, Lewis cabled back:

> It is the conviction of the CIO that both labor and employers should abide by the decisions of legally constituted authorities in democratic nations. . . . I see no reason why labor and employers in Mexico should not abide by this principle. When both sides have submitted their case to the tribunals of the land, then both should submit to the decision.[33]

Lewis remained firmly behind the Cárdenas government throughout the dispute, which ended in the nationalization of the companies. When the American and British oil companies, using their control of the world's tanker fleet, imposed a worldwide boycott on Mexican oil, Lewis arranged for a friend of his, an independent oilman named William Rhodes Davis, to go to Mexico and work out a barter deal by which, with Davis as the middleman, the Mexicans could exchange oil for tankers from Italy. Lewis arranged for Davis's introduction to the Mexican government through Lombardo Toledano.[34]

By 1938, Lewis appears to have been convinced that the CTM was indeed the counterpart of the CIO in Mexico, and that the program of the Cárdenas government was the Mexican counterpart of the New Deal. In a sense, he was right. Like Roosevelt and the CIO, Cárdenas and Lombardo represented a leftward departure from the system that prevailed in the 1920s. However, the Mexican political system, since the Revolution, had functioned on a plane considerably to the left of U.S. politics, and both Cárdenas and Lombardo were considerably to the left of FDR and Lewis. Although he did not consider himself a Marxist, Cárdenas was a strong nationalist, and in Latin America this frequently leads to a similar end— the nationalization of foreign-owned property. In addition, Cárdenas was a firm believer in the promise of the Revolution to carry out land reform. Under his administration more land was expropriated and redistributed than under all the previous revolutionary governments combined. It takes a great leap of the imagination to conceive of Roosevelt trying to ameliorate the agrarian misery of the South and Southwest in a similar fashion.

Lombardo was a Marxist, and Lewis was not. Lombardo looked upon unionism primarily as political tool, to be used where the real gains would be made—in the arena of national politics. The CTM was to be merely a tool for producing the broader social changes, and eventually the revolution, that would bring the real benefits. Lewis, although very adept at using unionism as a political force, was still in the Gompers tradition. He saw the major gains of the working classes accruing from purely "union action," the use of the strike to gain concessions from employers. In spite of any surface similarities, they represented, ideologically, the two poles of the traditional dichotomy between "political" unionism and "economic" unionism. Thus, Lewis's comparisons, shrewdly cultivated in him by the Mexicans, were rather farfetched.

Lewis's support for the CTM and Cárdenas was climaxed publicly by his triumphal appearance at the founding convention of the Confederación de Trabajadores de América Latina (CTAL) and the International Labor Congress against War and Fascism, held consecutively in Mexico City in September 1938. Cárdenas, who was a strong antifascist, had suggested the latter congress at the latest CTM convention, and the CTM had set about organizing one. The CTM was also strongly antifascist, and Lombardo, who had close relatives in Italy to whom he had pledged to carry on the antifascist fight in the 1920s,[35] was completely committed to the cause. Lombardo had visited Lewis twice in the late spring of 1938 and had succeeded in convincing him to attend both the founding convention of CTAL and the antifascist congress.[36] Lewis's attendance at the two functions would publicly demonstrate his support for the Latin American confederation of labor, the CTM, and the Cárdenas government, which had just nationalized the oil industry.

To highlight Lewis's progressive nature and to embarrass the AFL, an invitation was issued to William Green, Matthew Woll, and other AFL officials to attend as well. Lombardo and the CTM made the invitation on the assumption that the AFL would decline it, and decline it Green did.[37] Green issued a statement condemning the CTAL founding convention as an attempt to spread communist propaganda among the labor movements of Latin America.[38] "Given the personality of the person who convoked it," he said, "it could not be more than an act of communist propaganda." [39] This gave the CTM the chance to add to their indictment against Green and the AFL the charge that they were the enemies of hemispheric proletarian unity.[40]

Lewis's attendance at the two meetings in Mexico City was a coup for Lombardo, and the CTM lost no opportunity to publicize it. Indeed, he was the most honored of the foreign guests. His train was very late, and he did not arrive until early morning of the day the CTAL convention opened. Nevertheless, the CTM leaders were at the station to greet him, accompanied by a crowd of banner-equipped unionists and a squad of militiamen to clear a path through the crowd.[41] The

CTM's daily newspaper greeted Lewis as the champion of hemispheric proletarian unity, the voice of hopes for the liberation of the exploited of the United States, and the man whose organization stood up for Mexico in the most critical moments of the oil controversy.[42]

In his major address to the founding congress of the CTAL, Lewis emphasized the identity of interests of the workers of the world. "The workers of the whole world," he said, "always have the same adversaries: the great corporations voraciously exploiting the workers of the world constitute the common adversaries of the workers of the whole Earth." Lewis pointed out, however, that in Mexico and the United States two great statesmen had appeared who had extended a helping hand to labor—Presidents Roosevelt and Cárdenas. He said that if the workers of the rest of the continent would organize, the same waves of reform that had taken place in Mexico and the United States could and would take place in the rest of Latin America as well.[43] Lewis's speech was indeed a triumph of tact and diplomacy. Although he emphasized that the workers of the United States and Latin America had common enemies, he did not take the obvious next step and suggest that they band together to fight them. Instead, the emphasis of his speech was upon what each labor movement could do in its own country to combat the pernicious influence of large corporations. His advice to the workers of Latin America, he said, was exactly the same as that of the CIO in the United States: "Organize, organize!" [44] This meant to organize within their own countries and among themselves. It did not mean to join in a common hemispheric organization with the CIO.

Lewis did not publicly intervene again in the actual workings of the congress. Lombardo arranged personal interviews with President Cárdenas for him and Léon Jouhaux of the French Confédération Général de Travailleurs (CGT). After talking with Cárdenas for thirty minutes, Lewis emerged and declared: "He's an extraordinary man; a great statesman; a great democrat with magnificant valor and splendid qualities." [45] Lewis was becoming as effusive about Cárdenas as Green and the AFL had been about Calles.

At the International Labor Congress against War and Fascism, Lewis was again a featured speaker. Havana cigar in hand, he stood before 30,000 people in Mexico City's bullring and again emphasized the common interests of the workers of all countries. This time the emphasis was upon their common interest in defending democratic institutions against the threat of fascism. He said that reactionary employers in the United States were trying to prevent workers from organizing. Although these employers as yet had not made a clear attempt to form a fascist organization, the CIO expected that they would try to do so when they thought it would serve their interests. At present, however, they were using the methods of fascism to fight unionism. He pointed out that there were organized fascist groups in the United States, such as the Silver Shirts, the Ku Klux Klan, and the Ranchers Association of the Imperial Valley of California, which the CIO was fighting. After showing that the United States, too, faced an internal fascist threat and that the CIO was fighting it, he said that the workers of the hemisphere and of the world must work together to defend peace and democracy and fight fascism. [46] Lewis was not very explicit on exactly how the workers of the world should unite to fight fascism and what, aside from attending antifascist congresses, they could do about it.

Lewis appears to have been impressed with what he learned about conditions in Latin America during his stay in Mexico City. When the CTAL congress closed, after having elected Lombardo Toledano as its first president, Lewis issued a statement calling the formation of the CTAL "one of the most significant events that have happened for a long time." He continued:

> The revelations of the economic and social conditions in various countries made at this conference are in some respects astonishing. They show conclusively that large foreign corporations in various

countries are exercising their influence on the different governments to impose miserable wage structures and degraded working and social conditions on the workers.

When a correspondent asked him if he thought that Latin American workers should fight for their rights by demanding higher wages or by "throwing out" American business firms, Lewis replied that the organized labor movements should support the "justifiable policies" of their governments. The correspondent remarked that this did not answer his question and Lewis replied: "No, it leaves it to the people of the several countries to determine what are justifiable policies." [47]

Because of the rise of stronger labor movements in many Latin American countries, especially in Argentina, the CTAL was a much stronger and more influential group than the PAFL had ever been. It was also considerably to the left of the PAFL. In participating in its founding convention, the CIO was giving its blessing to an organization that was calling for profound social changes in Latin America. The two main principles of the organization's program were antifascism and the replacement of "the social regime that [prevailed] in the majority of the countries of the world" by a regime of "justice, based on the abolition of the exploitation of man by man," democracy, and the solidarity of all the people of the world.[48] But more important than the resounding phrases of the manifesto was that Lombardo, by excluding American unions, had ensured that the CTAL would be dominated by the next-strongest labor movement in the hemisphere, the CTM. As the AFL had dominated the PAFL, so the CTM, as the organization that underwrote the expenses, would dominate the CTAL. CIO support for Lombardo, the CTM, and the CTAL thrust hemispheric international labor relations into the context of the duel that was taking place in the United States between the AFL and the CIO. It aroused the AFL to a new interest in Mexico and Latin America. The CIO clearly was beginning to challenge the dominance of the AFL in foreign as well as domestic affairs, and the AFL could not stand by unconcerned.

The AFL had been watching the progress of Lombardo's attempt to form a Latin American labor confederation from the time of the founding of the CTM. Santiago Iglesias, in particular, was apprehensive about the proposed new confederation, especially about the distinction it made between workers north and south of the Rio Grande. At the 1936 AFL convention, two years before the CTAL was actually formed, he introduced a resolution condemning the whole project. He said that the new confederation was to be organized under "almost the same principles as the Pan-American Federation of Labor," but that it was based upon a distinction between Latin and Anglo-Saxon workers that amounted to racial prejudice. He also charged that it represented a dual organization aimed at the PAFL and called upon Latin American labor to support the PAFL.[49] However, the PAFL by that time was moribund, and the question devolved upon whether the Executive Council of the AFL saw fit to take steps to revive it. In its report to the 1936 convention, the council lamented its inability to distinguish which were the "free" trade unions of Latin America through correspondence alone. It suggested that an AFL commission be sent to tour Latin America to investigate the labor movements of the various countries and invite the "free" ones to the much-delayed Sixth Convention of the PAFL, to be held at some undetermined date.[50]

The AFL's hopes of reviving the PAFL received a setback in 1937 when its major ally in Latin America, the remnants of CROM, split again. Morones had returned from exile in the United States under a general amnesty issued by Cárdenas in 1937, but he remained an implacable enemy of Cárdenas. Cárdenas was in the process of forming a new government political party, and the CROM split over the issue of supporting Cárdenas's effort, with Morones holding out for the revival of the Mexican Labor party.[51] The split was finally formalized in April 1938, when those CROM members, led by Ricardo Treviño, who participated in the founding convention of the new political party were expelled from CROM by the Morones-dominated National Committee.[52]

By the time Lewis went to Mexico in September 1938, CROM was split into the Treviño and Morones factions, but the founding of the CTAL and Lewis's prominence there forced the AFL into action. In October the Executive Council dispatched Matthew Woll and Chester Wright to Mexico to assess the situation there. They spoke with leaders of both factions. According to Treviño, Woll asked him about reports of Morones to the AFL Executive Council that Cárdenas intended to install a communist regime in Mexico, and that the oil expropriation was proof of this. Treviño denied this charge to Woll and said that his faction of CROM supported the expropriation of the oil industry.[53]

When the Executive Council of the AFL held its next meeting, in February 1939, Woll was ready with a report on Mexico. Santiago Iglesias and Dan Tracy, the head of the Electrical Workers Union, had already presented independent recommendations that the PAFL be revived.[54] Woll reported that, although the CROM was torn with dissension, steps should be taken to revive the PAFL. He said that the CTM was "wholly political, extremely radical in character with communistic tenets." Lombardo Toledano, he said,

> is considered a mouthpiece of the Stalinites in Mexico. . . . His influence is considerable because of the courtesies extended him by President Cardenas and other political leaders. This assistance was extended to it because the government was unable to sway the CROM into deserting its policy of abstaining from politics rather than continuing along economic lines.

He called the CTM "entirely temporary in character" and expressed his confidence that the faction of CROM led by

Morones would emerge victorious in its contest with the CTM. He labeled Treviño's faction a "political labor movement" and made it clear that the AFL would continue to support Morones.

The Executive Council approved the idea of reviving the PAFL, and it was clear that the major motive was to combat the CIO's growing influence in Latin America.[55] The *New York Times* reported that the idea of reviving the PAFL was "understood to be another move in the effort to checkmate John L. Lewis, whose visit to Mexico placed him in close touch with many Latin American labor leaders."[56] When Woll made the announcement, he "strongly indicated" that this was a major object of the revival.[57] The attempt to revive the PAFL could certainly not be ascribed to conditions in Mexico and the rest of Latin America that favored its resuscitation. The CIO was challenging the traditional role of the AFL as the sole representative of "American labor" in international labor relations.

In his public attack on the CTM, Woll took care to point out that its leadership was "allied with" the CIO. He charged that the CTM was responsible for the expropriation of the railroads and the oil fields by the Mexican government, and said: "The CIO is sympathetic with this movement."[58] The attack drew an immediate response from Lombardo, who took the opportunity to charge that the AFL was in the service of the Standard Oil Company. He concluded that, since the Mexican oil problem was then one of the issues in the campaign for the presidency of the United States in 1940, "the attitude of the leaders of the American Federation of Labor must be considered an act of aggression against the sovereignty of Mexico and a threat to the independence of the people of Latin America." As for the revival of the PAFL, Lombardo charged that, in its brief period of existence, it had played the same role in international labor affairs as played by Theodore Roosevelt in international politics. He warned the workers of Latin America against it but asserted that he felt assured that the warning was unnecessary, for he was certain that they would laugh as heartily about the news of its proposed revival as he had upon reading Woll's statement the day before.[59]

Treviño's faction of CROM greeted the announcement with the same response. He charged that the AFL's statement had its parallel "in the traditional policy of American imperialist companies and politicians towards Mexico, that of supporting and financing the activities of the traitors who can be used to betray their countries, as in the case of Morones." He said that CROM (his faction) would adhere to its policy of giving full support to the revolutionary policies of Cárdenas.[60]

Morones met with Green, Woll, and Iglesias in a meeting of the PAFL Executive Council in Washington in May 1939. It was decided that the PAFL would hold an international conference in Havana in early 1940, the object being to unite all unions of "good faith" against certain unions of nazi, fascist, and communist tendencies.[61] Morones also took the opportunity to clarify the position of his faction of CROM on the oil expropriation issue. When asked about it by newsmen, he said that CROM supported the expropriation of the industry and considered the attitude of the Mexican government perfectly just.[62]

Morones's announcement that the PAFL would hold a convention was derided by Lombardo, who declared:

> The political cadaver of Luis Morones declared yesterday in Washington, in the name of the defunct Pan-American Federation of Labor, that this shadow of dead labor Pan-Americanism of the epoch of Theodore Roosevelt proposes to revive the tactic hated in all of Latin America, that of organizing the workers of its nations in order to subordinate them to the policies of the labor leaders of the United States who are in the service of the imperialist forces.

Lombardo charged that the real intention behind the move was to create an alliance of the enemies of Franklin Roosevelt and Cárdenas to participate in the upcoming presidential elections in the United States and Mexico. "Fortunately," he concluded, "Morones has about as much power in the social life of Mexico as he has in the Dominican Republic." [63]

The plans to reconstitute the PAFL received a severe blow less than a month later, when the newly formed Cuban Confederation of Workers (CTC) rejected the PAFL invitation to be the host union. The Cuban organization, formed with the backing of President Fulgencio Batista (then considered a left-winger), encompassed some labor organizations that had been members of the PAFL. The CTC announced it would join the CTAL and rejected the PAFL invitation. In replying to the PAFL, the CTC pointed out that those of its member organizations that had belonged to the PAFL had been requesting that the much-postponed PAFL Sixth Congress, which was supposed to have been held in Havana in 1930, be convoked. Their requests had been repeatedly ignored. It was only when the CTAL was formed, they charged, that the Executive Council of the PAFL, jealous of the new organization's prestige and control over the masses, remembered that the PAFL still existed and decided to call the congress. The calling of the congress had received the plaudits of the reactionary press throughout the continent, they said. The AFL had received the applause of the reactionary capitalists of the United States as well, they added, when, in the Mexican oil expropriation, instead of condemning the efforts of the reactionaries, the AFL supported them.[64]

In spite of this setback, Morones and the AFL kept up their efforts. At its convention in the fall of 1939, Morones urged the AFL on. In his major address, he attacked Lombardo Toledano. He said that the intellectuals, led by Lombardo, "came and set themselves down at the banquet table when the banquet table was ready, but when there was trouble, that is when these intellectuals left the table." They were being used by the Communists, he said, to destroy the only genuinely free trade-union organization in Mexico. He urged the AFL to continue the work outlined by the PAFL Executive Council in May.[65]

Almost immediately after the AFL convention, Iglesias was sent on a tour of Latin America to organize support for the reconvening of the PAFL. He conferred with CROM groups in Mexico and went on to Cuba, where he was to attend the Havana conference of the International Labor Organization as an observer and try to drum up Latin American support for the PAFL. Unfortunately, he died in Havana of an illness he had contracted in Mexico.[66]

Iglesias's death dealt another severe blow to the PAFL. Not only had his mission been an important one, but he himself had played an important role in raising hopes for reviving the PAFL. One hope remained for the AFL: that Morones and the CROM would be able to return to power. Morones was backing General Almazán, the right-wing candidate, in the contest to succeed Cárdenas as President, and the CTM was supporting Gen. Manuel Ávila Camacho, the choice of Cárdenas and his party, a man more in the center of the political spectrum. Chester Wright was sent to Mexico to investigate. He conferred with Morones and was taken to meet Almazán, who was campaigning in Guerrero.[67]

At that time, it appeared that Almazán had at least a chance to win the presidency. As the months passed however, it became obvious that no matter what his popular support, he would not win the presidential election for one simple reason: the government, which controlled the election machinery, would not allow him to do so. When Ávila Camacho was declared the winner, Almazán's last hope was to resort to traditional methods—to raise an armed revolt to nullify the official electoral count. When he failed to do this, he was politically dead; so was Morones, and so were the AFL's hopes of reviving the PAFL.

At first, it did not appear so. Upon his accession to power, President Ávila Camacho made friendly gestures to CROM and the AFL and ceased government support for attacks on

CROM.[68] However, rather than being indications that Ávila Camacho was thinking of displacing the CTM with CROM, these really were veiled threats to the CTM to replace Lombardo Toledano with someone closer to the center.

While the AFL had been trying to revive the PAFL, the CIO, making use of its status as friend of the CTAL and defender of the CTM and Cárdenas, had continued to cultivate its contacts with Latin American labor. In seeking to strengthen CIO cooperation with Latin American labor, John L. Lewis was motivated both by a desire to outflank the AFL in international labor affairs and by his general assessment of the trend of world affairs. In a speech to the 1939 CIO convention, he elaborated upon the need for closer cooperation with the labor movements of Latin America. Lewis said that Japan was closing the open door in the Orient and that Germany was undercutting U.S. markets in the Mediterranean, Scandinavia, and Latin America through the barter policy she was practicing. The United States, he said, was "gradually being driven out of trade relationships with the various markets of the world. . . . The Jap is on the march in Asia and the 'open door' is no more, and the British lion will have his tail clipped in the Orient, just the same as Uncle Sam's salesmen." Europe could not be counted on to make up for the lost markets, said Lewis, because the war there would diminish the buying power of that continent. The time had come for U.S. manufacturers, exporters, and the State and Commerce departments to turn to the Western Hemisphere.

Lewis proposed that the CIO work to strengthen the labor movements of Latin America and that the U.S. government extend credits to Latin American governments for the purchase of goods manufactured in the United States in a program to raise the standard of living in Latin America, to increase its purchasing power, and to make up for the markets' being lost to the United States in the rest of the world. The strengthening of the labor movements of Latin America would raise the incomes of the workers and provide a larger market for American goods.[69]

The CIO convention of 1939 set up a standing committee on Latin America, which operated on a permanent basis. By 1940 it claimed to be in "immediate contact with all bona fide labor movements in Latin American countries." [70] Lombardo invited the CIO to send "fraternal delegates" to the June 1940 meeting of the Executive Committee of the CTAL in Mexico City to study the attitude of the working class of the hemisphere "in relation to the European war and the economic offensive of imperialism in the Americas." [71] Katheryn Lewis, chairman of the CIO Latin American Affairs Committee, and Joe Curran of the National Maritime Workers Union were sent to represent the CIO. At the meeting, Lombardo called for the formation of a united front of American labor against the menace of fascism. As an example of measures that had already had been taken to ensure closer cooperation among the workers of the hemisphere he pointed to the formation of the CIO committee on Latin America.[72]

Thus, by mid-1940 it seemed as if the CIO and the CTM were on their way to monopolizing control of international labor relations in the hemisphere. The AFL-CIO domestic conflict had been expanded to the field of foreign affairs, and in Latin America the AFL had met its first major defeat.

NOTES

1. Moises Poblete Troncoso, *El movimiento obrero latinoamericano* (Mexico: Fondo de Cultura Económica, 1946), p. 227; Roberto Blanco Moheno, *Crónica de la Revolución Mexicana* (Mexico: Editorial Diana, 1967), III, p. 117.

2. Vicente Lombardo Toledano, *Teoría y práctica del movimiento sindical mexicana* (Mexico, D.F.: Editorial Magisterio, 1961), pp. 62–64.

3. Ibid., p. 67.

4. CTM, *CTM 1936–1937, Informe del Comité Nacional* (Mexico: CTM, 1938), pp. 63–65; Robert Millon, *Vicente Lombardo Toledano,* trans. Jesús Lozoyo-Solis (Mexico: Libreria Madero, 1964), pp. 131–132; Lombardo Toledano, *Teoría y práctica,* pp. 68–71; Blanco Moheno, *Crónica de la Revolución,* III, pp. 345–359.

5. CTM, *CTM 1936–1941, Anales históricos* (Mexico: CTM, 1941), pp. 67–71; Lombardo Toledano, *Teoría y práctica,* p. 72.

6. Lombardo Toledano, *Teoría y práctica,* p. 81.

7. CTM, *CTM 1936–1937, Informe del Comité Nacional,* pp. 74–75.

8. Dirección General de Estadística, *50 Años de Revolución Mexicana en Cifras* (México: Presidencia de la República, 1963), p. 61.

9. Ibid; Poblete Troncoso, *Movimiento obrero,* p. 230.

10. Lombardo Toledano, *Teoría y práctica,* p. 71.

11. Interview with Vicente Lombardo Toledano, Mexico City, Mar. 25, 1965.

12. *Memoria de la CROM,* julio de 1935 al julio de 1937, pp. 46–51.

13. Lombardo Toledano, *Teoría y práctica,* p. 72.

14. Vicente Lombardo Toledano, *La Confederación de Trabajadores de América Latina* (Mexico: Editorial Popular, 1964), p. 7.

15. Interview with Lombardo Toledano, Mar. 25, 1965. The Communists made an attempt at forming a Latin American confederation in 1929, when they formed the Confederación Sindical Latinoamericana, but only Brazil, Mexico, Uruguay, and Ecuador had Communist unions with any claim to existence, and the organization went out of business in 1936, when dual unionism was abandoned and the Communist party line changed to that of the "Popular Front." ORIT-CIOSL, *15 Años de sindicalismo libre interamericano,* 2d ed. (Mexico: ORIT, 1963), p. 7.

16. Lombardo Toledano, *Confederación de Trabajadores,* p. 16.

17. *Mexican Labor News* (hereafter referred to as *MLN*) (Sept. 30, 1936).

18. Ibid. (June 2, 1937).

19. Interview with Lombardo Toledano, Mar. 25, 1965.

20. At that time Morones was in exile, along with Calles, in the United States. When the CROM and the Confederación General de Trabajadores mounted a drive to brand the CTM as Communist, the CTM pointed out the similarity of this campaign to the one being carried out by the AFL against the CIO. It also pointed out that Morones was still "persona grata" with the Executive Council of the AFL. *MLN* (Dec. 9, 1936).

21. Interview with Lombardo Toledano, Mar. 25, 1965.

22. *MLN* (Nov. 18, 1936).

23. Ibid.

24. CTM *CTM, 1936–1937, Informe del Comité Nacional,* p. 101; *MLN* (July 1, 1936).

25. *MLN,* passim.

26. Ibid. (June 30, 1937).

27. Ibid. (Dec. 16, 1937).

28. Ibid.

29. Ibid. (Nov. 15, 1936).
30. Ibid. (Jan. 6, 1937).
31. Ibid. (Oct. 14, 1937).
32. For example, see *El Popular* (Mexico City), Oct. 20, 1938.
33. *MLN* (Mar. 24, 1938).
34. Interview with Lombardo Toledano, Mar. 25, 1965.
35. Ibid.
36. *MLN* (May 5, July 7, 1938); *Excelsior,* Sept. 3, 1938.
37. Interview with Lombardo Toledano, Mar. 25, 1965.
38. *MLN* (Aug. 25, 1938).
39. ORIT-CIOSL, *15 Años de sindicalismo libre,* p. 169.
40. *El Popular,* Sept. 5, 1938.
41. Ibid., Sept. 6, 1938.
42. Ibid., Sept. 5, 1938.
43. Ibid., Sept. 6, 1938; *Excelsior,* Sept. 6, 1938.
44. *Excelsior,* Sept. 6, 1938.
45. *El Popular,* Sept. 10, 1938.
46. *Excelsior,* Sept. 12, 1938; *El Popular,* Sept. 12, 1938.
47. *MLN* (Sept. 8, 1938).
48. *Excelsior,* Sept. 7, 1938.
49. AFL, *Proceedings,* 1936, p. 225.
50. Ibid., p. 200.
51. *MLN* (Apr. 28, June 20, 27, 1938).
52. Ibid. (Apr. 28, 1938).
53. Ibid. (Oct. 20, 1938, Feb. 18, 1939).
54. *New York Times,* Feb. 8, 1939.
55. Ibid., Feb. 12, 1939.
56. Ibid., Feb. 8, 1939.
57. Ibid., Feb. 12, 1939.
58. Ibid.
59. *El Popular,* Feb. 14, 1939.
60. *MLN* (Feb. 15, 1938).
61. *El Popular,* May 18, 1939; AFL, *Proceedings,* 1939, p. 229.
62. *El Popular,* May 18, 1939.
63. Ibid.
64. Lazaro Pena, secretary-general, and Juan Arevalo, secretary of organization of the CTC, to Santiago Iglesias, secretary of the PAFL, June 6, 1939, in ibid., June 18, 1939.
65. AFL, *Proceedings,* 1939.
66. Ibid.
67. *MLN* (Nov. 16, 1939).
68. AFL, *Proceedings,* 1941, pp. 218, 614.
69. Congress of Industrial Organizations, *Proceedings of the Convention of 1940* (hereafter referred to as CIO, *Proceedings*), pp. 270–272.
70. Ibid., p. 105.
71. *MLN* (May 16, 1940).
72. Ibid. (June 20, 1940).

11

World War II

THE OUTBREAK of war in Europe in September 1939 did not at first usher in any profound changes in direction or policy in American-Mexican labor relations. All of the unions involved had been antifascist before the outbreak of the war, and all had continually emphasized the necessity of preventing the rise of fascist influence in the hemisphere. As the war dragged on, however, it became increasingly apparent to many that the United States would sooner or later be drawn into it. Even before the official entry of the United States into the war in December 1941, antifascist unity became the dominant issue in Latin American international labor relations. From 1939 on, everyone, from the State Department to the AFL and CIO to Lombardo's CTAL, was thinking in terms of hemispheric defense and hemispheric unity. Thus the war itself brought a short truce in the battle that had been shaping up over control of Latin American international labor relations, and all the interested parties worked for the one goal they had in common —the defeat of the Axis Powers.

Germany's invasion of Poland and the response of Britain and France provoked an immediate response in Mexico as well.

The CTM issued a manifesto in which it declared that no country would be able to remain neutral in the war, that sooner or later all the countries of the hemisphere would participate either directly or indirectly. "Mexico likewise will be involved, an event that will be no more than the natural result of its entire international position as a defender of democracy and peace." It called upon all labor unions to wage an unceasing battle against fascism.[1] Shortly thereafter, Lombardo declared that the workers of Mexico could not be neutral. This was not, said Lombardo, like World War I. It was not merely a struggle for markets and colonial possessions. It was a war between fascism and democracy throughout the world. The working classes had to fight on the side of the capitalist democracies because the democracies permitted the free development of the labor movement. The fascist regimes, on the other hand, destroyed all working-class liberties and rights.[2] The right-wing press in Mexico thereupon charged that Lombardo was trying to get Mexico to abandon neutrality and enter the war. Lombardo denied the charge,[3] but obviously it had some justification. The day after the invasion, the newspaper Lombardo controlled had declared: "We can't adopt an attitude of false, hypocritical, or cowardly neutrality." [4]

The period of the "phony war" set Lombardo and the CTM into rethinking their position on the war. By October the situation in Europe was still unclear, but the war was not assuming the proportions of the crusade for democracy that had been predicted at its outset. In early November the CTM issued a policy statement saying that, in view of the quiescent and undetermined nature of the war, it would be unwise for Mexico to abandon neutrality at that time. There was the possibility that the Allies might acquiesce to Germany's conquest of Poland or that Fascist Italy might join the war on the Allied side. The CTM statement concluded that, unless the war assumed a definite ideological shape, Mexico should remain out of it. If it remained what it appeared to be, another capitalist war over spoils, Mexico should remain neutral.[5]

As the war in Europe heated up, the CTM continued to advocate neutrality, as did the AFL and the CIO in the United States. However, as the entry of the United States into the war became increasingly likely, and after the adhesion of Italy and Japan to the Axis gave it an increasingly ideological tone, the labor movements increased their emphasis upon the need for cooperation to combat fascism.

Early in 1941, Lombardo began to side with President Roosevelt's firm support of the Allied cause and expressed the hope that the United States would enter the war. Later that year, just before the Nazi attack on the Soviet Union, he suggested that a continental democratic movement be formed to fight fascism and imperialism. With the entry of the Soviet Union into the war, the nature of the war changed, said Lombardo. With Russia in the war it was no longer an inter-imperial war.[6] Lombardo and the CTAL then embarked on a program of all-out support for the Allied cause.

Lombardo's campaign to garner labor support for the Allies centered around an attempt to achieve labor unity in support of their war effort. Thus the quarrel between the AFL and CIO, which had previously worked in favor of the CTAL, was now viewed as an impediment. The CTAL congress in November 1941 called for the unification of the AFL and CIO and closer relations between the workers of the United States, Britain, and the Soviet Union.[7]

Meanwhile, Lombardo's power within Mexico was rapidly dwindling. In 1940, as it became apparent that Ávila Camacho would become the next President and the Mexican government would move to the right, opposition to his leadership grew within the CTM. Throughout 1940, rumors flourished that he had been overthrown.[8] It was obvious that if the CTM was to retain its privileged position in the governing elite, Lombardo would have to go. (The CTM had come to represent "labor" in the reshuffling of the government party that took place under Cárdenas.) He held on to his position as secretary-general of the CTM until late 1941, when his five-year term expired. When he resigned, because the CTM constitution prohibited his reelection, he was unable to retain control of the organization.

Ávila Camacho set the pattern for handling the labor unions of Mexico, which has prevailed until the present. He allowed the CTM to retain its dominant position within the labor sector of the tripartite government party [9] and remain by far the largest and most powerful labor confederation in the country. However, in order to keep the CTM in line, and remind it that there were alternatives, he went out of his way to show his sympathy with the other, smaller confederations.[10] Thus, at the same time as he attended the 1941 CTAL congress, and gave Lombardo's work in international relations his benediction,[11] he was assiduously cultivating CROM as well, and letting Morones know that he was no longer persona non grata around the presidency. The contrast between Morones's description of the state of the unions in Mexico to the 1940 and 1941 AFL conventions is striking. Morones, in November 1940, shortly after the failure of his candidate, Almazán, unfolded a tale of government persecution of CROM. Its headquarters had been repeatedly searched, his house had been searched, and his family had been "molested." Many CROM members had been assassinated. The government was persecuting CROM, said Morones, because it refused to join the government-controlled labor unions. It had recently passed a law turning all unions into political clubs, which was probably the first step toward setting up a dictatorship, and was putting through another that would permit the existence of only one labor union in Mexico.[12]

In 1941, after Ávila Camacho's accession to the presidency, Morones had a much different tale to tell. "I am happy to tell you," he told the AFL convention, "that our fate has changed." CROM was now cooperating with the new government, he announced, without having lost its independence.[13] The AFL Executive Council, in its report, waxed joyful about the reconciliation as well. It praised the keen interest Ávila Camacho had shown in the PAFL and AFL ("to such an extent that he has sent a most cordial letter of greetings to President Green which was duly acknowledged") and pointed out that he had granted Matthew Woll an audience in Mexico City, expressing the goodwill he felt towards the United States and the AFL. Now that the persecution of the previous government had ceased, reported the Executive Council, CROM had been consistently gaining strength. The council concluded:

> This regaining of power, influence and prestige designates clearly the general trade union character of the C.R.O.M. We are indeed happy to note that the present Mexican government has realized these facts and that it seems willing and ready to give it the opportunity for further development.[14]

Morones and the AFL Executive Council were being overoptimistic. Ávila Camacho was in no mood to overturn the labor balance of power again. He did not have to. The prime necessity of governments in Mexico is control of the labor movement, and this he could achieve simply through subtle shifts in the balance of power. Lombardo's successors, his former aide Fidel Velásquez and the group surrounding him, got the message. The CTM grew much more pliant to the will of the government and began the slow movement toward the center of the political spectrum that has characterized its subsequent history. In June 1942, shortly after Mexico's entry into the war, it formally acknowledged the new multilateral union order by acceding to the wishes of the government and signing a labor unity pact with CROM, the CGT, and other minor confederations and independent unions. They pledged to suspend, for the duration of the war, all labor conflict, especially strikes, and to cooperate with the government in promoting the war effort.[15]

Lombardo undoubtedly was discomfited by the CTM's rightward shift and his increasing isolation in national politics. He had made many personal enemies, including former President Emilio Portes Gil, still a powerful figure in the government party, and was regarded by many cabinet members, including the President's brother, as too far to the left for comfort.[16] Thus, for him to concentrate almost totally on international affairs was the most comfortable path for all concerned. It coincided with his interests and with his conception of the labor movement as ultimately an international political movement. Lombardo's vision and interests had always gone far beyond the borders of Mexico, and here was a chance for him to participate in an important way in the great worldwide drama that was unfolding. For the Camacho government, his representing Mexican labor in international affairs was a suitably innocuous diversion, and it was happy to aid him as he traveled around the world trying to organize support for the Allied war effort. In a sense, it was a continuation of the Latin tradition of appointing embarrassing intellectual opponents to diplomatic posts in embassies abroad. Lombardo, however, did not turn his position as president of the CTAL into a sinecure.

Meanwhile, in the United States, changes in leadership were occurring as well. John L. Lewis had opposed the election of Roosevelt for a third term in 1940. When Roosevelt was elected, Lewis resigned as president of the CIO and withdrew his United Mine Workers from the organization. He too was replaced by a former protégé, Philip Murray of the United Steel Workers Union.

Murray in many ways was the ideal president for the CIO in those years, divided as it was politically. An incipient explosion of communists versus anticommunists was being held in check only by their common goals during the war and the communists' support of Roosevelt and the war effort. He was widely respected by both sides, both because of his personality and because he was somewhat remote from the intense conflicts over international affairs that raged among his more political associates. The conduct of international affairs in the CIO under Murray tended to follow the pattern established in the AFL under Green. Individual members of the Executive Council who had a great interest in international affairs tended to play a large role. In the AFL it was people like Matthew Woll, George Meany, and David Dubinsky. In the CIO it was people like Walter Reuther, Sidney Hillman (and his successor as head of the Amalgamated Clothing Workers, Jacob Potofsky), and O. A. Knight, president of the Oil and Chemical Workers.

Lombardo's campaign to rally Latin American labor behind the Allied cause received strong support both from the CIO and the U.S. government. Even before American entry into the war, Nelson Rockefeller, the young, energetic Coordinator of Inter-American Affairs, had been concerned about the lack of impact of American propaganda in Latin America. In a conference with Henry Luce, the publisher of *Time,* in the fall of 1940, he expressed his concern about the problem, saying that the only concept they were trying to "sell" to the world at the moment was "Democracy," and that this might boomerang in Latin America, since most of the governments there were dictatorships. The only theme available for use there, he said, is the concept loosely called the "good neighbor." The memorandum of their conversation continued:

Mr. Luce felt that the theme should grow out of the "necessity for America to expand." He explained that by expansion he meant not military expansion but expansion of trade, of commerce, and of the ideas important to us. Until the World War, he said, we were concerned with expansion within our own country and felt, in general, that the development of the world was not our job. Now, he said, we felt the world closing in on us and it was essential for us to spread our way of life, which he called Democracy. Mr. Rockfeller said that this concept might be presented to Latin America by calling it "The principles of Bolivar and Washington." He felt that Mr. Luce's philosophy would meet a natural psychological urge of this country, as it is happy only when going ahead.[17]

By June 1941, Rockefeller had become interested in using the AFL and CIO to improve the image of the United States among the Latin American masses. Carl B. Spaeth, an assistant of his, wrote Lawrence Duggan, Chief of the Division of American Republics of the State Department, that they believed that the AFL and CIO might be interested in inviting "certain Latin American trade union leaders" for visits to the United States. Each would invite its own leaders and entertain them separately, at different times. Spaeth wrote:

> As to financing, it might be assumed that both the CIO and AFL would be willing to supply certain funds; moreover, in most cases it would be expected that the invited union leaders would make some contributions. If more money were still needed, it is conceivable that this office could provide it though without advertising its participation.

The union leaders would be taken on the grand tour of industrial plants and other sights. "Details would have to be worked out," he continued, "so as to eliminate all possibility of the guests returning with anything but an enthusiasm for the American way of life." [18] After the United States entered the war in December of that year, the promotion of this type of visit became a major function of the OIAA. A labor division emerged in it, and a special labor newsletter, *Inter-American Labor Notes and Labor Letters,* was distributed to trade unionists throughout Latin America.[19]

The OIAA was more successful in promoting interchanges than Spaeth had hoped. It succeeded in getting the AFL and

CIO to work together during 1942 and 1943, jointly sponsoring visits such as that of Bernardo Ibañez, head of the Chilean Confederation of Workers, to the United States, where the AFL and CIO both acted as his hosts, and the return visits of combined AFL and CIO delegations to Latin America.[20] It also granted funds to the Division of Labor and Social Information of the Inter-American Union and to the Bureau of Labor Statistics to finance studies of Latin American labor that might be of interest to American unions.[21]

AFL–CIO cooperation in 1942 and 1943 was greatly facilitated by a softening of the AFL line towards the CTAL in late 1941. After attempting during 1941 to continue Iglesias's last mission, the revival of the PAFL,[22] the AFL abandoned this forlorn hope and began to feel out the possibility of reaching a modus vivendi with the CTAL. In November 1941, while in Mexico City for a meeting of the International Labor Organization, George Meany and the AFL representatives took the opportunity to sound out the CTAL, also meeting in Mexico City at that time, on the possibility of mutual cooperation in furthering the war effort. The AFL Executive Council felt that this meeting had provided a sound basis for further cooperation in the future.[23]

Securing the cooperation of the labor movements of Latin America in increasing the production of war materials was but one of the concerns of the AFL in again seeking closer ties with the labor movements to the south. The Executive Council of the AFL was also concerned about the great increase in U.S. investment in Latin America and the distinct possibility that U.S. manufacturers would take advantage of cheap labor in Latin America to produce their goods there for export to the United States, thus depriving American workers of jobs. The AFL was especially concerned about the possible effects of this trend in the postwar era. Thus, in 1942 the AFL's Executive Council decided to ask for U.S. government cooperation in calling a Pan-American labor conference to consider not only increasing the production of war materials in Latin America, but to formulate plans for a postwar economic program to raise working and living standards in Latin America.[24]

The AFL's call for a Pan-American labor conference was not taken up by Rockefeller and the OIAA. It would have undercut the influence of the CTAL and Lombardo, with whom they were cooperating quite successfully. The willingness of Rockefeller, an heir of the Standard Oil fortune, to cooperate with Lombardo, the man looked upon as being responsible for the nationalization of the Mexican oil industry, was based on a rather sound analysis of the Mexican political scene. As succinctly stated in an OIAA report in 1943, the OIAA saw Ávila Camacho as standing between the right and the left. It continued: "The Right, however, is opposed to the reformism inherited from the previous Cárdenas administration and would give the United States only minimum cooperation; the Left stands for the contrary policies." [25]

As for Lombardo, who had spent much of his life denouncing the Standard Oil Company and imperialistic American capitalists, in 1965, after he had gone back to his old "anti-American" stance, he still recalled having had very good relations with Rockefeller during the war. He said that, at the end of the war, when Rockefeller personally thanked him for the aid he had rendered, he replied that he had not done it to aid the United States, but to help his own country. Lombardo had been told by British Intelligence, and had subsequently confirmed through sources of his own, that if Hitler won he intended to divide Mexico in two, with the part to the north of the Tropic of Cancer going to the United States and the part to the south being merged with Central America to form a new nation.[26] Undoubtedly, there was a little more to it than that.

Lombardo was given more than cordial treatment by the U.S. government during the war. He conferred frequently with Rockefeller, spent some time visiting Roosevelt's friend, former ambassador to Mexico Josephus Daniels, in retirement in Raleigh, North Carolina,[27] and, after one visit to the United States in 1942, he reported to the CTM that Vice-President Henry Wallace had told him that Roosevelt was disposed to urge recalcitrant Latin American governments [28] to aid him in organizing the CTAL.[29]

The Roosevelt administration, sensitive to the fears of the AFL and CIO that the plethora of war contracts being let in Latin America would lead to the undercutting of American wages and standards by cheap Latin American labor, acceded to their demands that the Office of Economic Warfare include protective labor provisions in its Latin American contracts.[30] However, these were not strictly enforced, and the labor organizations had to keep constant pressure on the government to make sure that attempts would be made to adhere to them.[31]

Although the AFL and CIO continued to cooperate throughout most of the war in drumming up Latin American labor support for the war effort, the AFL's detente with Lombardo and the CTAL could not last for long. In the end, Lombardo was too much to stomach for such fervid AFL anti-Communists as Matthew Woll and George Meany. In the spring of 1942, Lombardo flew twice to Washington, conferring with Rockefeller and Philip Murray about the possibility of setting up a United Nations labor union, which would include both the AFL and CIO. The idea was endorsed by the United Steel Workers convention and the CIO Executive Committee, but the *New York Times* reported that the AFL was unwilling to go along because of its reluctance to have anything to do with an organization in which Lombardo would play a prominent role.[32] Rockefeller's office declined to provide the $40,000 necessary to hold the convention of United Nations labor somewhere in the hemisphere, presumably at least in part because of the AFL's unwillingness to go along.[33]

During 1942 and most of 1943, when the fortunes of the Allies in the war looked bleakest, the AFL-CIO rivalry in Latin

America remained muted. Their common interest in supporting the war effort in Latin America forced a certain amount of
cooperation. The rivalry continued in other spheres of foreign
affairs, especially with regard to the exclusion of the CIO from
the ILO, but the dominance of the CTAL in Latin America,
and the CIO's close ties to it, made any attempt by the AFL
to compete with them in Latin America appear not only fool-
hardy but harmful to the war effort. However, this quiescence
did not last long. By late 1943, the AFL was laying the groundwork for a renewal of the contest once the war was over.

By early 1944, the Central Committee of the CTAL was
attacking the AFL for trying to undermine it. It charged that
the AFL was maneuvering to break the unity of the CTAL
by trying to establish direct contacts with its member organizations, bypassing the CTAL and its president. Complement-
ing this, charged the CTAL, were a series of small maneuvers:
"systematic propaganda, direct and indirect, against the President of the CTAL"; favorable and "hypocritical" publicity
about other members of the organization combined with invitations to them to visit the United States; the sending of anti-
Lombardo unionists on tours of Latin America—all these
underlined the AFL's hostility to the president of the CTAL.[34]
Lombardo tried to respond to the assault that was building
up by tightening his control over the foreign relations of the
member organizations. They were reminded that, according
to the CTAL constitution, international relations were the
responsibility of the president and he and the Central Committee now forbade them to accept any invitations from the
AFL.[35]

By mid-1944, with the Allied landings in Normandy bringing the prospect of certain victory in the war against Germany,
the AFL offensive to spread anti-Communist unionism throughout the world began in earnest. The Free Trade Union Committee, headed by Vice President Matthew Woll, was set up,
directed at establishing "free trade unionism" in the liberated

countries of Europe and the rest of the world. The executive secretary, the man who directed its day-to-day operations, was Jay Lovestone, a leader of the American Communist party in the 1920s who, after his expulsion from the party, had drifted rightward and had become a rabid anticommunist. He had been an assistant to David Dubinsky, head of the International Ladies Garment Workers Union, specializing in international affairs, and now, with the support of such powerful people as Woll, Dubinsky, and Meany, was ready to direct an anticommunist crusade along a broad front.[36]

In late 1944 the AFL convention called for the establishment of a new hemispheric labor organization, and George Meany immediately went to Mexico, ostensibly on vacation. The *New York Times* reported that he was also "to confer with important Mexican labor leaders to lay the groundwork for a 'new deal' between the AFL and the trade unions south of the border." Lombardo was at a CTAL congress in Colombia, so Meany was certainly not conferring with him.[37]

Meany did not have much success in Mexico, and the AFL's efforts to undermine the CTAL in the rest of Latin America made only halting progress during the rest of the war. But the cold war soon immeasurably strengthened the hands of Woll, Meany, Lovestone, and company. They were "cold warriors" before the cold war had even begun. Once it began, they were prepared for it.

NOTES

1. *MLN* (Sept. 7, 1939).
2. Ibid. (Sept. 14, 1939).
3. Ibid.
4. *El Popular,* Sept. 2, 1939. This point must be explained in some detail because it is frequently said that on this question Lombardo followed the Communist party line to the letter and immediately opposed

the war as an imperalist war. See Robert Alexander, "Union Movements in Latin America," *Labor and Nation* (Summer 1951): 36. This is obviously not true.

5. *MLN* (Nov. 9, 1939).

6. Millon, *Lombardo Toledano,* p. 123.

7. Amaro del Rosal, *Los Congresos Obreros Internacionales en el siglo XX, 1900–1950* (Mexico: Editorial Grijalvo, 1963), p. 387.

8. *New York Times,* July 20, Nov. 17, 1940; Millon, *Lombardo Toledano,* p. 150.

9. Under Camacho, the army was eliminated as an official "sector." The three remaining were "labor," "peasants," and the "popular" sectors, which supposedly represented civil servants, large and small business, and everyone not included in the first two sectors.

10. Mainly CROM and the CGT, the Confederación General de Trabajadores, a small confederation founded in the 1920s which was to the left of CROM in the 1920s but to the right of the CTM in the 1930s, as far as anyone can decipher.

11. CTAL, *CTAL 1938–1948, Resoluciones de sus asambleas* (Mexico: CTAL, 1948), p. 79.

12. AFL, *Proceedings,* 1940, pp. 616–617.

13. Ibid., 1941, p. 614.

14. Ibid., p. 218.

15. Moises Poblete Troncoso, *El movimiento obrero latinoamericano* (Mexico: Fondo de Cultura Económica, 1946), p. 236. This agreement was not particularly effective in obtaining real cooperation, either among the labor unions themselves, or between the unions, management, and government. See Frank Jellinek, "Watch Mexico," *The Nation* 158 (Mar. 25, 1944): 364.

16. *New York Times,* May 5, 8, 1942.

17. Minutes of Meeting of Policy Committee of Cultural Relations Division of Coordinator's Office, Sept. 27, 1940, Papers of the Office of Inter-American Affairs, National Archives (hereafter referred to as OIAA Papers), Box 5.

18. Carl B. Spaeth to Lawrence Duggan, June 6, 1941, OIAA Papers, Box 322.

19. "History of the OIAA," passim., OIAA Papers.

20. AFL, *Proceedings,* 1943, p. 154.

21. Ibid., 1944, p. 624.

22. Ibid., 1941, p. 219.

23. Ibid., 1942, pp. 233–234; interview with Lic. Vicente Lombardo Toledano, Mexico City, Mar. 25, 1965; interview with Sr. José Ortiz Petricioli, private secretary to the late Luis Morones, Mexico City, March 12, 1965. The recollections of the latter two conflict somewhat on exactly when Meany came to Mexico and how much contact he had with the CTAL. Lombardo remembered Meany's being in Mexico at the time but claimed that he himself did not meet with him. Petricioli claimed that

Meany sought out Lombardo and the CTM and did not bother to look up Morones, thus inflicting a slight on Morones and CROM which they never forgot nor forgave. The AFL, *Proceedings,* speak of a meeting in November 1941 between representatives of the AFL and "the representatives of the Latin American National Labor Federations, members of the Confederation of Latin America." This would appear to be applicable only to the CTAL.

24. AFL, *Proceedings,* 1942, p. 233.

25. "Activities of the Office of the Coordinator of Inter-American Affairs: Mexico, Political" [June 1943], OIAA Papers, Box 2. The report called Cárdenas and Toledano the leaders of the Left and the President's brother, Maximino Ávila Camacho, Miguel Alemán, and Vejar Vásquez, the Minister of Education, the leaders of the right.

26. Interview with Lombardo Toledano, Mar. 25, 1965.

27. Vicente Lombardo Toledano, Introduction to Millon, *Lombardo Toledano,* p. xiv.

28. Those of Brazil, Argentina, Venezuela, and Guatemala.

29. *New York Times,* April 24, 1942.

30. AFL, *Proceedings,* 1943, p. 165; CIO Committee on Latin American Affairs, press release, May 19, 1943, Papers of the Amalgamated Clothing Workers of America, New York, N.Y. (hereafter referred to as Amalgamated Papers), Latin American File.

31. CIO, *Proceedings,* 1943, p. 100.

32. *New York Times,* June 28, 1942. Another reason would have been the AFL's unwillingness to establish relations with the Soviet trade unions, which it didn't consider authentic unions. Lombardo and Murray had attacked the AFL on this point and supported the inclusion of the Soviets. *New York Times,* Feb. 11, 1942.

33. *New York Times,* June 28, 1942.

34. CTAL, *CTAL 1938–1948, Resoluciones,* pp. 130–132.

35. Ibid., p. 132.

36. *AFL Weekly News Service* (Dec. 9, 1947); "Labor and the Cold War," *The Nation* (Dec. 10, 1955).

37. AFL, *Proceedings,* 1944, p. 624; *New York Times,* Dec. 13, 1944.

12

Cold War Unionism

It was relatively easy for people like Lovestone, Dubinsky, and Meany to celebrate the end of the crusade against fascism by embarking on a new crusade against communism. Since the Bolshevik revolution, communist unionism had appeared to represent a threat to AFL unionism. During the 1920s, the Communists had tried to take control of the labor movement in the United States, first by "boring from within" existing AFL unions and then by setting up competing unions, gathered in the Trade Union Unity League. Dubinsky's International Ladies Garment Workers Union, a union dominated by Socialist party of America sympathizers whose largely Jewish membership was generally rather left-wing, was a prime target of both campaigns.

After the Communists abandoned "dual unionism" in late 1935 and switched to the "Popular Front" line, it appeared obvious to many that, beneath their protestations about the necessity for "antifascist unity," they were merely switching back to "boring from within." To many AFL unionists, it appeared that the Communists had been all-too-successful in infiltrating CIO unions. Until 1948, one of the major barriers

186

to healing the rift between the two confederations was the presence, in the CIO, of an influential minority of Communists and Communist-dominated unions.

For people who had spent much of their lives fighting an internal battle against Communist unionists, and then had participated in an international struggle against "fascism," it was easy to blend the two impulses and wage an international battle against communism. The rhetoric of the struggles, the battle cries, and the casts of mind demanded by the wars against fascism and communism were frighteningly similar. In both cases, it was a life-or-death struggle for the survival of "democracy," "liberty," and "free trade unionism" against a "totalitarian" enemy who represented dictatorship, oppression, and slave-labor camps. In both cases, the enemy was a centrally directed, worldwide conspiracy, which worked through "puppet regimes" and "fifth columns" to achieve its obvious goal—the conquest of the world. The AFL anticommunists hardly took the time to catch their breath (or rethink their clichés) before turning from one monster conspiracy to confront the next.

During the war, the British Trades Union Congress had created an alliance of sorts with the Soviet trade union organization. From this basis they formed, in 1945, a new international trade union organization, which was to include every significant "democratic" national labor confederation in the world. The new organization, the World Federation of Trade Unions, was to be a labor counterpart to the solid links developed among the "democracies" during the war. Its unity lasted only slightly longer than those rapidly crumbling links. The CIO joined the WFTU, but the AFL, continuing its policy of having no intercourse with the Soviet unions, demurred. It soon mounted a counterattack and began to organize a rival body which would represent only "free" trade unions.[1]

The CTM belonged to the WFTU, and the CTAL was associated with it as well. Thus one of the first aims of the AFL was to break the control of the CTAL over Latin American international labor relations. In 1946, Serafino Romualdi, an antifascist, anticommunist Italian who spoke Spanish well, was appointed full-time Latin American representative of the AFL.[2] An assistant to Lovestone in the Ladies Garment Workers Union during the war, Romualdi was now given the formidable task of destroying the CTAL and constructing a new, AFL-led, Latin American labor confederation. He set out on his mission with zest and energy, traveling through Latin America cultivating the support of dissident groups in the CTAL and small organizations that were not members of the CTAL.[3]

By late 1946, Romualdi had managed to round up representatives of anti-CTAL organizations in eight countries to attend the AFL convention. A whole afternoon was set aside for Latin America. The Latins were regaled with speeches emphasizing the necessity of resisting communism and its leader in Latin America, Lombardo Toledano.[4] Mexico was one of the eight countries represented, but by neither the CTM nor CROM. The Mexicans were from two more minor confederations and an independent electrical workers union.[5] CROM, the AFL's ancient ally, was not represented because relations between the two had cooled considerably during the war, and Morones was now supporting the Peronist CGT in Argentina, a firm enemy of the AFL.[6]

In 1947, Romualdi made two more trips to Latin America, attempting to line up organizations willing to participate in the proposed new confederation.[7] In Mexico he met with little success. He met with a group of leaders of all the major labor organizations, including the CTM, CROM, and the Railway Workers, but to little avail. According to Morones's private secretary, they received him with appropriate courtesy, but he proceeded to treat them like schoolchildren, telling them that they had done nothing for Latin American labor unity and that he held the future of Latin America in his hands.[8]

Still, CROM was at least ambivalent about the new venture. When a formal invitation to attend the founding conference of the new confederation in Lima, Peru, in January 1948 arrived in CROM headquarters, Morones decided that before accepting or rejecting it, he should go to Washington to speak with William Green. He flew north and met with Green, arguing for a reestablishment of the Pan-American Federation of Labor (and, presumably, his important role in it). Green told him the affair was not in his hands and sent him to Dubinsky. Dubinsky repeated Green's disclaimer and sent him to Romualdi, whom he had already met and disliked. Romualdi told him that everything was already arranged, that it was too late to change plans, and that Bernardo Ibañez of Chile was to be the first president of the new organization. Incensed, Morones returned to Mexico saying that the conference was a prefabricated one.[9] That Morones was not one of the architects of the prefabricated structure no doubt fed his outrage even more.

Upon his return to Mexico, Morones received a letter from the Costa Rican Federation of Labor saying that they had been invited to the Lima conference but that they knew the Argentinian CGT had not. They asked what CROM thought of this situation. Morones wrote to Ibañez, in Washington at that time, asking why the CGT and the unions of the Dominican Republic had not been invited, but never received an answer.[10]

Morones was enraged. He was convinced that the new organization would just be a tool of the AFL and the State Department. Still, he was not one to quietly crawl back into the woodwork and ignore the whole affair. He decided to go to Lima and expose the nature of the proceedings at the conference itself. At Lima, Romualdi and those who controlled the conference, aware of what Morones intended to do, declared him a traitor to the workers and had him expelled before he had a chance to speak. When he left the theater where the conference was being held, he was taken into custody by two policemen, who escorted him to the police station, where he was given twenty-four hours to leave the country.

He took a plane to Chile, where he received the same treatment. He then proceeded to Argentina, where he had been
invited by the CGT, and was received royally by the CGT
as the man who had defended them against the Americans.
The loose ties between the CGT and the CROM were
thenceforth greatly strengthened.[11]

In spite of Morones's attempt to disrupt the proceedings, the
new organization, the Confederación Interamericano de Trabajadores (CIT) was founded on schedule and according to
plan, with Ibañez as president and Serafino Romualdi as
secretary-treasurer. The only Mexican organization represented
was the small Confederación Proletaria Nacional.

It was clear from the outset that the main purpose of the
new organization was to combat the influence of Lombardo
Toledano and the CTAL in Latin America. The cold war had
been getting increasingly colder, and Lombardo was attacking
American policy and generally supporting the Soviets on cold
war issues. To George Meany, he was "Stalin's chief Lieutenant
in the Western Hemisphere."[12] William Green said that it was
especially important that the new confederation be formed in
view of the renewal by Lombardo "and his so-called confederation" of their prewar attempts to undermine American prestige
in the hemisphere. "They are now busily engaged in smearing
the United States in South America and Central America and
they are also trying to lure the workers of our countries into
the communist camp," said Green.[13]

In founding the CIT, leaders of the AFL were not thinking
merely of the effects it would have in Latin America. They
were also thinking of the worldwide international labor scene.
In reporting favorably on the proposition to the 1947 AFL
convention, the International Relations Committee said: "No
doubt the effective functioning of such a federation as a loyal
champion of the workers' interest, rather than a slavish lackey
of Russian, or another imperialism, is bound to have the
profoundest repercussions in the WFTU itself."[14]

Attempts to use the CIT as a base for the formation of a worldwide competitor of the WFTU began almost immediately after its formation at an ILO meeting in July 1948, when Romualdi, in his capacity as secretary-treasurer of the CIT, set up a joint secretariat with Liu Sun-sen, the representative of the newly formed Asian Federation of Labor. The secretariat was to serve, said Romualdi, "not only . . . for liaison purposes, but to take joint action towards calling, as soon as possible, an international conference to form a genuine international confederation of free trade unions." [15]

Thus, with the coming of the cold war, the dominant theme of AFL policy in Latin America became the kind of strident anticommunism that has distinguished it to this day. In the atmosphere of the cold war, there was no need to sugarcoat this aim for Latin American and AFL unionists by emphasizing that the CIT would bring all sorts of practical "bread and butter" benefits to members of its constituent unions. To the AFL, the CIT was helping them achieve the necessary basis for these practical benefits—"free trade unionism." Unfortunately, "free trade unionism" all too often appeared simply to coincide with nothing more than anticommunist unionism.

The AFL anticommunist and anti-CTAL drive received a great impetus from divisions within the CTM and CIO. The conflicts within these two movements and the defeat of the left-wing forces in them paved the way for them to join with the AFL in a crusade to make the hemisphere safe for "free trade unionism."

Once the war had ended, Lombardo and the Mexican government began to diverge in their pronouncements on foreign policy. While the Ávila Camacho government was attempting to perpetuate and strengthen the rapprochement with the United States constructed during the war, Lombardo lapsed back into his old ways. In December 1945 he caused the government great embarrassment by charging that "certain U.S. firms" were smuggling arms to the right-wing Sinarquista

Union to foment a revolution and set up a pro-American "Quisling" as President of Mexico. The American ambassador, George S. Messersmith, incensed by the charges, lodged an official protest with the Ministry of Foreign Affairs. This gave the government an opportunity to hand Lombardo a sharp rebuff. In an official statement it announced, "The Government of Mexico does not associate itself with or support the statements of Lombardo Toledano." Mexican government agencies of all kinds then set about refuting Lombardo's charges.[16] The government's statement seriously weakened Lombardo's prestige, to the great satisfaction of the U.S. embassy.[17]

However, Lombardo continued to play the game of Mexican politics from within the consensus, represented in this case by the all-powerful ruling party, the Partido Revolucionario Institucional (PRI). He accepted Ávila Camacho's choice for the presidential succession in 1946, Miguel Alemán, even though Alemán was further to the right than Camacho. A CIO delegation, headed by Jacob Potofsky, president of the Amalgamated Clothing Workers and chairman of the CIO Latin American Affairs Committee, was invited by the CTM to attend Alemán's inauguration. There, in a luncheon speech, Potofsky praised Lombardo as "a great internationalist, a great intellectual, and spiritual leader" and described Alemán as "a great humanitarian and champion of the people's rights." [18] Alas, it soon became clear that, whoever Alemán was championing, it was not going to be Lombardo and left-wing unionism.

Still, Lombardo hung in there, trying to act as a moderating influence on the more militant left-wing unionists and defending Alemán against the rapidly burgeoning charges that he was an "enemy" of labor.[19] In 1947, when Fidel Velásquez's term as secretary-general of the CTM expired, the organization split along generally left-right lines in the contest to name his successor. The moderate Velásquez group, the so-called reformist faction, had the support of Alemán, Lombardo, and the large majority of the union leaders who made up the CTM. When it became apparent that they were going to lose the struggle, the left-wing faction, led mainly by Communists, withdrew from the convention and the organization.[20] The control of the CTM by the Velásquez faction was thus strengthened and solidified by the elimination of a strong opposition group. It owed much of its power to the increasingly open intervention of the Alemán and subsequent governments in union affairs and paid off much of this debt by henceforth becoming almost totally subservient to the government.[21]

Although Lombardo had supported the "reformist" candidate for secretary-general, he too soon made a false move and was crushed. Falling into increasing disfavor with the Alemán government, which was determined to move the Mexican Revolution sharply to the right, he had been trying to form a new political party, the Partido Popular, to give the left more leverage within the Mexican power structure. The National Council of the CTM at first had supported the idea, but under government pressure it turned about and came out in opposition to it. Lombardo was expelled from the CTM, and the CTM withdrew from the CTAL, of which he remained the president.[22] The CTAL line in international affairs was now running counter to the Alemán government's alignment with the United States in the cold war, and the CTM reacted accordingly. In withdrawing from the CTAL, the CTM made no move to turn its back on the CIO, its old ally in the United States, and join the AFL-dominated CIT.

During the same period, the CIO was being divided on issues more directly related to foreign policy. A conflict between the unions on the left and right of the CIO had been shaping up ever since the end of the war, when the foreign policy of the Truman administration began to diverge from the policy of friendship toward the Soviet Union and strengthening of Big Three unity, which the Communists and many

others in the CIO wanted to see followed. The conflict
came to a head at the 1947 convention on the question of
whether the CIO should support the proposed Marshall Plan,
which would accept the fact of a divided world and rebuild
Western Europe as a bastion against communism, or whether
American aid should be given in the context of Big Three
unity through the United Nations without ideological strings
attached. In the struggle that ensued, the Communists and
their supporters were obviously the weaker group.

Although no formal decision was made at the convention,
when the Marshall Plan was initiated, the majority of CIO
unions gave it their support. In March 1948, the CIO International Affairs Committee sent O. A. Knight of the Oil Workers International Union to Mexico City to attend a CTAL
meeting and urge that body to support the Marshall Plan. His
mission was advertised as an attempt to counteract Communist
propaganda, to show that the plan was not "a creature of Wall
Street" but had the support of American trade unionists.[23]
What was really at stake was the continuance of CIO support
for the CTAL, which had been a prime denouncer of the plan
in Latin America. The CTM had withdrawn from the CTAL,
and the CIO was preparing to drop its support as well.

In 1948, Lombardo's CTAL, deprived of the financial support it had been receiving from the CTM, had joined the
WFTU. Thus, during 1948, when it still officially remained
a member of the WFTU, the CIO had an obligation to continue rendering at least lip-service support to the CTAL.
When, in January 1949, it withdrew from the WFTU, the
CIO was free to abandon the CTAL totally. This it did with
alacrity. However, it was unwilling to turn about abruptly and
join the CIT, which it had been attacking since its inception.
Thus, in 1949, when the AFL and CIO jointly underwrote the
founding of the new rival of the WFTU, the International
Confederation of Free Trade Unions (ICFTU), it was decided
that, rather than taking the CIT in as the Latin American

"regional organization," it would be better to disband the CIT and form a new Latin American labor confederation, consisting only of IFCTU members. This would also make it easier to recruit the major non-CIT member whose membership the AFL and CIO coveted: the CTM.[24]

The CTM proved relatively easy to recruit, but there were signs that the sailing would not be smooth. The resolution of the CTM National Council in October 1950, in approving the new international policy, described it as working for the establishment of the hemispheric labor organization "on the bases of equality, unity, open opposition to communism and capitalism, and the inclusion of all the workers' centrals of America." [25] The drawback was the latter reference, for it soon developed that the CTM would hold out for the inclusion of those mortal enemies of the AFL and CIO, the only labor movement in Latin America of equal potency to the CTM— the Argentinian CGT.

When the founding convention of the Organización Regional Interamericano de Trabajadores (ORIT) met in Mexico City in January 1951, the support of the Alemán government for the venture was obvious. Alemán himself addressed the opening session, and the CTM was there at the head of a united front together with CROM and CPN.[26] The support of the U.S. government was obvious as well. Alas, all did not proceed as planned thereafter.

The opening of the convention was marked by confusion and bickering. In order to convince Morones and CROM to participate in the new organizations, the labor attachés of the U.S. and British embassies, in an all-day conference with him, had promised that the Argentinian CGT would be invited as well. The CGT was invited, and both the CROM and the CTM believed that this meant that they had been invited to be members of the new organization.[27] However, when the Congress opened, they were told that the CGT people had not been invited as delegates, but only to attend the inaugural ceremonies, that their right to be seated as delegates would have to be voted upon after the Constituent Assembly of the organization had formed itself. Morones and Fidel Velásquez, who was president of the congress, decided to make a fight out of it.[28] So did the AFL and CIO. Jacob Potofsky, head of the CIO delegation, declaring himself opposed to "representatives of totalitarianism—whether to the right or left," announced that he would withdraw the CIO if the CGT were seated.[29] Rumors abounded that the Americans were acting under State Department direction.[30]

When the vote on the admission of the CGT came, the Mexicans found only themselves voting for the Argentinians. Thereupon, Fidel Velásquez resigned as president of the congress, and representatives of CROM and CTM walked out. In his resignation speech, Velásquez pointed out the hollowness of the AFL and CIO arguments against the CGT. The CGT was not admitted because it was reputedly not a "free" labor movement, but was merely a puppet of the Perón government. Velásquez pointed out that the CGT had a history of fifty years of independence. He asked, "Why discriminate against them?" Why, he asked, say that the CGT was worse than the Brazilian unions, members in good standing of the CIT and ORIT, "who were born with the stigma of putative sons of the State?" They were created by order of the dictator Getulio Vargas, and at that very moment, the executive committees of all the unions in Brazil were being reshuffled by the government in order to maintain the control of the pro-Vargas elements.[31] The answer to Velásquez's questions seemed obvious: the CGT was discriminated against because it supported the Perón government, and Perón had been incurring the wrath of the U.S. government since World War II.

The next day, upon announcing the withdrawal of the CTM from ORIT, Velásquez said: "This organization has no Latin American head or feet. It is merely the instrument of the United States State Department, to be manipulated by the big three United States labor organizations and their Cuban satellites." [32] Later, in a report to the CTM National Council, he said that a majority of the delegates to the congress were apocryphal; they were paid and instructed by agents of the North American leaders and acted like a mafia.[33]

Immediately after their withdrawal from the convention, the CROM organized a large mass meeting in Mexico City in support of the CGT and began laying plans for the formation of yet another Latin American labor confederation. The only Mexican organization that remained in ORIT was the CPN, which claimed a membership of 300,000.[34]

During the next two years, the CTM found itself courted diligently from two sides and pushed not too gently from its backside. The CGT asked it to send delegations to Argentina and itself sent delegations to the CTM. The CTM remained friendly but not effusive. It received the CGT delegations cordially, but did not reciprocate the visits.[35]

Then, when CROM invited the CTM to join with it and the CGT in the new Latin American labor organization, it politely refused to join in even the preliminary discussions.[36] When the official invitation came to join the new organization, the Asociación de Trabajadores Latino Americanos (ATLAS), the CTM turned down the offer, supposedly because it saw little chance for success in the venture.[37] The displeasure that the government would display at such a step likely was no mean factor in the decision.

Meanwhile, the CIO and ORIT were alternately courting and cajoling the CTM. Close contacts with the CIO and AFL, especially on the immigration problem, continued,[38] and ORIT continued to send CTM unions propaganda, bulletins, and pamphlets, obviously hoping to break the CTM front against joining.[39]

While ATLAS and ORIT were doing some pulling and tugging, the Mexican government was behind, doing some not-too-subtle kicking. The CTM suddenly found itself unable to send delegates to the 1951 conference of the International Labor Organization in Geneva because the government refused to pay the fares of its delegates, as it usually did.[40] The next year, when the CTM man went to pick up the money for that year's ILO conference at the office of the Secretary of Labor, he was shunted about from official to official, all of whom professed ignorance as to the proper procedures to follow. Before he could get the money, he was told by his travel agent that it was impossible to get air reservations so that he could arrive at the conference on time. Once again the CTM was unrepresented at Geneva.[41]

By mid-1952, the various forces pushing and pulling the CTM into ORIT were having their effects. In July, Velásquez and Alfonso Sánchez Madariaga went to the CIO congress in Atlantic City to discuss reentry.[42] By September, arrangements had been made for Velásquez to attend a meeting in Denmark of the World Food Organization of the United Nations as head of a CTM delegation.[43] From there he went to Hamburg at the invitation of Ernest Schwartz of the CIO, the Western Hemisphere representative of the International Secretariat of Food Industry Unions, to attend a convention of that organization.[44] Schwartz took him to Brussels, for a conference with J. H. Oldenbrock, the secretary-general of the ICFTU, at which the three laid the groundwork for the reentry of the CTM into the ICFTU and ORIT. The CTM was invited to send representatives to the ORIT convention in December in Rio de Janeiro, and it subsequently rejoined.[45]

The CTM was never precisely clear as to why it rejoined ORIT. Upon his return to Mexico from Europe, Velásquez said that the ICFTU leaders told him that they weren't happy with the way ORIT was functioning without the CTM, implying that the CTM was joining to save ORIT.[46] But given his previous descriptions of the nature of ORIT, he should have been overjoyed about this and content to watch it wither away. The CTM newspaper's editorial on the subject was equally vague. It interpreted Velásquez's trip as a demonstration of international recognition of the importance of the CTM and the greatness of Fidel Velásquez. In typical fashion, it concluded:

> In that way, the renown which Fidel Velásquez has in the labor world was established once more, thanks to his great intelligence, his firm love for the cause of those dispossessed of their own fatherlands, and his unbreakable firmness, which has enabled him to overcome the dangers and provocations to which the CTM has been submitted during its heroic life.[47]

This may have been true, but it did not help explain why the CTM was to rejoin ORIT.

After the meeting at Rio de Janeiro, the CTM again claimed great victories for its observers there, saying that they "succeeded in having acknowledged most of the errors committed in Mexico [in 1951] and that [the CTM] would be given the place which it deserved" in ORIT.[48] Again, it is not clear exactly what this meant. Aside from having the site of the headquarters of ORIT changed back from Havana to Mexico City there is no indication of any clear concessions or gains. Even today, CTM participants in the negotiations are unclear and vague about any concessions made to the CTM.[49] One thing is clear: no concessions were made on the issue that provoked the CTM walkout in January 1951. There was no thought of inviting the Argentine CGT to join.

NOTES

1. *AFL Weekly News Service* (Dec. 9, 1947); "Labor and the Cold War," *The Nation* (Dec. 10, 1955).
2. *New York Times,* Feb. 1, 1946; AFL, *Proceedings,* 1946, p. 401.
3. AFL, *Proceedings,* 1946, pp. 401, 404; Robert J. Alexander, "Union Movements in Latin America," *Labor and Nation* (Summer 1951): 37.

4. AFL, *Proceedings,* 1946, pp. 400–403; *New York Times,* Oct. 12, 1946.

5. AFL, *Proceedings,* 1946, p. 400.

6. Interview with Sr. José Ortiz Petricioli, Morones's private secretary, Mexico City, Mar. 12, 1965.

7. AFL, *Proceedings,* 1947, p. 191.

8. Interview with Sr. Petricioli, Mar. 12, 1965.

9. Ibid., Mar. 9, 1965.

10. Ibid.

11. Ibid.

12. *AFL Weekly News Service* (June 8, 1948).

13. Ibid. (Nov. 25, 1947).

14. AFL, *Proceedings,* 1947, p. 472.

15. *AFL Weekly News Service* (July 6, 1948).

16. *New York Times,* Dec. 18–22, 1945.

17. Ibid., Dec. 22, 1945.

18. *CIO News* (Dec. 16, 1946).

19. *New York Times,* Dec. 24, 27, 1946.

20. Vicente Lombardo Toledano, *Teoría y práctica del movimiento sindical mexicano* (Mexico: Editorial Popular, 1964), pp. 82–83.

21. The government in turn repaid the leaders of the CTM for their support when it stepped in to crush the next major threats to the power of the Velásquez group in 1959 and 1961.

22. Robert P. Millon, *Vicente Lombardo Toledano,* trans. Jesús Lozoyo-Solis (Mexico: Libreria Madero, 1964), p. 154.

23. *New York Times,* Feb. 28, 1948; *CIO Reporter* (Mar. 20, 1948).

24. Alexander, "Union Movements," p. 37.

25. CTM, *Memorias del XL Consejo Nacional de la CTM celebrado en Mérida, Yuc.,* del 4 al 6 de octubre, 1950 (hereafter referred to as CTM, *Memorias del Consejo Nacional),* p. 83.

26. *Excelsior,* Jan. 9, 1951.

27. Interview with Sr. Petricioli, Mar. 9, 1965.

28. Ibid.

29. *New York Times,* Jan. 11, 1951.

30. Murray Kempton, "How Clean a Smell," *New York Post,* Jan. 29, 1951.

31. CTM, *Informe al XLII Consejo Nacional,* 1951, pp. 63–65.

32. *New York Times,* Jan. 13, 1951.

33. CTM, *Informe al XLII Consejo Nacional,* 1951, p. 9.

34. *CIO News* (Jan. 22, 1951). It should be pointed out again that Mexican labor confederation membership claims are usually highly inflated, especially those of smaller confederations. The CTM at that time was claiming 1.25 million (ibid.), which likely was somewhat closer to the mark than the CPN's claim.

35. CTM, *Informe al XLII Consejo Nacional,* 1951, p. 65.

36. CTM, *Informe al XLIII Consejo Nacional,* 1951, p. 44.

37. CTM, *Informe al XLIV Consejo Nacional,* 1952, p. 42.

38. Ibid., p. 42; CTM, *Informe al XLV Consejo Nacional,* 1952, p. 42; AFL, *Proceedings,* 1953, p. 416; *New Republic* (Sept. 24, 1951): 7.

39. CTM, *Informe al XLII Consejo Nacional,* 1951, p. 43.
40. Ibid.
41. CTM, *Informe al XLIV Consejo Nacional,* 1952, pp. 43–44.
42. Ibid., pp. 14, 52.
43. *Ceteme* (Oct. 17, 1952).
44. CTM, *Informe al XLVII Consejo Nacional,* 1953, p. 9.
45. Ibid.
46. *Ceteme* (Oct. 17, 1952).
47. Ibid. (Oct. 12, 1952).
48. CTM, *Informe al XLVII Consejo Nacional,* 1953, p. 9.
49. Interview with Bernardo Cobos, Secretary of Education of the CTM, Mexico City, July 16, 1967.

13

Braceros
and Wetbacks

THE POSTWAR period witnessed the revival of the "immigration question" for unionists on both sides of the border, but in a slightly different form than in the 1920s. During the war, supposedly as a temporary, wartime response to the labor shortage in the United States, the U.S. and Mexican governments had initiated the bracero program. Its continuance after the war and into the 1960s, along with the heavy postwar influx of legal and illegal immigration of Mexicans to the United States, evoked some responses similar to those of the 1920s.

The bracero program essentially was an agreement between the U.S. and Mexican governments for the recruitment of temporary contract laborers in Mexico to work in specific occupations in the United States. The 1943 agreement, entered into in late 1942, served as the model for all subsequent agreements, with relatively minor changes. Under the agreement, a contract was signed with individual Mexican workers by a U.S. government agency (the Farm Security Administration in 1943, the Agriculture and Labor departments later) in which the laborer agreed to provide his services for a certain specified period (usually one year) and return to Mexico immediately upon the termination of his contract. He also promised to work only in certain specified occupations, usually agriculture. In return, the U.S. government provided transportation expenses to and from Mexico, guaranteed the workers the "prevailing wage" for the particular work they were engaged in, and ensured that they would receive adequate housing and medical services. It also guaranteed that they would be provided with employment for at least 75 percent of the working days covered by the contract. The U.S. government would then contract with employers' organizations in the United States for the hiring of the braceros in groups. The contract with the employers could be canceled and the workers withdrawn if the employers did not comply with the standards set.[1]

Most employers would have preferred that the United States work unilaterally and regulate the flow of laborers simply by adjusting its immigration laws. This would eliminate the necessity for including the guarantees demanded by the Mexican government. But it was generally recognized in Congress that this was impossible. The Mexican government could retaliate in many ways, most obviously by refusing to allow the braceros to return to Mexico.[2] It was all right to have the braceros come to the United States for a year while they were young, strong, and ingenuous, but to have them stay permanently was another matter.

During the war, the agreement worked well for both sides and encountered little opposition. The United States was provided with help in harvesting its crops, and Mexico was provided with a kind of free unemployment insurance. The Mexican government usually dictated from where the workers would be recruited and in 1944, for example, recruited most of the 75,000 braceros from the section of the state of Michoacán that had been devastated by volcanic eruptions.[3]

During the war, there were isolated examples of local opposition to braceros on the part of American workers, as when 300 AFL members in Huron, South Dakota, struck in December 1944 against the employment of braceros on farms.[4] For the most part, however, American unionists did not object to the program.

Most of the trouble the program encountered came from the Mexican side, on the old question of discrimination against Mexicans in the United States. During the war, the popular press fed the Mexican public a steady diet of horror stories about the maltreatment of Mexicans, Indians, and Negroes in the United States.[5] In an effort to alleviate the plight of Mexicans in the Southwest, the Mexican government tried to use the leverage of the bracero program to force the southwestern states to abandon discriminatory policies. On July 30, 1943, the Mexican government declared Texas out of bounds to contract laborers because of the racial discrimination that existed there.[6] Texas refused to reform and remained on the blacklist until after the war, with Texas farmers finding ways of evading the restriction,[7] but there were some minor repercussions. The cotton farmers in neighboring Arizona, fearful of the same thing happening to them, set up a special Mexican Labor Committee to try to alleviate discrimination.[8]

After World War II, the farming interests succeeded with relative ease in having the wartime bracero program extended, with an annual average of 100,000 men imported from Mexico, mainly to work in agriculture.[9] The wartime legislation was renewed in 1947 and 1948, and in 1949 negotiations were entered with the Mexican government for the signing of an entirely new executive agreement that would extend the program for two years more.[10] During the negotiations, the Mexican government tried to have assurances against discrimination written into the agreement.[11] The CIO supported them on this and recommended a series of measures to ensure the braceros equal treatment and redress of grievances, including the full participation of labor unions in all negotiations concerning them.[12] But when the Mexicans tried to negotiate the renewal of their right to withdraw braceros from any area declared discriminatory, the U.S. government successfully held out for local farmers' associations merely to sign a pledge not to discriminate when they signed their contracts.[13]

For the most part, until 1950, the pressure on the program from within the United States came, not from the labor unions and people who thought that it was being administered without due regard for the rights of the Mexicans, but from farm interests who thought the opposite and sought the extension of the program and an expansion in the number of braceros. When a subcommittee of the House Agricultural Committee, very sympathetic to the program, held hearings on it in the South and Southwest in 1950, the main complaint was that the U.S. Employment Service, which administered the program, was dominated by labor unionists, "CIO types," who wanted to turn the United States into a "welfare state" and adopt "Russian" agricultural methods.[14]

Along with the bracero program, the postwar agricultural boom in the Southwest had also brought a renewal of legal and illegal immigration from Mexico. The illegal immigration rapidly became the most spectacular phenomenon of all. Dubbed "wetbacks," because of their propensity to take the easiest and coolest route across the border, wading the Rio Grande, illegal Mexican immigrants swarmed across the border to earn the relatively high wages being paid farm laborers. There is no way of estimating how many people did this or how many of them stayed. Often they were recruited by agents of the large farmers, whose protection they enjoyed, and were not apprehended by local law-enforcement agencies. But in 1952, the first time a concerted attempt was made by federal agencies to round them up, over 600,000 Mexicans were deported.[15]

The dangers inherent in both the bracero program and the wave of "wetbacks" were first made apparent in the spring of 1950, when a drop in farm prices coincided with and helped create an oversupply of farm labor in the Southwest. "Thousands of workers were unemployed; families were stranded in hundreds of labor camps; eight or nine infant deaths were reported in California; relief officials were up in arms over the burden that had suddenly been saddled on rural counties." [16] Governor Earl Warren of California and President Harry Truman appointed the usual commissions to investigate. Before anything was done, however, the Korean War boom brought a lifting of controls on cotton acreage, and the San Joaquin Valley went "cotton crazy." The "relief crisis" suddenly turned into another "manpower shortage," and the demands for more braceros were on again. [17]

This time, the labor unions and many liberals in the United States tried to make a fight of it. It was obvious that there was not nearly enough support in Congress to make a frontal attack on the bracero program worthwhile. Anyway, the AFL and CIO had never opposed that program per se. The main attack centered on the wetbacks, and a campaign was mounted to have the U.S. government impose penalties on those found guilty of smuggling and harboring them. [18] President Truman was enlisted on the side of the campaign, but the administration and the labor unions were unsuccessful in having the penalties included in the legislation for the renewal of the bracero program passed by Congress in July 1951. Rather than veto the legislation, Truman signed it reluctantly, admitting that it hardly touched the basic problem, the wetbacks, and called on Congress to pass supplemental legislation providing criminal penalties for those in the wetback trade. [19]

Faced with this setback in Congress, and responding to increasing pressure not only from the traditional sources of Southwest labor union opposition to Mexican immigration but also from the aspiring AFL National Agricultural Workers Union, [20] William Green, still president of the AFL, fell back on the tactic he had employed unsuccessfully in the 1920s. He decided to call on the Mexican unions for aid. [21] Again, there was only one union with influence enough in the government to be of any real aid. This time it was not CROM, but the CTM, which had quit ORIT in a huff just seven months before. Undaunted, Green called for a meeting of the AFL and CTM to explore the possibility "that Mexican workers, admitted under the U.S.-Mexican agreement, would cross the border under the protection of the AFL and the Mexican Federation of Labor." [22] Meanwhile, the CIO was also in touch with the CTM on the bracero question, but mainly to obtain information about the CTM's stand on the question. The CTM's position was essentially the same as that of the Mexican government—that the program was fine as long as the braceros were well treated and not discriminated against.[23] Later in the year, the CTM asked the help of the CIO in ensuring fair treatment for the braceros.[24]

By the time discussions between the CTM and AFL were initiated in 1952, the campaign against the wetbacks had been successful in obtaining passage of more stringent "anti-wetback" legislation, and the AFL–CTM contacts revolved increasingly around the negotiations over ORIT. In late 1952, with the CTM's reentry into ORIT in sight, the AFL convention passed a resolution calling for discussions with the CTM to work out a joint program to deal with the problems caused by illegal Mexican immigration into the United States.[25]

In 1953, after the CTM joined ORIT, talks were initiated among the AFL, CIO, and CTM to see what the three of them could do about the bracero and wetback problems. Again, as in the 1920s, in the reports to their memberships, there was a discrepancy in the ways in which the Mexicans and the Americans described the nature of the problems dealt with. The Mexicans spoke of finding the best ways to protect the braceros against exploitation and discrimination,[26] whereas the AFL described the problem as that of illegal immigration.[27] It was decided that the formal negotiations should take place under the auspices of ORIT,[28] presumably to mitigate the charge that ORIT had no function except to propagate American foreign policy.

When the delegates to the meeting met and dispersed in Mexico City in December 1953, the resolutions they left behind them had a familiar ring. They agreed that the exchange of information and observers between counterpart unions on each side of the border should be encouraged; that unions in the two countries active in the same industry develop a method for the interchange of union cards, with full rights and privileges being granted immediately to the foreigner; and that another committee be set up, a Joint U.S.–Mexican Trade Union Committee, to facilitate cooperation between the labor movements of the two countries.[29]

The recommendations of the meeting were as much of a dream as they had always been, and for the same general reasons. In the 1950s the national labor confederations could not control the membership policies of their own national unions anymore than they could in the 1920s, and the unions who were members of the national confederations had equal difficulty with their own locals. In the end, the question of membership admission was so important and delicate at the local level that the only weapon a larger organization could wield over one of its smaller constituents to force it to comply was the threat of expulsion or a form of receivership. When the issue was racial discrimination, rather than power, union leaders were extremely reluctant to use these powers. Also, although the bulk of the problem lay in getting American unionists to accept Mexican union cards, in a few cases, the sword was now cutting both ways. In the same way as it was inconceivable for Dallas carpenters to gaily accept, in the spirit of brotherhood, the hundreds of Mexicans who would show up with Mexican carpenters' union cards, so would it be impossible to conceive of the Mexico City musicians union accepting, with alacrity, every itinerant American who showed up with an instrument and a card from the American Federation of

Musicians. In neither case could the national labor confederation do much to force the locals to commit suicide.

As is often the case, the agreement was more noteworthy for what was not agreed to than for what was agreed to. There was no mention of either the bracero or wetback questions. However, it seemed to be understood that the new committee would continue to explore the possibilities.

Clearly, there were few possibilities as creative as those of the 1920s. The Mexican government was committed to the bracero program, and the CTM was committed to the Mexican government. There could be little hope of obtaining CTM cooperation in having the program terminated. In the meetings that followed, all that could be agreed upon was that the labor movements of the two countries would work on their respective governments to ensure that the braceros received fair treatment.[30] As for illegal immigration, the American unionists simply continued to support more stringent punishment for those who trafficked in and employed illegal migratory workers [31] and succeeded in getting CTM backing for their efforts in the U.S. Congress,[32] for whatever that was worth.

Although the Mexicans made a clear distinction between the braceros and the wetbacks, the Americans often tended to link the two together. The AFL Executive Council stated in 1954 that the two were part of the same problem. This was shown, it said,

by the fact that thousands of contracted aliens have either "skipped" their contract or have continued to live in the United States after the expiration of their contracts. In either case they have automatically become "wetbacks" who work and live at the mercy of easy-money employers and unscrupulous labor contractors.

It has been amply shown that the Mexican contract National has an adverse effect on the employment security and work standards of American citizens who work as wage earners in agriculture. . . . It has also been established beyond doubt that Mexican

Nationals are used to depress wage rates and to prevent the organization of domestic workers into trade unions.[33]

The CIO was less prone to make the same connection, and when the two confederations merged in 1955, the new AFL-CIO refrained from demanding the abolition of the bracero program. It called for legislation to regulate labor contractors, to provide better housing and sanitary conditions for braceros, to end discrimination against American farm workers, and to guard against wetbacks. When the importation of foreign labor did prove necessary, said the AFL-CIO, it favored the use of international agreements, such as that which existed with Mexico.[34]

The Joint U.S.-Mexican Trade Union Committee continued to meet fairly regularly in the ensuing years, often discussing the bracero and wetback questions. Recommendations were made, some of which would have proved very useful in aiding both the braceros and the American farm workers. Most revolutionary, perhaps, was one calling for the organization of braceros into Mexican unions at the time they sought employment in the United States, with arrangements being made for the acceptance of their Mexican union cards for admission into American farm-workers' unions.[35] However, like most of the calls for cooperation along these lines, this proved to be a pipe dream. Although the CTM had always grudgingly claimed that it had the right to organize farm-workers' unions, this was clearly not its province in the tripartite Mexican political system. The farm workers were the bailiwick of the Confederación Nacional de Campesinos, which represented the peasants in the government political party and functioned more as a pressure group than as a labor union for farm workers. The CNC was rarely represented in the U.S.-Mexican Trade Union Committee. In a sense, because the braceros, for the most part, were Mexican peasants (often small landholders), the Americans were never really talking to the people who could organize them in Mexico.

The bracero program, combined with stricter enforcement of the immigration laws, practically eliminated the wetback problem in the later 1950s. However, it did so by assuming massive proportions. The measure that authorized the new wave, Public Law 78, had been passed during the Korean War, supposedly to meet the temporary labor shortage caused by the emergency, yet the number of Mexicans admitted under the program continued to rise precipitously long after the conclusion of the war, from approximately 200,000 in 1952 to over 500,000 in 1959.[36] The California AFL-CIO and the National Agricultural Workers Union had strenuously opposed the program, claiming that the braceros were driving native-born farm workers out of work,[37] but it wasn't until 1960 that the national AFL-CIO was moved to mobilize substantial resources to help solve the problem. The attempts of the NAWU to organize migrant workers had fallen flat. In early 1960 it had only 4,500 members.[38]

The AFL-CIO Executive Council stepped in and set up a broader Agricultural Workers Organizing Committee. It was endowed with $300,000 as a start and promised further "substantial" assistance from the federation. California was selected as the first target.[39] However, the Executive Council still found it difficult to come out openly and decisively for the abolition of the whole bracero program, at least in part because of its desire to avoid a split with the CTM over the issue.

In May 1960, shortly before the new organizing drive was launched, the Joint U.S.-Mexican Trade Union Committee met and discussed the question. The CTM, committed to supporting the Mexican government, could not be persuaded to support the abandonment of the bracero program. They would just join with the AFL-CIO in acknowledging "that excessive numbers of 'braceros' result in the displacement of domestic workers and depress wages of 'braceros' and domestic workers alike." [40] The Joint Committee also called for improved procedures for certifying the need for foreign workers in the United States and demanded for braceros a minimum hourly wage of one dollar along with greater health and insurance benefits and improved living standards.[41] It did not demand the abolition of the program.

The Agricultural Workers Organizing Committee drive soon faltered and fell apart, but the California AFL-CIO still maintained its opposition to braceros. By 1963, when Public Law 78 came up for renewal, the national AFL-CIO had swung over and was coming out openly for the ending of the program. The AFL-CIO called on the Kennedy administration, in which it had considerable influence, to oppose renewal of the law. The administration, caught between the demands of the AFL-CIO and church and charitable groups for ending the program and the pressure of the growers for a two-year extension of the program, tried to compromise by asking for a one-year extension.[42]

Characteristically, the administration had overestimated the strength of the "conservative" opposition. Over the years, the braceros had been increasingly concentrated in two states, Texas and California, and the base of die-hard support for the program had correspondingly narrowed. Also, increasing unemployment had made many urban congressmen more reluctant than usual to support their rural colleagues on this issue.[43] When the measure was brought to the floor of the House, it was defeated, 174 to 158.[44] The Senate passed a one-year extension of the act, with strings attached, assuring domestic migrant laborers the same benefits as braceros. The growers, however, regrouped their forces in the House and, pleading that it would take at least a year to adjust to the cutting off of the bracero supply, won House approval for a one-year extension, with no strings attached.[45] The Senate approved the House bill, but only after Senator Albert Ellender of Louisiana, chairman of the Senate Agricultural Committee, gave assurances that the act would be allowed to expire in December 1964.[46] Thus the bracero program died.

There is no indication that the AFL-CIO tried to enlist CTM support for the final assault on the bracero program, for the whole question was indeed embarrassing for the Mexicans. The Mexican governments of the 1950s and 1960s had become increasingly concerned, both at home and abroad, with projecting the image of Mexico as a dynamic, progressive, industrializing country with a rapidly rising standard of living. If Mexico was progressing so wonderfully, why was it so easy to annually recruit half a million young men to work for wages, which most Americans regarded as a pittance, at back-breaking stoop labor that most American migrant workers were even reluctant to do? However, the braceros sent most of their hard-earned dollars back to Mexico, approximately $30 million per year,[47] and these remittances, along with tourist dollars, were important factors in Mexico's ability to maintain a reasonable balance of trade. Naturally, the Mexican government was reluctant to see the program abandoned.

Generally, in trying to persuade Washington to continue the program, the Mexican government argued that the end of the program would bring about the resurgence of the wetback problem. When the expiration date of the program approached in December 1964, Foreign Minister Antonio Carrillo Flores again expressed his government's fears of a resurgence of the wetbacks and the consequent exploitation of them in the United States, but to no avail.[48]

With the end of the program, the most dire predictions of the growers were not borne out. Domestic labor combined with increased use of harvesting machinery to head off widespread famine. Also, Mexican agricultural workers continued to cross the borders on a temporary basis under various guises, although in nothing approaching the numbers of the bracero program. However, if the growers agreed with the AFL-CIO in assuming that the elimination of the braceros would help drives to unionize domestic agricultural workers, there are signs that some of their worst fears might be realized. The first successes of César Chavez's organizing efforts among the grape pickers of California would indicate that perhaps migrant workers are not as "unorganizable" as they have generally been assumed to be. Most striking is that Chavez was able to organize the group traditionally most resistant to union organization—workers of Mexican origin. Here, perhaps, is an important side effect of Mexican labor history on the United States. In the 1920s, one of the most common charges against Mexican immigrants was that they were ignorant of the value of unions. By the 1960s, after fifty years of noisy unionism, this no longer held true. It was almost impossible for anyone from Mexico to be totally unaware of unionism. Chavez and his followers showed themselves to be capable of exploiting this. The red-and-black flag of their union is the traditional flag of Mexican unionism. Their symbol, the stylized eagle, is the symbol of the CTM.

NOTES

1. Carey McWilliams, "They Saved the Crops," *The Inter-American* 2, no. 8 (Aug. 1943): 11.

2. U.S., Congress, House, Committee on Agriculture, *Hearings* on H.R. 5557, 81st Cong., 2d sess., 1950, p. 23.

3. *The Inter-American* 2, no. 12 (December 1943): 7.

4. Carey McWilliams, *North from Mexico* (Philadelphia: J. B. Lippincott, 1949), p. 270. McWilliams does not elaborate on what the Mexicans (or anyone, for that matter) were doing in South Dakota in December.

5. A favorite theme was frequently that of the U.S. claiming to be fighting a war against racism while practicing it at home. Hensley C. Woodbridge, "Mexico and U.S. Racism," *Commonweal* 42 (June 22, 1945): 234–236.

6. *The Inter-American* 2, no. 12, p. 7.

7. McWilliams, *North from Mexico*, p. 275.

8. U.S., Congress, House, Committee on Agriculture, *Farm Labor Investigations, Hearings* before the Subcommittee on Farm Labor, 81st Cong., 2d sess., 1950, p. 61.

9. AFL, *Proceedings*, 1952, p. 28.

10. House, Committee on Agriculture, *Hearings on* H.R. 5557, p. 3.
11. Ibid., p. 11.
12. *CIO News* (Mar. 7, 1949).
13. House, Committee on Agriculture, *Hearings on* H.R. 5557, p. 11.
14. House, Committee on Agriculture, *Farm Labor Investigations,* passim.
15. AFL, *Proceedings,* 1953, p. 153.
16. "Wetbacks, Cotton, and Korea," *The Nation* 172, no. 18 (May 5, 1951): 408.
17. Ibid.
18. AFL, *Proceedings,* 1952, p. 28.
19. *New Republic* (Sept. 24, 1951): 7.
20. AFL, *Proceedings,* 1952, p. 28.
21. *New Republic* (Sept. 24, 1951): 7.
22. Ibid.
23. CTM, *Informe al XLII Consejo Nacional,* 1951, p. 47.
24. Ibid., pp. 44–45.
25. AFL, *Proceedings,* 1953, p. 416.
26. CTM, *Informe al XLVI Consejo Nacional,* 1953, p. 9.
27. AFL, *Proceedings,* 1953, p. 416. The CIO, whose reports to its membership were much less voluminous and detailed than those of the AFL, did not report on the negotiations of that year in its annual report.
28. CTM, *Informe al XLVI Consejo Nacional,* 1953, p. 9.
29. AFL, *Proceedings,* 1954, pp. 245–246.
30. CTM, *Informe al LI Consejo Nacional,* 1954, p. 66; CTM, *Informe al LIV Consejo Nacional,* 1955, p. 57.
31. AFL, *Proceedings,* 1954, p. 112.
32. CTM, *Informe al LIV Consejo Nacional,* 1955, p. 57.
33. AFL, *Proceedings,* 1954, p. 113.
34. AFL-CIO, *Proceedings,* 1955, p. 37.
35. Ibid., 1957, pp. 178–179.
36. Ted Le Berton, "At the Prevailing Rate," *Commonweal* 67, no. 5 (Nov. 1, 1957): 122; Anthony Soto, "The *Bracero* Story," *Commonweal* 71, no. 9 (Nov. 27, 1959).
37. Le Berton, "At the Prevailing Rate."
38. "AFL-CIO Organizers Go After Farm Labor," *Business Week* (Sept. 24, 1960).
39. Ibid.
40. AFL-CIO, *Proceedings,* 1961, p. 118.
41. Ibid.
42. *New York Times,* March 30, 1967.
43. "The Fate of P.L. 78," *Commonweal* 78, no. 12 (June 14, 1963): 316.
44. *New York Times,* May 30, 1963.
45. Ibid., Aug. 15, 1963; "Another Extension," *Commonweal* 79, no. 8 (Nov. 15, 1963): 213.
46. *New York Times,* Dec. 5, 1963.
47. Ibid., Dec. 6, 1964.
48. Ibid.

14

The New
Internationalism

AFTER THE "FALL" of China and the outbreak of the Korean
War, the AFL's anticommunist world crusade moved into full
gear. With people like Joseph McCarthy rising to the fore as
staunch guardians against the worldwide Communist conspiracy, the AFL could now claim that it was one of the first to
become aware of and combat the danger. In 1952 the AFL
Executive Council proudly proclaimed:

> The AFL never had illusions in regard to the real nature and role
> of the Communist movement in China. To us, Mao Tse-Tung and
> his Moscow-trained and controlled political bosses never were
> anything but "inspired" or hired betrayers of the Chinese people.
> We have been unrelenting in our opposition to our government
> granting to this totalitarian regime of Communist quislings any
> form of de jure or de facto recognition. We are likewise opposed
> to even the slightest economic aid to the Peiping puppets. We
> unreservedly reject all proposals to support maneuvers for bringing
> Mao Tse-Tung into the U.N. or any of its agencies—through a
> back door or front entrance. . . . Communist China is a vast

prison house, with millions of slave laborers. Mao Tse-Tung and his associates are the catspaws of Russian imperial expansion in Asia. They are at the head of a regime guilty of savagery and bestiality unequalled even by their master in the Kremlin or by Stalin's partner of 1939–1941 (Hitler).[1]

This imparts some of the flavor of the thinking that dominated the international relations of the AFL until the merger with the CIO in 1955, and that continued to dominate the International Affairs department of the AFL-CIO into the late 1960s. The rhetoric and the manner of thinking are those of George Meany, his mentor on foreign policy Jay Lovestone, and their associates. Lovestone had been associated with Homer Martin, the head of the short-lived United Auto Workers–AFL, the rival of Walter and Victor Reuther's UAW-CIO in the late 1930s and early 1940s. For the Reuthers, Lovestone was a bit too much to accept as head of the International Relations department when the two federations first merged, and he was forced into the background, temporarily. But he continued to dominate AFL-CIO foreign policy because his outlook coincided almost exactly with that of the new president of the AFL-CIO, George Meany, and David Dubinsky, and he soon reemerged as official head of the International Affairs Department.

To the AFL's anticommunists, the world continued to be essentially a simple one, divided into the forces of good and evil, right and wrong. To murmured comments that perhaps their anticommunism was a bit excessive, they replied:

Just as we could not be too much anti-Nazi or too much anti-Fascist in 1939, so we cannot be too much anti-Communist totalitarian in 1952. To say that one could never be too much anti-Nazi and yet could be too much anti-Communist is to draw a false distinction between the two brands of totalitarian despotism and to give preference to the Communist form against the Nazi specie of anti-human tyrannical dictatorship. By drawing such false distinctions, one wittingly or unwittingly plays into the hands of Communism which has replaced Fascism as the main danger to democracy, world peace, and social progress. The American Federation of Labor warns against making such a false mistake. We stress that totalitarian Communism is synonymous with slave labor, ruthless dictatorship, human degradation, total intellectual enslavement, destructive social conflict, military imperialist aggression, genocide, and world war. To conduct a militant struggle against these reprehensible evils is not to engage in "mere negative" activities but to engage in the most positive constructive activities deserving of utmost support by free labor.[2]

In this grand and glorious battle to the death between two systems, there was to be no place in between. "Neutralism" was "a conscious or unwitting ally of Soviet imperialism." [3] Thus the job of the AFL-CIO was that of building up the "free labor movement" of the world—"free labor" being synonymous, not just with "noncommunist" but with "anticommunist." Although queasy about some of the methods employed by Lovestone and Meany, and some of their rhetoric, the Reuthers could not dissent from the policy, for they shared the same general assumptions about what was happening and what had to be done. Addressing the founding convention of the AFL-CIO, Walter Reuther announced to the "free workers of the world":

We will work with you, we will work together with free labor in the world in building the free labor movement in every country in the world, because the free labor movement of the world is the strongest anti-Communist force in the world.[4]

In Latin America, the chief instrument of this policy in the 1950s was ORIT. Until the success of the Castro revolution in late 1958, much of the anticommunist rhetoric seemed rather irrelevant in Latin America, both to Latin American unionists, who failed to perceive any real threat from Soviet "imperialism" in their homelands, and to Americans, who regarded Latin America as a secure American-held bastion in the cold war. To many Latin American unionists and intellectuals, the real threats to trade unionism and liberty came from the right, and not from the usually insignificant Communist parties of their countries. All too frequently, the U.S. government seemed to be the main prop behind these oppressive regimes. Thus, Serafino Romualdi and those who ran ORIT developed a peculiar rhetoric—reminiscent of the days of the Stalin-Hitler pact—which charged that, somehow or other, the right was in league with the left in opposing U.S. policy. Juan Perón was labeled a fascist, but one whose anti-American propaganda was supported by the Communists. Peronist propaganda, said Romualdi, was aimed at

> sabotaging the re-armament efforts of the democratic community, attempts to create dissension among the member-nations of the American family, advocates the so-called "third neutral position," slanders the heroic United Nations soldiers who are fighting and dying in Korea, and practically condones every aggressive move of Soviet imperialism. This is done by emphasizing that the only real danger for Latin America lies in the policies of "North American imperialism," whatever that means. . . .[5]

This attempt to link the right and the left, and make the left threat seem relevant in Latin America, reached one of its more absurd heights in 1958. A spokesman of the U.S. Chamber of Commerce had declared that American union leaders were at fault for the lack of democracy in union life in the United States, and that the same could be said for the rest of the hemisphere. ORIT accused him of taking part in a double offensive, "tacitly or expressly combined," of the "communist or crypto-Soviet" groups and "reactionary and authentically anti-democratic groups" against the trade union movement.[6]

With Fidel Castro's overthrow of the Batista dictatorship in Cuba, ORIT was given a more tangible enemy. It was clear from the start that the leaders of the Confederación de Traba-jadores Cubana (CTC), many of whom had collaborated actively with the Batista regime, would be replaced by pro-Castro men. The old leaders were also solid supporters of ORIT, and it was obvious that the days of the "new" CTC in that organization were numbered. Thus, ORIT and the AFL-CIO joined the first riders on the anti–Castro bandwagon.

In early February 1959, the Executive Committee of ORIT held an emergency meeting in Mexico City, in which, in anticipation of the outcome of the new elections being held in the CTC, it laid the theoretical groundwork for labeling the CTC an unfree union. Its "basic principle," the Executive Committee said, was that the organizations it supported must have complete independence, and that "the authority of their leaders must be derived exclusively from the will of the members. In other words, the unions cannot be dominated by outside forces, be they of a governmental character, political parties, employers, or others." [7] If these criteria had been applied to the CTM, it would not have remained a member of ORIT for long. In late 1959, after pro-Castro men won control of the CTC, the CTC beat ORIT to the punch by denouncing it as a State Department stooge and withdrawing.[8]

Until the Castro revolution, the CTM's membership in ORIT and its close relations with the AFL-CIO caused it little trouble. Moreover, it derived some benefits, not least of which were frequent all-expense paid trips abroad for many of its leaders. Fidel Velásquez thought that the CTM had established a special relationship, based on "affinity of ideals and community of interests," with the AFL-CIO. This was shown, he said, by the many visits they had exchanged and the interchanges they had had on the various problems which confronted them.[9]

With regard to foreign policy, although the CTM was never quite as rabid as Meany, Lovestone, and Romualdi in pressing the world anticommunist crusade, its leaders had little trouble adjusting it and toning it down to suit Mexican palates. Soon after rejoining ORIT and the ICFTU, Velásquez and the CTM joined in the current ICFTU attack on the International Labor Organization for not being anticommunist enough. For the first time, Velásquez began to speak of the dangers that the "World of the Democracies" faced from the "World of the Dictatorships." [10] By the later 1950s the international news columns of the CTM's newspaper, *Ceteme,* appeared to consist mainly of handouts from the U.S. embassy.[11] However, this was tempered by a subtle shift in emphasis from the ORIT line. While Serafino Romualdi talked of the communists of Latin America as "our principal enemy," the CTM often emphasized the evils of the right-wing dictatorships that abounded in Latin America.

In its reports to its members, the CTM interpreted "free" and "democratic" unionism to mean antidictatorial unionism, and tended to play down pure anticommunism.[12] It also counteracted its growing passivity in foreign and domestic relations with occasional displays of rhetorical militancy. The front page of the May Day 1958 issue of *Ceteme* was festooned with portraits of the eight anarchists executed because of the Haymarket Square bombing of May 1, 1886, complete with the story of the strike, quotes from the anarchists, and a large headline that read: "AS LONG AS SOCIAL INJUSTICE CONTINUES TO EXIST, THERE WILL BE CLASS STRUGGLE." [13]

However, rhetorical militancy was not enough, and in 1958 and 1959 the Velásquez group faced a serious challenge to its control of the CTM from more militant left-wing groups in various unions. The militants were headed off by the timely intervention of the government of the new President, Adolfo López Mateos, which culminated in the arrest of several hundred people, including the communist leaders of the Railway Workers Union.[14] This close call led to a shift in the CTM position on Latin American affairs after 1958, and Velásquez and the CTM began to move closer to the ORIT line, linking the left-wing threat in Mexico with a more generalized communist threat in Latin America.[15] But they could not go too far, especially on the question of Cuba, because in the end they had to support the foreign policy of the López Mateos government.

Confronted with the rapid leftward shift of the Castro regime, and its burgeoning conflict with the United States, the López Mateos government was placed in a delicate situation. On the one hand, there was intense U.S. pressure to participate in ostracizing Cuba from the hemisphere. On the other hand, there was a strong segment of the official party, led by the still-influential ex-President Lázaro Cárdenas, which opposed the U.S. policy on Cuba and was generally pro-Castro. In addition, there were many people in the party and in the country who, although not enthusiastic about Castro, remembered that Mexico had faced U.S. intervention and pressure in the process of carrying out its revolution of 1910 and believed that the Cubans should be able to proceed with theirs without foreign intervention. For López Mateos to plump for either a pro-Castro or anti-Castro stance would have been disastrous in many senses, not the least of which was the threat that either would split the PRI wide open. Thus a posture based on the old principle of "nonintervention," which had been conveniently espoused by Mexico's favorite President, Benito Juárez, the Liberal Indian President of the 1850s and 1860s, proved to be the safest course to follow. The left was placated by Mexico's becoming the only Latin American country that retained diplomatic relations and a tenuous air link with Cuba. The right was placated by making it so inconvenient for foreigners and Mexicans taking the flight as to discourage its use as a real link to the mainland.

Mexican agents openly record the *vitae* and take individual photographs of those on the flights. Returning Mexicans are searched for "Communist propaganda," [16] and returning foreigners must leave the country within a short time. The U.S. government was partially placated by allowing American agents to obtain full information on anyone flying to Cuba, by not encouraging efforts to expand trade with Cuba, and by acting as if Juárez's principle of "nonintervention" was something peculiar to Mexico. There is little record of the Mexican delegations at the various OAS conferences having worked energetically to persuade other Latin American countries to follow its lead in opposing the ostracism of Cuba.

It was this policy of passive, and somewhat smug, nonparticipation in the movement to boycott Cuba that the CTM had to follow. Thus, while it gave a home to ORIT in its headquarters building, and helped disseminate ORIT's anti-Castro propaganda, the CTM could not participate in any overt acts that would conflict with the policy of the Mexican government. In 1965, when the Venezuelan delegates to the Sixth Continental Congress of ORIT proposed a boycott of the ships of countries that were trading with Cuba, Fidel Velásquez opposed the move, saying that the CTM would not participate in actions that "infringe on the sovereignty and self-determination of peoples." [17] As the original proponent of the boycott, the AFL-CIO supported it.[18]

In the 1960s the CTM made it clear that its role in foreign affairs was simply to support the policies decided upon by the Mexican government. In domestic policy, Velásquez would describe the relationship of the CTM to the government as reciprocal, each helping the other and thereby strengthening the Revolution.[19] In foreign policy, however, he asked no such reciprocity. In a speech in 1962, when the López Mateos government was walking the tightrope on Cuba and seeking to improve its relations with the "Third World," he reiterated a favorite theme:

> The responsibility for external affairs is solely in the hands of the Government, and the people must maintain themselves united behind it, confident of the capacity of its chief to overcome all the dangers and in his loyalty and patriotism in defending the interests of the nation. . . . We Mexicans will gain nothing by dividing ourselves on international questions. Although they interest us and demand an opinion on our part, the best road is not to make [foreign policy] in isolation, but to give that power to the person who, by virtue of law and reason, has it.[20]

The relationship between the foreign policy of the AFL-CIO and that of the U.S. government was not so clear and explicit. Before their merger, both the AFL and the CIO had tended to demand a role in the shaping and execution of foreign policy at the same time as they affirmed their independence of the government. On the surface, this would appear to involve a grave contradiction. How can organizations which, in the words of George Meany, must "display initiative in helping our government to mold and carry out a sound, peaceful and democratic foreign policy," also claim independence from the policies they have helped to mold? The way out of the dilemma lay in Samuel Gompers's old dictum: It was precisely because the labor movement was independent of the government and represented the "common man" that it could be a very effective force in carrying out the government's foreign policy. Thus, Meany reasoned, "In all these international activities, labor cannot make its full contribution, either at home or abroad— unless it plays a completely independent and distinct role from the government." [21]

The CIO was echoing similar sentiments at that time, and raising with great vigor Samuel Gompers's old demand for labor participation in the shaping and execution of foreign policy. Jacob Potofsky, chairman of the CIO's International Relations Committee, said that progress in the fight against communism abroad would be much greater if the State Department would heed labor's voice when it made policy decisions. State Department planners, he said, "haven't the feel of what hurts the man on the street abroad." Foreign policy planning, he complained, was dominated by "bankers and Wall Street fellows" who could not anticipate the reactions of the "plain people" abroad.[22] Later, he was more explicit.

> The United States deals with very many countries that have either labor governments or influential labor movements. We must go beyond conventional diplomacy if we are to understand and evaluate the factors which have given rise to these forces of world labor.
>
> Labor participation in foreign policy means more than just calling occasionally upon American trade unionists for token advice. Men and women trained in the ranks of labor must be appointed to important positions in planning, policy, and operations divisions of the State Department, as well as other agencies dealing with the conduct of our foreign affairs.[23]

When the AFL and CIO merged in 1955, President George Meany reasserted not only the right but the duty of labor unionists, as citizens, "to take part in shaping the policies of our government." The AFL-CIO, he said, had "a special interest in seeing to it that our government makes its full contribution to the preservation of human freedom everywhere on this earth where it is possible to make such a contribution."[24]

Obviously, neither the AFL nor the CIO leaders concerned with foreign policy agreed with every foreign-policy decision of the U.S. government, and they reserved and exercised the right to dissent from these decisions. In the words of Meany, "The international policies of American labor, or of any other free trade union movement, need not and must not necessarily coincide with those of the government at any particular moment." [25] However, never did the labor movements dissent from the main outlines of the foreign policies of the Truman, Eisenhower, Kennedy, and Johnson administrations, which were based on premises shared by the AFL and CIO—namely, that the United States was gravely threatened by a force called "communism," which threatened to overrun much of the world. Thus, the labor movement could, and often did, dissent on the tactics used to fight the menace, and often questioned the zeal and competence of those running the battle. Meany and Lovestone, however, never wavered in their conviction that the war being waged was of the utmost importance.

The complex relationships that developed between the AFL-CIO and the U.S. government, as they waged the same war, led to some curious circumstances, which caused some embarrassment to the AFL-CIO. In 1967 the AFL-CIO was rocked by the revelation that the international activities of certain member unions had been secretly funded by the Central Intelligence Agency, acting through "dummy" foundations. Allegations that the AFL-CIO was working with the CIA had been voiced before,[26] but this was the first time that unionists were forced to admit publicly that they had accepted CIA money. While leaders of the various unions acknowledged that they had received CIA money, George Meany stoutly denied that the AFL-CIO had been on the CIA payroll. His repeated denials often were met with a certain amount of incredulity, and the Reuther brothers tried to use the revelations to force Meany's resignation.[27] But technically, Meany may have been telling the truth. There was no proof that the AFL-CIO International Affairs Department itself ever directly received CIA money.

The striking thing about the uproar over the CIA subsidies was how it generally missed the point. The implication of much of the criticism of the AFL-CIO was that the union somehow was being secretly "bought" by the CIA, and that its foreign policy therefore was being directed by the CIA. This is not true. As was pointed out, the AFL opened a cold war of its own before either the term or the CIA had been invented. The foreign policy of the AFL-CIO was the product of the predilections of the leaders of the organization, supported by a largely passive membership. The AFL and CIO had been cooperating with the government in the execution of foreign policy since at least World War II. The economic aid of the U.S. government had been apparent all the way through, from the OIAA's aid in bringing Latin unionists on visits to the United States to the more elaborate program of Point Four in the 1950s, which brought Latin unionists to the United States for ORIT, as part of the U.S. technical-aid program.[28]

The helping hand of the U.S. embassy was all-too-obvious when ORIT was founded in Mexico in 1951, and the relationship between the two institutions has always been extremely close, to say the least.[29] This was never a secret, and Meany had never abjured this kind of "cooperation." In 1952, speaking of the AFL's independence in foreign affairs, he said:

> Though we consider this independent role as a *must,* we do not exclude cooperation with and help to our government and its agencies in furtherance of some specific policy or objective with which we are in agreement.[30]

Thus in 1961, when the AFL-CIO set up the American Institute for Free Labor Development, to give "leadership training" courses to Latin American unionists, it did so with the open aid of the U.S. government. The institute was supposed to represent a joint venture of U.S. labor and corporations, and boasted J. Peter Grace, head of W. R. Grace & Co., as chairman of the board. However, the venture was soon blessed with U.S. government help. In May 1962, Chairman Grace and Vice-Chairman Meany proudly announced the receipt of a $250,000 grant from the Agency for International Development. They declared that the aim of the institute was not simply to train Latin American trade unionists, in the narrow sense, in such skills as collective-bargaining procedure and contract administration. In addition, the training would "embrace the broader concepts of the trade union as an essential element in a democratic society, and will include schooling in the defense of unions from infiltration by Communists, Fascists, or crooks." [31] According to the institute, its 1963 budget was made up of approximately $300,000 from the AFL-CIO, $300,000 from business and $500,000 from the U.S. government.[32]

The U.S. government was not the only government contributor to the AIFLD. At the behest of the CTM (and presumably, the Mexican federal government), the governor of the state of Morelos donated the tract of land on the outskirts of Cuernavaca where the AIFLD constructed its Holiday Inn-like training facility and the Mexican government granted it tax exemption.[33]

Along with training unionists, the AIFLD was also active in obtaining Alliance for Progress backing for loans to trade-union housing projects in Mexico, Peru, and El Salvador. In Mexico, this involved having AID guarantee a $9.569 million loan to the Graphic Arts Workers Union from AFL-CIO welfare funds to underwrite the John F. Kennedy housing project in Mexico City.[34] In announcing the project, William C. Doherty, head of the AIFLD's Social Projects Department, proudly added that "workers in several unions had deposed Communist leadership after the institute had advised them that no assistance would be forthcoming as long as they were led by non-democratic elements." [35]

Given its long history of accepting open government aid in its dealings with Latin America, the AFL-CIO with relative equanimity could face the charges of accepting covert aid. The uproar aroused by the revelations in the United States revolved around a relatively fine distinction between overt and covert government aid. Although the distinction can be important, in this instance it is not, for no one would be foolish enough to charge that it was secret government aid that turned Meany and Lovestone into anti-Communists, and one would have to be naïve to think that the AFL-CIO was totally immune from government contacts and government support.

Whatever the merits of the moral and practical arguments for and against unions accepting covert (or overt) government aid, one thing is clear: in Mexico, the controversy caused little stir. In the first place, there was little publicity given to the charges in the government-dominated press. Second, and more important, most Mexicans involved in union affairs do not perceive any great moral distinction between receiving overt and covert aid. In Mexico, favored unions had always expected and received both kinds of aid, and it would have been hypocritical and self-destructive for the CTM, for instance, to pretend that it was shocked by the charges. The CTM pursued the most logical course for it: it ignored the charges. When asked for their opinion on the matter, CTM officials usually claim ignorance of the complexities of the U.S. political system. For the CTM, the revelations were nothing more than an embarrassing little incident. They did not change the leadership's attitude towards the AFL-CIO. It was obvious that the AFL-CIO was receiving overt government aid, and it was assumed therefore that it was also receiving covert aid.

In a sense, the postwar foreign policy of the labor movement in the United States represented a return to the old nineteenth century tradition of labor internationalism. The difference is that the international labor movements of the nineteenth century thought of their interests as being firmly tied to the interests of international socialism or anarchism. Those who directed AFL-CIO foreign policy thought of their interests as being tied to those of international capitalism. In the same way as nineteenth century socialists and anarchists saw direct links between the success or failure of left-wing movements abroad and their own success or failure, so did the leaders of the AFL-

CIO draw a direct connection between the interests of American trade unionism and of American capitalism throughout the world. This connection was frequently garbled, as it was lumped in with the other, more traditional references to how low wages abroad are a threat to American workers, but it was usually there, in one form or another. Speaking to the 1961 AFL-CIO convention, Meany managed to lump them all together.

> You can't be a trade unionist unless you are an internationalist. You can't be a real trade unionist unless you think of workers wherever they happen to be, and unless you realize that substandard conditions and poverty anywhere in the world is a threat to good conditions and comparatively good standards anywhere else in the world, just as the loss of freedom any place in the world is a threat of some kind to the freedom of those who have freedom everywhere else in the world.
>
> This is the reason we have always tried to participate in international trade union work, to work with trade unions in other countries, not because we want to influence the other countries, not because we expect to get any members in these other countries, but because we realize that if we can develop free trade unions in the newly merging [sic] countries that we are erecting a bulwark of democracy in every such country where that happens, because the Commies can't take over where there is a strong trade union movement. And where there is not a strong trade union movement, they can and do take over. So our attitude isn't all altruistic.[36]

Gone were those old relics of socialist internationalism, the Iglesias-style pleas of the necessity for international labor organization to combat international business organization. Now the pleas were to business to join in combating the common enemy. Speaking to the Chicago Executives Club in 1963, Meany recognized some of the changes that had taken place.

We have come a long way from the days of the banana republics, when American companies . . . made their deals with local tyrants, without regard to the welfare of the population. Mr. Grace and others like him are well aware that the choice today is between democracy and Castroism; and that if democracy is to win, it must meet the needs and desires of the people, starting with a high standard of living. . . . While unions and management may quarrel over the terms of a contract, while the AFL-CIO and business spokesmen may be deeply divided on a wide range of domestic issues, from fiscal policy to federal housing, they should stand together in the great struggle of our times, the struggle that will determine the future and perhaps the survival of mankind.[37]

The road from international labor cooperation to combat international capitalism to business-labor cooperation to combat communism may have seemed, in some senses, a long one. But it was not really that long, and it was not really that different. It was implicit, all along, in Gompersian unionism. From the moment the AFL was founded, on the basis of working from within the capitalist system to meliorate some of the problems of workers within it, the assumption was always that it was only within this type of system that a union such as the AFL could function. The Bolshevik revolution and the creation of labor unions that did not have "free collective bargaining" in the American sense appeared to substantiate this. This rise of right-wing dictatorships with union movements similarly deprived of their collective bargaining function confirmed this. The experience of the twentieth century, in other words, would tend to confirm the AFL assumption that only within a system that resembles today's American capitalism could a labor movement such as the AFL-CIO today survive and retain its power and independence. It is understandable, then, that its leaders, sensing a threat to the system as a whole, should rush to defend it, allying themselves with anyone who seemed prepared to defend it, including the government and business.

NOTES

1. AFL, *Proceedings,* 1952, p. 120.
2. Ibid., p. 111.
3. Ibid., p. 112.
4. AFL-CIO, *Proceedings,* 1955, p. 7.
5. AFL, *Proceedings,* 1952, pp. 385–386.
6. *Ceteme* (Aug. 16, 1958).
7. Confederacion Internacional de Organizaciones Sindicales Libres, *Informe de Actividades,* 1957–1959, p. 59.
8. *New York Times,* Nov. 19, 1959.
9. CTM, *Informe al LIII Consejo Nacional,* 1955, p. 10.
10. CTM, *Informe al XLVII Consejo Nacional,* 1953, pp. 56–57.
11. For example, *Ceteme* (1958), passim.
12. For example, CTM, *Informe al LII Consejo Nacional,* 1955, p. 66.
13. *Ceteme* (May 1, 1958).
14. *New York Times,* Aug. 26, Sept. 3, 1958; Robert E. Scott, *Mexican Government in Transition,* rev. ed. (Urbana: University of Illinois Press, 1964), pp. 164–168. The leaders, including artist David Siquieros, were sentenced to indefinite terms under Mexico's interesting law against preaching or practicing "social dissolution," which can be interpreted to be almost anything. Siquieros was released along with some others in 1964, but, as of 1968, three others were still in jail. The release of prisoners held under the "social dissolution" law was a major demand of the leaders of the student strike of 1968.
15. CTM, *Informe al LXIII Consejo Nacional,* 1960, p. 11.
16. One returning student had *Das Kapital* confiscated in 1965.
17. CTM, *Informe al LXIX Consejo Nacional,* 1965, p. 22.
18. AFL-CIO, *Proceedings,* 1965, II, p. 106.
19. CTM, *Informe al LVIII Consejo Nacional,* 1958, p. 4.
20. CTM, *Informe al LXIII Congreso Nacional,* 1962, p. 19.
21. AFL, *Proceedings,* 1952, p. 118. At the AFL's 1952 convention, both presidential candidates praised the AFL's international fight against communism and recognized labor's unique role in foreign policy. General Eisenhower thanked the AFL for its help "over there in the workshops, on the docks, in the mines and in the union halls—in all the places where battle is hardest" (ibid., p. 364). Adlai Stevenson said, "To the workers of other nations, yours is perhaps the clearest voice America has. . . . Ambassadors in overalls can be the best salesmen of democracy" (ibid.).
22. *Wall Street Journal,* Nov. 2, 1951.
23. *CIO World Affairs Bulletin* 1, no. 5 (February 1952).
24. AFL-CIO, *Proceedings,* 1955, p. 26.
25. AFL, *Proceedings,* 1952, p. 118.
26. For example, "Labor and the Cold War," *The Nation* (Dec. 10, 1955); Sidney Lens, "Lovestone Diplomacy," *The Nation* (July 5, 1965); Dan

Kurzman, "Lovestone's Cold War—The AFL-CIO Has its Own CIA," *New Republic* (June 25, 1966).

27. Much to their embarrassment, it was soon revealed that Victor Reuther had accepted $50,000 from the CIA in the late 1950s, to be spent in Berlin.

28. CTM, *Informe al LVI Consejo Nacional,* February 1957, pp. 69–70.

29. For example, the U.S. Information Agency was enlisted to make a documentary film on the achievements of ORIT to be shown to workers throughout Latin America (*Ceteme,* May 24, 1958). The U.S. embassy in Mexico began printing a pro-ORIT anti-CTAL labor newspaper, *El Obrero,* in 1956, with a circulation of 25,000 aimed at workers' leaders in Mexico and Central America (*New York Times,* May 6, 1956).

30. AFL, *Proceedings,* 1952, p. 118.

31. *New York Times,* May 30, 1962.

32. Stanley Meisler, "Meddling in Latin America," *The Nation* 198, no. 7 (Feb. 10, 1964).

33. ICFTU-CIOSL, *Informe del Octavo Congreso Mundial,* Amsterdam, 11–15 de julio, 1965, p. 173.

34. *New York Times,* Sept. 17, 1963.

35. Ibid.

36. AFL-CIO, *Proceedings,* 1961, I, pp. 21–22.

37. Quoted in Meisler, "Meddling in Latin America."

15

Conclusion

THE PERIOD SINCE the 1930s saw great changes in the nature of the relationship between the U.S. and Mexican labor movements. The rise of fascism and communism as apparent threats to the nature of both American and Mexican society, and therefore as threats to the nature of unionism in each country, led to a blurring of the lines between foreign and domestic policy. What had previously been thought of as "foreign affairs" became translated into a fight for domestic survival. This attitude had been a consideration in the past, especially when AFL unionists had contemplated the possibility of a revolutionary union movement arising on their back doorstep, but in the late 1930s it became the dominant consideration.

In this context, the nature of Mexican-American labor relations changed as well. The dominant consideration in both countries now became relations with Latin America as a whole. What had been a unique relationship between the two labor movements now became one relationship among many. The easing of tensions between the United States and Mexico also played a great role in changing the nature of the relationship. As we have seen, one of the consistent reasons for the desire of the Mexicans to develop close relations with American labor was to ensure its support for Mexico in the recurring crises between the two countries. After 1940, when the Mexican Revolution took what appeared to be a permanent rightward course, and an "era of good feeling" was initiated between the United States and Mexico, the crises, and the threat of them, were virtually eliminated. But eliminated as well was one of the traditional reasons for the Mexicans to continue their close ties with the American labor movement. Thus, although both movements continued to retain an interest in foreign policy and both continued to serve their governments in this field, American interest rose as Mexican interest fell. Perhaps a key indicator of the change that had taken place was the immigration problem. In the 1920s the AFL subordinated all other major international considerations to the desire to obtain an agreement with CROM on this question. In the 1940s and 1950s the AFL and CIO tended to subordinate their desires for elimination of the bracero program to the need for enlisting CTM support on broader issues of international policy.

The decline of interest in pragmatic considerations would appear to indicate that if their cold war against the Soviet Union, China, Cuba, and other dangerous regimes ever ended, then the AFL-CIO's interest in ORIT and Latin America would decline precipitously. Certainly the AFL-CIO and ORIT would likely be deprived of much U.S. government support, both financial and otherwise, they have had for continuing their activities. In a sense not peculiar to the United States at present, the men who staff and participate in ORIT have an almost professional interest in prolonging the cold war and the mentality that it has bred.

If there was one key event that allowed the present situation to develop, it was the defeat of the left wing in both the CIO and the CTM in the postwar years. Given the rise of the cold war and the nature of the two organizations, it was inevitable that conflict would arise. Given the real versus the imagined

strength of the left in both movements, it was almost inevitable that they should be defeated. The defeat of the left-
wing unions, and their departure from the organizations, meant
that there was no longer any force within them strong enough
to exert a countervailing force against the anticommunist
excesses of those who remained in control.

The withdrawal of the CTM from the CTAL dealt the latter
a crushing blow, and with the demise of the CTAL, so withered
away the hopes, at least for the 1940s and 1950s, of developing
a hemispheric labor organization in the no-man's-land between
the battle lines of the cold war. The postwar CTAL by no
means was perfect in this respect. Indeed, the voice of the
CTAL quite often was indistinguishable from the voice of
Moscow. But the original premise behind its creation was
certainly a sound one: any hemispheric labor organization
that included the huge, wealthy, American labor organizations
was bound to be completely dominated by them. Lombardo
hoped that Latin American labor as a whole, organized into
a single confederation, would be able to develop enough
weight to deal with the American labor movement on an equal
basis.

If the postwar CTAL appeared to be following the line of
Moscow too often for the taste of the Americans, there was
good reason. First, Lombardo, along with most other Latin
American progressive intellectuals, believed that Latin America
faced a much greater threat from American imperialism than
from Soviet imperialism. It would be hard to deny that he had
just cause for concern. Second, the withdrawal of the CTM
forced the CTAL to look for another source of funds—in this
case, the WFTU—and the influence of Moscow-oriented Communists on the CTAL was thereby greatly increased. Lombardo's subsequent political path would indicate that, if the
CTAL had been assured of continued support from the CTM,
and if it had not had to face a massive onslaught from the
American labor movement, it might have evolved into an

organization that was independent of either side in the cold war. If he did not abandon his militant stance against American imperialism, neither did he become a tool of Moscow.

The history of ORIT, which appears to have borne out the predictions of its opponents, such as Luis Morones, that it would be nothing more than a puppet of the AFL and CIO, would seem to leave no grounds for assuming that it could have been otherwise. The combined strength of the Latin American labor movement is still not great enough to hold its own in a test of strength against the labor movement of the United States, especially when the latter is paying the bills.

Frequently, factors are as noteworthy by their absence as by their presence. Perhaps the most striking absentees in this story are the vast majority of union members on both sides of the border, who played virtually no active role in the proceedings. For the most part, international affairs were conducted by small groups of men acting on their own predilections. The general nature of their constituencies did play a role in setting the outer limits of the framework within which the leaderships could operate, but beyond this passive role—the role of just existing—there were few pressures upon the leaderships to act or not act in certain ways. There were exceptions to this, such as the cries of the Catholic opposition in the United States during the 1910s and 1920s, but the remarkable thing is how little, rather than how much, these affected AFL policy in Mexico.

One of the results of the remarkably free hand they were thereby given is the continual wavering of the leaders on both sides of the border on the question of what U.S.-Mexican labor relations existed for. In certain periods, as during the ascendancies of Gompers, Toledano, and Meany, broad considerations of international politics dominated relations. At other times, as during the 1920s, more pragmatic considerations came to the fore. However, it would be simplistic to say that the leaders simply were responding to the major considerations of the times, and that in times of international crisis broader considerations naturally came to the fore. People like Gompers, Toledano, and Meany tended to interpret every period as a time of international crisis. Even during the 1930s, when the Great Depression created an intense preoccupation with domestic affairs throughout the world, Lombardo expended much of his energy in Latin American and international affairs. Also, the people who determined labor foreign policy in both countries were usually affected by a mixture of motives—some narrow, some broad. Among them, one senses a general uncertainty, especially on the part of the Americans, about what international labor relations were supposed to accomplish. Perhaps this is best exemplified by the "internationalist" Gompers's uncertainty with regard to Mexico after World War I.

As was pointed out at the outset, this lack of a consistent and clear rationale for participating in international labor activities is natural to unions that reject the idea of international working-class revolution. Lombardo was able to work out an ideological framework that enabled him to fashion a "revolutionary" union in a bourgeois framework, but events showed that he had been deluding himself. His successors were under no such delusions. In the previous chapter, the peculiar obversion of the international ideal that the present leadership of the AFL-CIO has worked out was described. Perhaps, after the departure of the present leadership, this idea will not survive many more years of détente in the cold war. But it could, for by now it has become a deeply ingrained tradition, with a history stretching back at least into the 1930s. Whatever its attractions in the United States, it would appear to have little relevance to unionists in less industrialized countries.

There certainly exists a need for continuing contact between the labor organizations of the United States and Mexico to help solve some of the union problems that arise from having contiguous borders. But if the experience of the 1940s and

1950s is any guide, most of these problems are handled most efficiently at the local level, through the negotiations of state and local federations on both sides of the border. The powers that the national confederations are able and willing to exert over the locals are generally too limited to justify elaborate organizational contacts between Washington and Mexico City. On the broader scale, it would seem that the continuing internationalization of American corporations necessitates increased cooperation among unions in different countries working for the same company. However, the union that presently is most affected by this trend, the United Auto Workers, which since 1965 has taken steps toward organizing a truly international auto workers union, has found it most convenient to ignore the ICFTU and ORIT. Indeed, its withdrawal from the AFL-CIO, and therefore from the international organizations, in 1968 would indicate that it felt that nonmembership in them would not place great obstacles in the way of its ambitions.

If one looks back on the "bread-and-butter" benefits that have accrued to Mexican and American unionists because of their close relationships, one is forced to conclude that they could have been achieved as well if organizations such as the PAFL and ORIT had never seen the light of day. The justification for maintaining large, active, well-endowed international organizations of labor confederations must come from an ideology that sees a direct link between the interests of workers in all countries and can project common goals that hold promise for them all. The socialist and anarchist international organizations at least had the ideology. Samuel Gompers and his successors have spent their lives trying, unsuccessfully, to come up with attractive substitutes.

Bibliography

Manuscript Collections

American Alliance for Labor and Democracy. Copied Letters. AFL-CIO Archives, AFL-CIO Building, Washington, D.C.
Amalgamated Clothing Workers of America Papers. Amalgamated Clothing Workers of America Building, New York, N.Y.
Borah, William. Papers. Library of Congress.
Committee on Public Information. Files. National Archives.
Creel, George. Papers. Library of Congress.
Daniels, Josephus. Papers. Library of Congress.
Gompers, Samuel. Papers. AFL Collection, State Historical Society of Wisconsin, Madison, Wis.
———. Copied Letters. AFL-CIO Archives, AFL-CIO Building, Washington, D.C.
———. Copied Letters. Confidential and Official. AFL-CIO Archives, AFL-CIO Archives, AFL-CIO Building, Washington, D.C.
Green, William. Papers. AFL Collection, State Historical Society of Wisconsin, Madison, Wis.
———. Copied Letters. AFL-CIO Archives, AFL-CIO Building, Washington, D.C.
Office of Inter-American Affairs. Files. National Archives, Washington, D.C.
Taylor, Paul. Papers. Bancroft Library, University of California, Berkeley, Calif.

U.S. Department of State. Papers Relating to Mexico 1910–1929, Internal Affairs. National Archives.
———. Papers Relating to Mexico 1910–1929, Relations with the U.S. National Archives.

Interviews

Cobos, Bernardo. Personal interview, Mexico, D.F., August 15, 1967, with the author.
Lombardo Toledano, Lic. Vicente. Personal interviews, Mexico, D.F., March 25, April 2, 1965, with the author.
Petricioli, José Ortiz. Personal interviews, Mexico, D.F., March 9, 12, 1965, with the author.
Salazar, Rosendo. Personal interviews, Mexico, D.F., various dates, 1964 and 1965, with the author.

Public Documents

American Federation of Labor, *Proceedings of the Annual Conventions.* 1907–1955.
———. *Labor and the War.* Washington: American Federation of Labor, 1918.
American Federation of Labor-Congress of Industrial Organizations. *Proceedings of the Conventions.* 1955–1966.
Confederación Internacional de Organizaciones Sindicales Libres. *Informe de Actividades.* 1957–1959.
———. *Informe del Octavo Congreso Mundial.* Amsterdam, 1965.
Confederación Regional Obrera Mexicana. *Memorias de los trabajos llevados a cabo por el Comité Central.* 1934–1943.
Confederación de Trabajadores de América Latina. *C.T.A.L. 1938–1948. Resoluciones de sus asambleas.* Mexico, D.F.: CTAL, 1948.
Confederación de Trabajadores de Mexico. *CTM 1936–1941, Anales históricos.* Mexico, D.F.: CTM, 1941.
———. *CTM 1936–1937, Informe del Comité Nacional.* Mexico, D.F.: CTM, 1938.
———. *Informes a los Consejos Nacionales Ordinarios.* 1950–1967.

Congress of Industrial Organizations. *Proceedings of the Conventions.* 1938–1955.

México. Departamento de Trabajo. *Memoria del Departamento de Trabajo, 1935–1936.*

——. *Segunda Memoria del Departamento Autonomo del Trabajo (1933–1934.)*

México. Presidencia de la Republica. *50 Años de Revolución Mexicana en cifras.* Mexico, D.F.: Presidencia de la Republica, 1963.

Pan American Federation of Labor. *Proceedings of the Conventions.* 1919–1927.

U.S. Congress. House. Committee on Agriculture. *Farm Labor Investigations. Hearings* before the Subcommittee on Farm Labor, 81st Cong., 2d sess., 1950.

——. *Hearings* on H.R. 5557, 81st Cong., 1st sess., 1950.

——. *Hearings* on H.R. 3480, 83d Cong., 1st sess., 1953.

——. *Hearings* on H.R. 3822, 84th Cong., 2d sess., 1955.

U.S. Congress. Senate. Committee on Foreign Relations. *Revolutions in Mexico. Hearings* before a Subcommittee pursuant to S. R. 335, 62d Cong., 2d sess., 1913.

——. *Investigations of Mexican Affairs.* S. Doc. 285, 66th Cong., 2d sess., 1919–1920.

——. Committee on the Judiciary. *The Immigration and Naturalization Systems of the United States.* Report pursuant to S. Res. 137, 80th Cong., 1st sess., 1950.

Newspapers

El Popular (Mexico City)   *New York Times*
El Pueblo (Mexico City)   *New York Post*
El Universal (Mexico City)   *Wall Street Journal*
Excelsior (Mexico City)

Periodicals

AFL Weekly News Service
American Federationist
Ceteme

CIO News
CIO Reporter
CIO World Affairs Bulletin
Commonweal
CROM
Fresno (California) *Labor News*
Mexican Labor News
New Republic
Pan- American Labor Press
The Inter-American

Selected Secondary Works

"AFL-CIO Organizers Go After Farm Labor." *Business Week* (Sept. 24, 1960).

Alba, Victor. *Historia del Movimiento Obrero en América Latina.* México: Libreros Mexicanos Unidos, 1964.

Alexander, Robert J. *Communism in Latin America.* New Brunswick: Rutgers University Press, 1957.

————. *Organized Labor in Latin America.* New York: The Free Press, 1965.

————. "Union Movements in Latin America." *Labor and Nation* (Summer 1951): 37–40.

"Another Extension." *Commonweal* 79 (Nov. 1, 1963).

Ashby, Joe C. *Organized Labor and the Mexican Revolution under Lázaro Cárdenas.* Chapel Hill: University of North Carolina Press, 1967.

"Auto Labor Goes Multinational." *Business Week* (June 11, 1966).

"Ávila Camacho Steals the Show." *Time* 37 (Mar. 10, 1941): 33, 34.

Bernstein, Irving. *The Lean Years: A History of the American Worker, 1920–1933.* Boston: Houghton Mifflin, 1960.

Blaisdell, Lowell. *Desert Revolution.* Madison: University of Wisconsin Press, 1961.

Blanco Moheno, Roberto. *Crónica de la Revolución Mexicana.* Mexico: Editorial Diana, 1967.

Brissenden, Paul F. *The I.W.W.: A Study of American Syndicalism.* New York: Russel and Russel, 1920.

Capetillo, Alonso. *La Rebelión sin Cabeza*. Mexico: Imprenta Botas, 1925.

Clark, Marjorie R. *Organized Labor in Mexico*. Chapel Hill: University of North Carolina Press, 1934.

Cline, Howard F. *The United States and Mexico*. Rev. ed. New York: Atheneum, 1963.

Cumberland, Charles C. *Mexican Revolution: Genesis under Madero*. Austin: University of Texas Press, 1952.

Daniels, Josephus. *The Cabinet Diaries of Josephus Daniels*. Edited by E. David Cronon. Lincoln: University of Nebraska Press, 1963.

Fabela, Isidro, ed. *Documentos históricos de la Revolución Mexicana: Revolución y Régimen Constitucionalista*. 3 vols. Mexico: Fondo de Cultura Económica, 1960–1962.

Galenson, Walter. *The CIO Challenge to the AFL*. Cambridge: Harvard University Press, 1960.

Gompers, Samuel. *Seventy Years of Life and Labor*. 2 vols. New York: E. P. Dutton, 1925.

Gonzales Ramirez, Manuel. *La revolución social de México: Las ideas—la violencia*. Mexico: Fondo de Cultura Económica, 1960.

Kurzman, Dan. "Lovestone's Cold War—The AFL-CIO Has its Own CIA." *New Republic* (June 25, 1966).

"Labor and the Cold War." *The Nation* (Dec. 10, 1955).

LeBerthon, Ted. "At the Prevailing Rate." *Commonweal* 67 (Nov. 1, 1957).

Lens, Sidney. "Lovestone Diplomacy." *The Nation* (July 5, 1965).

Link, Arthur S. *Wilson*. 4 vols. Princeton: Princeton University Press, 1947–1964.

Lombardo Toledano, Vicente. *La Confederación de Trabajadores de América Latina*. México: Editorial Popular, 1964.

———. *Teoría y práctica del movimiento sindical Mexicano*. México: Editorial Magisterio, 1961.

Lorwin, Lewis L. *The American Federation of Labor*. Washington: The Brookings Institute, 1933.

———. *The International Labor Movement*. New York: Harper and Brothers, 1953.

Madison, Charles A. *American Labor Leaders.* New York: Harper and Brothers, 1950.

McWilliams, Carey. *North from Mexico.* Philadelphia and New York: J. B. Lippincott, 1949.

Meisler, Stanley. "Meddling in Latin America." *The Nation* (Feb. 10, 1964).

Millon, Robert P. *Vicente Lombardo Toledano: Biografía intelectual de un Marxista mexicano.* Translated by Jesús Lozoyo-Solis. Mexico: Libreria Madero, 1964.

Morales Jiménez, Alberto. *Hombres de la Revolución Mexicana.* México: Biblioteca del Instituto Nacional de Estudios Histórcos de la Revolucion Mexicana, 1960.

Morris, George. *CIA and American Labor.* New York: International Publishers, 1967.

Petricioli, Jose Ortiz. *Cincuentenario de la Casa del Obrero Mundial.* Mexico: Casa Ramirez Editores, 1962.

Poblete Troncoso, Moises. *El movimiento obrero latinoamericano.* Mexico: Fondo de Cultura Económica, 1946.

Rettinger, J. H. *Morones de México,* México: Biblioteca de Grupo Acción, 1927.

Romualdi, Serafino. "Free Labor's Struggle in Latin America." *New Leader* (April 16, 1956).

Rosal, Amaro del. *Los congresos obreros internacionales en el siglo XX: 1900–1950.* Mexico: Editorial Grijalvo, 1963.

Salazar, Rosendo. *La Casa del Obrero Mundial.* Mexico: Costa-Amic, 1962.

———, and Escobedo, José G. *Las pugnas de la gleba.* Mexico: Editoral Avante, 1923.

———. *Samuel Gompers, presencia de un líder.* Mexico: Artycom, 1957.

Scott, Robert E. *Mexican Government in Transition.* Rev. ed. Urbana: University of Illinois, 1964.

Silva, Jesús. *Breve história de la Revolución Mexicana.* 2 vols. México: Fondo de Cultura Ecónómica, 1960.

Snow, Sinclair. "The Pan-American Federation of Labor." Ph.D. dissertation, University of Virgina, 1960.

Soto, Anthony. "The Bracero Story." *Commonweal* 71 (Nov. 27, 1959)

Stimson, Grace H. *The Rise of the Labor Movement in Los Angeles.* Berkeley: University of California Press, 1955.

Taft, Philip. *The AFL in the Time of Gompers.* New York: Harper and Brothers, 1957.

——. *The AFL from the Death of Gompers to the Merger.* New York: Harper and Brothers, 1959.

Tannenbaum, Frank. "Samuel Gompers' Last Convention." *The Survey* (Jan. 1, 1925).

Taylor, Paul. *Mexican Labor in the United States.* 3 vols. Berkeley: University of California Press, 1928–1934.

Toth, Charles William. "The Pan-American Federation of Labor." Master's thesis, University of Illinois, 1947.

Trachtenberg, Alexander, ed. *American Labor Yearbook, 1916.* New York: The Rand School of Social Science, 1916.

——. *American Labor Yearbook, 1917–1918.* New York: The Rand School of Social Science, 1919.

"Wetbacks, Cotton and Korea." *The Nation* (May 5, 1951): 408.

Windmuller, John P. *American Labor and the International Labor Movement, 1940 to 1953.* Ithaca: The Institute of International Industrial and Labor Relations, 1954.

Wolman, Leo. *Ebb and Flow in Trade Unionism.* New York: National Bureau of Economic Research, 1936.

Woodbridge, Hensley C. "Mexico and U.S. Racism." *Commonweal* 42 (June 22, 1954): 234–236.

Index

Acción Mundial, 38
AFL (American Federation of Labor), 4; alliance with Casa del Obrero Mundial, 21; anticommunism in, 186–187, 191; commission to Mexico, 67–68; at Eagle Pass conference, 45–46; El Paso Convention, 1924, 109–110; founding of, 13; Gompers and, 5; government role of, 94–05; International Relations Committee, 132–133; and La Casa del Obrero Mundial, 13–28; Laredo conference, 1918, 78–90; Latin-American delegates of, 89; Marxist unions and, 14; membership, 51; Mexican immigrants and, 97–100; Mexican proposals for merger in PAFL, 80–81; and Mexican Revolution, 9–10; new interest in Mexico and Latin America, 160–161; opposes armed intervention, 15; and PAFL revival, 161; Socialists in, 5; support of Carranza by, 17, 30; wartime economy and, 56; wetbacks and, 206–207; *see also* Gompers, Samuel
AFL-CIO, on capitalism, 230–231; cooperation between, 179–182;

foreign policy of, 224, 227–230; merger of, 217–281, 225
AFL-CIO International Affairs Department, 226
AFL Convention, Atlantic City, 1916, 53–54
AFL-CROM alliance, 104–105, 108–111, 124–143; *see also* CROM
AFL-CROM conference on immigration, 117
AFL Executive Council, 39, 116, 124, 133, 142, 163, 179, 209, 216; and Casa del Obrero Mundial, 25; as dabblers, 17; and Pan American organization of labor
Agency for International Development (AID), 227
Agrarian Code, 150
Agricultural Workers Organizing Committee, 212
AIFLD (American Institute for Free Labor Development), 227–228
Almazán, Gen. Juan Andreu, 166
Alvarado, Salvador, 44
Amalgamated Clothing Workers Union, 177, 192
American Alliance for Labor and Democracy, 73
American Federationist, 36, 57, 135

249

*Labor Organizations in the
United States and Mexico* was composed
in Linotype Baskerville with Bulmer display
type and printed by offset lithography by
Port City Press, Inc., Baltimore, Maryland.
The book was bound by Arnold's Book Bindery,
Reading, Pennsylvania.